**Stratification and Inequality Series**

The Center for the Study of Social Stratification and Inequality,
Tohoku University, Japan
Volume 1

# Inequality amid Affluence

**Stratification and Inequality Series**

The Center for the Study of Social Stratification and Inequality,
Tohoku University, Japan

Inequality amid Affluence: Social Stratification in Japan
*Junsuke Hara and Kazuo Seiyama*

Intentional Social Change: A Rational Choice Theory
*Yoshimichi Sato*

Constructing Civil Society in Japan: Voices of Environmental Movements
*Koichi Hasegawa*

**Stratification and Inequality Series**

The Center for the Study of Social Stratification and Inequality,
Tohoku University, Japan
Volume 1

# Inequality amid Affluence

## Social Stratification in Japan

### Junsuke Hara

and

### Kazuo Seiyama

Translated by
Brad Williams

First published in Japanese in 1999 by Tokyo Daigaku Shuppankai as *Shakai kaisō: Yutakasa no naka no fubyōdō*
This English edition first published in 2005 by
Trans Pacific Press, PO Box 120, Rosanna, Melbourne, Victoria 3084, Australia
Telephone: +61 3 9459 3021  Fax: +61 3 9457 5923
Email: info@transpacificpress.com
Web: http://www.transpacificpress.com

Copyright © Trans Pacific Press 2005

Designed and set by digital environs Melbourne. enquiries@digitalenvirons.com

Printed by BPA Print Group, Burwood, Victoria, Australia

**Distributors**

**Asia and the Pacific**
Kinokuniya Company Ltd.

*Head office*:
38-1 Sakuragaoka 5-chome, Setagaya-ku, Tokyo
156-8691, Japan
Telephone: +81 (0)3 3439 0161
Fax: +81 (0)3 3439 0839
Email: bkimp@kinokuniya.co.jp
Web: www.kinokuniya.co.jp

*Asia-Pacific office*:
Kinokuniya Book Stores of Singapore Pte., Ltd.
391B Orchard Road #13-06/07/08
Ngee Ann City Tower B
Singapore 238874
Telephone: +65 6276 5558
Fax: +65 6276 5570
Email: SSO@kinokuniya.co.jp

**Japan**
Kyoto University Press
Kyodai Kaikan
15-9 Yoshida Kawara-cho
Sakyo-ku, Kyoto 606-8305
Telephone: (075) 761-6182
Fax: (075) 761-6190
Email: sales@kyoto-up.gr.jp
Web: http://www.kyoto-up.gr.jp

**UK and Europe**
Asian Studies Book Services
Franseweg 55B, 3921 DE Elst, Utrecht,
The Netherlands
Telephone: +31 318 470 030
Fax: +31 318 470 073
Email: info@asianstudiesbooks.com
Web: http://www.asianstudiesbooks.com

**USA and Canada**
International Specialized Book
Services (ISBS)
920 NE 58th Avenue, Suite 300
Portland, Oregon 97213-3786
USA
Telephone: (800) 944-6190
Fax: (503) 280-8832
Email: orders@isbs.com
Web: http://www.isbs.com

**Australia and New Zealand**
UNIREPS
University of New South Wales
Sydney, NSW 2052
Australia
Telephone: +61(0)2-9664-0999
Fax: +61(0)2-9664-5420
Email: info.press@unsw.edu.au
Web: http://www.unireps.com.au

ISBN   1-8768-4314-4 (Hardback)
ISBN   1-8768-4315-2 (Paperback)

# Contents

# List of tables

# List of figures

# Preface to the Japanese Edition

'Social stratification' was once one of the undoubted research problems for sociology and the social sciences. An examination of occupational stratification before World War II – for instance, between white-collar workers (*shokuinsō*), blue-collar workers (*kōinsō*) and peasants – clearly reveals the existence of disparities in socio-economic living conditions in Japan. During this time, 'poverty' and 'starvation' were real problems. A book written by junior high school students from a mountain village in northern Japan entitled *Echoes from a Mountain School* (*Yamabiko Gakkō* – Muchaku 1951) depicts a level of poverty unimaginable today. It should be noted that this story was not set in pre-war Japan.

However, the situation surrounding social stratification in Japan changed radically, particularly in the period of high economic growth. During the twenty years of high economic growth in Japan (1955–1975), GNP and GNP per capita increased by 5.4 and 4.3 times in real terms, respectively, resulting in the virtual elimination of 'poverty' and 'starvation.' Moreover, differences in attire and lifestyle, once evident among occupational strata, were no longer so obvious. Many Japanese came to see themselves as being in the 'middle.' 'Strata' lost much of its reality for most people.

This does not mean, however, that the differences among strata had been eliminated and that Japan had witnessed the birth of an equal society. In this book we refer to tangible and intangible objects, which have become the object of people's desires, as 'goods' (*zai*). We have further divided 'goods' into 'basic goods' (*kisozai*) and 'upper goods' (*jōkyūzai*). It is appropriate to refer to a situation in which most Japanese have attained a level of income in which they no longer suffer from 'poverty' and 'starvation' and the majority of Japanese children advance to high school as the equalisation of 'basic goods.' However, at the same time, there has been no progress whatsoever towards the equalisation of 'upper goods.' For instance, the difference in incomes among strata has instead widened, while the disparity among strata in terms of university advancement rates has not decreased.

What should we discuss regarding 'stratification' under these conditions?

Since Japan has not realised a completely equal society, it is possible to investigate the actual disparity among strata and the factors that have brought about it. Certainly, if we conduct surveys examining various indices and coefficients, there are several figures which show that Japan is by no means equal. However, at a time today when 'stratification' is no longer a serious issue, what significance does it hold? Recently, the mass media has been continually focusing on the trend towards expanding income disparity in Japan. However, we believe the argument that Japanese people's 'middle' consciousness is merely an illusion and that an extremely unequal society will re-emerge in Japan either ignores or makes light of the fact that Japan has attained an equalisation of 'basic goods' and only propagates an erroneous image of Japanese society.

What about simply ceasing all discussions of 'stratification'? Within the diverse fields of sociology is rural sociology. In a society in which farm workers comprised nearly half of the workforce and urban and rural life was believed to be completely different, rural sociology was the most active field in Japan, boasting many researchers. However, with the advance of industrialisation and urbanisation today, rural sociology's former prosperity is no longer evident. Young researchers' interest in rural sociology has waned due to the absence of new and clear fields of inquiry. It is possible that research into stratification will experience a similar fate to rural sociology.

What we have aimed for in this book is an approach different to that discussed above. While the reality of 'stratification' in its former sense may have become lost, the same cannot be said of the significance of research into stratification itself. This is because many of the problems that have arisen in Japanese society, which is in many ways in disarray and has reached a turning point, in fact depend largely on stratification (inequality). For instance, there is the problem of 'liberalisation,' which, as is often discussed, is not only a stratification issue in the sense that it can only lead to the discarding of the socially weak, but also a problem in the sense that regulations that should be relaxed have until now enhanced the profits of a limited strata of society. It can also be argued that an education-conscious society, gender disparities and the status of minorities, beginning with foreign workers in Japan (which, unfortunately, are not sufficiently dealt within this book), are precisely stratification problems.

Moreover, even after the period of high economic growth in Japan, there exists data showing that people's sensitivity towards stratification and status has by no means diminished. However, approaching the issue of stratification in contemporary Japanese society using pre-existing analytical frameworks is problematic. Instead, a new framework focusing on societies that have achieved an equalisation of 'basic goods,' or, in other words, inequality in 'affluent' societies is called for. We would like to demonstrate this.

This book is structured in the following manner. First, after presenting an overview of the changes in Japanese society and the problems associated with existing research on stratification, we examine the four issues of an education-conscious society, occupational careers, class consciousness, and gender focusing on the problems arising in an affluent society. Finally, we consider the meaning of 'stratification' in contemporary 'affluent' society.

The arguments posited in this book are based largely on data collected in the National Survey of Social Stratification and Social Mobility (*Shakai Kaisō to Shakai Idō Zenkoku Chōsa*). This survey is called the SSM Survey and has been conducted every ten years since 1955 by Japanese researchers of stratification. The most recent of these is the fifth survey, which was carried out under the leadership of one of this book's authors, Seiyama Kazuo, in 1995. The survey features a series of questions, including those inquiring about the respondents' and their family's attributes such as academic background and occupation and awareness of stratification, and is a valuable source of information otherwise unobtainable from government statistics (Hara 1998c). It is possible not only to trace the changes in Japan during the 40 years that have elapsed since 1955, but also to reconstruct people's circumstances before 1955 to a certain extent using detailed information regarding the respondents' occupational careers since their first jobs. However, it should be noted that the first three surveys only examined males – females were polled from the fourth survey onwards. As a result, we highlight the fact that many longitudinal analyses have only focused on males (refer to ch. 5).

Without the SSM Surveys, it would have been impossible to write this book. There are no other examples of longitudinal surveys of stratification over 40 years on a national scale in Japan. As such, this book should be well received overseas. These surveys have continually received the support of many individuals. While the number of respondents who have kindly provided extremely private and valuable information has not been uniform for each survey, it has risen to 20 423. The authors were added to the survey team from the time of the third (1975) and fourth (1985) surveys. Many of our teachers and university seniors, beginning with Odaka Kunio (Tokyo University, deceased), Nishihira Shigeki (Institute of Statistical Mathematics), Yasuda Saburō (Tokyo University of Education, deceased), Tominaga Ken'ichi (Tokyo University) and Naoi Atsushi (Osaka University), previously promoted these surveys.[1] Many of our friends, including Imada Takatoshi (Tokyo Institute of Technology), Umino Michio (Tohoku University), Kōsaka Kenji (Kwansei Gakuin University), Kondō Hiroyuki (Osaka University) and Shirakura Yukio (Osaka University) shared the hardship of conducting and analysing the 1995 survey. We express our heartfelt gratitude to all these people.

Because we have conducted wider-ranging research into stratification based on the results of a data analysis of the 1995 SSM Survey, in addition to thanking our friends and colleagues, we would also like to announce that overall project was published as a six-volume series by Tokyo University Press in 2000 under the title of *Stratification System in Japan* (*Nihon no Kaisō Shisutemu*). In addition to the aforementioned names, this series features the work of many young researchers who have each provided their own perspective of stratification in Japan.

Among the four topics covered in this book, Hara initially prepared drafts on occupational careers and awareness of stratification, while Seiyama drafted chapters on an education-conscious society and gender. Seiyama wrote chapters one and six, and Hara wrote the remaining sections. However, after repeatedly exchanging and revising manuscripts, we believe the final product approaches something akin to a co-authored book.

The research project from which this book was written was supported by a Grant-in Aid from the-then Japanese Ministry of Education (special research promotion) and a research grant from the Casio Foundation. The authors have received permission from the 1995 SSM Research Association for the use of the data in this book.

Hara Junsuke and Seiyama Kazuo
July 1999

# Preface to the English Edition

## Center for the Study of Social Stratification and Inequality

Japan's Ministry of Education, Culture, Sports, Science and Technology has fundamentally changed its position regarding university administration since the end of the 20th century. The Ministry has moved away from its previous approach of standardised protection and regulation of what has been referred to pejoratively as 'the convoy' (*gosō sendan*). It now encourages competition between universities and researchers and provides funding on a selective basis. The Twenty-first Century Center of Excellence (COE) Program, which was established in 2002, is representative of this new policy. The COE program attempts to select internationally competitive research and education centres and provide them with extensive funding. Chosen as a COE in the field of social sciences, the Graduate School of Arts and Letters at Tōhoku University established the Center for the Study of Social Stratification and Inequality (CSSI) in 2003.

This center organises a diverse range of activities, including running both international and domestic workshops, providing academic and financial support to postdoctoral research fellows and postgraduate students and creating links with domestic and foreign research institutes. The publication of the 'Research Series on Social Stratification and Inequality' is also an important part of CSSI's activities. This book, entitled *Inequality amid Affluence: Social Stratification in Japan*, is the first volume in this series.

This book was first published in 1999. Therefore, it cannot lay claim to being an original research finding for CSSI. However, this book represents the attainment point of previous Japanese research on social stratification. One of the authors is a key member of CSSI. In addition, the 1995 SSM Survey constitutes an important source of data used in the analysis of this book. Since 1955, this survey has been conducted by researchers interested in stratification every 10 years. CSSI established its own '2005 SSM Survey Preparation Office' and will continue to support this survey on a formal basis.

Thus, this book is a springboard and departure point for CSSI's activities. It is for this reason that it is included in the 'Research

Series on Social Stratification and Inequality.' Following on from the findings of this book, CSSI will include analyses of such topics as 'minorities,' 'fairness,' and 'East Asia' in addition to focusing on 'structure and change.' The Center aims to theoretically and empirically elucidate issues related to 'new' inequality within an affluent society.

## Formation of Strata in Japan

The Japanese edition of this book has received many reviews and comments. While it is not the objective here to respond to every one, there is one point we would like to supplement.

One of the criticisms directed at the book was the lack of clarity regarding the outcome of depicting Japan's 1995 strata structure as briefly as possible. At the heart of such doubts is a general sense of dissatisfaction that this book does not show diagrams of strata structure in the form of pyramids or diamonds. However, a meticulous reading of this book will reveal that one of its major claims is that such simple diagrams are not possible. That said, we do recognise that our explanation as to why this is so may be somewhat insufficient. It is this point that we would like to supplement.

For our basic occupational strata categories we have adopted a general classification comprising the eight categories that appear in table 0.1. This is a combination of job type, employee status and employee numbers (refer to the glossary). Among the various classificatory methods, we think that this best reflects the differences between people's strata position (status, lifestyle and consciousness etc). However, this does not mean that these eight categories have been ranked one-dimensionally in the manner of a pyramid or diamond. Even regarding the individual dimensions, the difference in strata position among the categories is ultimately one of averages with significant mutual overlap. We seek to demonstrate this using several indicators.

Table 0.1 shows the mean and median values, as well as the rank order, for each occupation in regards to occupational prestige (SSM Occupational Prestige Score), academic background (number of years of school attendance), income (individual and household) and strata identification.[1] This table can be said to show the average position for each occupational strata category.

From this table it is clear that the ranking differs according to each indicator. Therefore, the strata ranking is not one-dimensional. Examining it more closely, on the whole, professionals, white-collar

*Table 0.1: The mean value of strata indicators by occupation (1995)*

| Occupation | Distribution percentage | Occupational prestige | Years schooling | Individual income | Household income | Strata identification |
|---|---|---|---|---|---|---|
| Professionals | (11.9) | 62.1 (1) | 15.0 (1) | 478.7 (3) | 690.8 (3) | 3.19 (3) |
| White-collar workers in large companies | (17.5) | 52.0 (3) | 13.7 (2) | 575.2 (1) | 740.9 (2) | 3.25 (1) |
| White-collar workers in SMEs | (12.6) | 52.7 (2) | 12.7 (4) | 390.4 (5) | 561.8 (6) | 3.06 (4) |
| Self-employed white collar workers | (12.7) | 47.4 (4) | 12.8 (3) | 514.6 (2) | 831.8 (1) | 3.24 (2) |
| Blue-collar workers in large companies | (9.2) | 38.9 (6) | 11.6 (5) | 391.7 (4) | 570.0 (5) | 2.89 (6) |
| Blue-collar workers in SMEs | (20.0) | 37.8 (8) | 10.8 (6) | 278.9 (7) | 452.6 (8) | 2.78 (8) |
| Self-employed blue-collar workers | (10.3) | 39.7 (5) | 10.8 (7) | 376.2 (6) | 646.6 (4) | 2.86 (7) |
| Farmers | (5.9) | 38.8 (7) | 10.1 (8) | 202.0 (8) | 469.5 (7) | 2.96 (5) |
| Total | (100.0) | 46.7 | 12.3 | 358.5 | 581.1 | 3.04 |

Note: Occupational prestige: SSM Occupational prestige score; Individual and household income: Annual income (¥10,000). The figures in parenthesis following mean value denote ranking.
Source: SSM Survey data. Only for males aged between 20–69.

workers in large companies and self-employed white-collar workers who occupy a high ranking can be referred to as the upper tier group while the other occupations can be called the lower tier group.

Among the upper tier group, professionals have extraordinarily high occupations and academic backgrounds but in terms of incomes and strata identification do not reach the level of white-collar workers in large companies and self-employed white-collar workers. On the other hand, the occupational prestige, academic background and strata identification of white-collar workers in medium and small companies in the lower tier group are high but in terms of incomes are much lower than the upper tier group and, as such, cannot be included in this group. Although there are many instances in which agriculture ranks the lowest for these indicators, it ranks fifth for strata identification.

Next, figures 0.1 through 0.4 show the distribution for the strata indicators appearing in the table for each occupational category. We find that the distribution of each indicator overlaps considerably and that the position of each occupational strata in table 0.1 is literally an 'average.'

This is the real image of the strata structure of Japanese society. It can be said to consist of a kind of overlapping, multi-dimensional hierarchy and certainly does not represent a uni-dimensional pyramid structure.

*Figure 0.1:   Distribution of occupational prestige scores by occupation
(1995)*

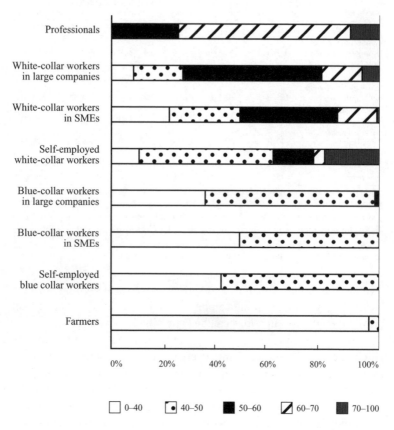

Source: SSM Survey data. Only for males aged 20–69.

## Expansion of Disparities?

It has already been 10 years since the aforementioned SSM Survey
was conducted and preparation for the 2005 survey is proceeding at a
rapid rate. The most significant change in stratification over the last 10
years is the growing recognition in Japanese society of an 'expansion
of disparities.' This is a change that we initially failed to predict in the
Japanese edition of this book. In recent times, Japanese society has
been affected by a severe and seemingly endless economic recession,
massive government debt and financial deficit and an aging population

*Figure 0.2:  Distribution of academic backgrounds by occupation (1995)*

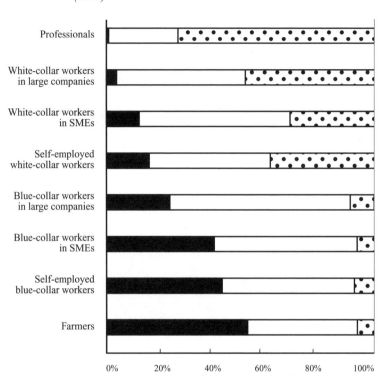

Source: SSM Survey data. Only for males aged 20–69.

combined with a diminishing number of children. The prospects for the immediate future appear bleak. As a result, a sense that it is appropriate to feel obstructed, or simply put, uneasy, is permeating Japanese society. Against the backdrop of this, the claim that Japanese society is becoming increasingly unequal is attracting considerable interest.

Many of those who adhere to the 'disparities are expanding' thesis are, in fact, merely generalising local phenomena, such as corporate restructuring (employment adjustment) and performance-based hiring that are taking place in some companies and industries, to

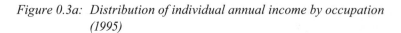

*Figure 0.3a: Distribution of individual annual income by occupation (1995)*

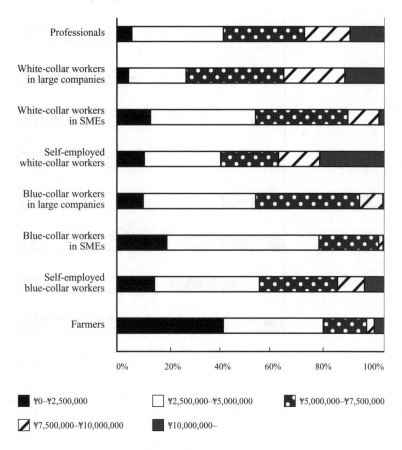

Source: SSM Survey data. Only for males aged 20–69.

Japanese society as a whole. However, there are not a few scholars who argue this thesis is based on reliable data and analyses of high quality, to a certain extent. Hence, we believe some comments have to be added about them here.

**Income Disparities**

Tachibanaki Toshiaki's *Economic Disparities in Japan: Income and Assets* (1998) raises the issue of income and asset disparities, comparing Japan with the other advanced industrialised societies. It argues

*Figure 0.3b: Distribution of household annual incomes by occupation (1995)*

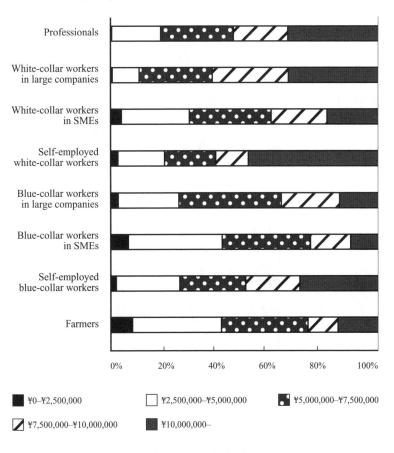

Source: SSM Survey data. Only for males aged 20–69.

that Japanese society is not as egalitarian as it has been claimed and that since the 1980s disparities have been widening rapidly. His book provided a strong blow to Japanese society. Because the manuscript of our original version of this book was mostly complete by the time Tachibanaki's work was published, we did not comment on it. In addition, there is a difference in topics covered in that the issue of asset and income disparities is only part of the strata problems our book deals with. However, in relation to Tachibanaki's claims, we emphasised the inequality inherent in Japanese society from various angles and elucidated the fact that while income disparities declined greatly

*Figure 0.4:   Distribution of strata identification by occupation (1995)*

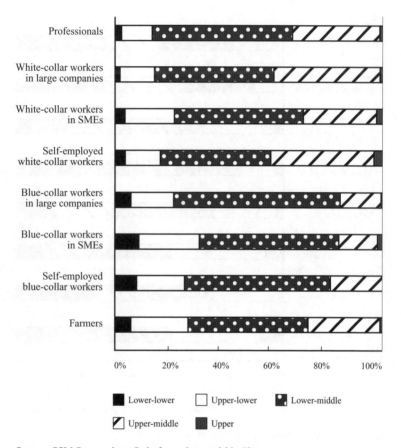

Source: SSM Survey data. Only for males aged 20–69.

between 1955 and 1975, there has been virtually no change thereafter. The difference between Tachibanaki and our research lies in whether one argues that since the 1980s there has been a 'rapid expansion of disparities' or basically 'continuing disparities' at the same level.

Many scholars were critical of Tachibanaki's claims. The criticisms centred on the following two points. First, the concept of 'income' used for each country's data is not necessarily uniform. When you adjust for this, Japan's level of inequality ranks it in the middle of the advanced industrialised countries. Second, while the level of inequality appears to increase when all age groups are included, this does not necessarily mean that income disparities have widened between those from the same age group. In fact, for most age groups, income disparity seems to remain virtually constant. However, one cannot deny that the income disparities among those aged 65 and over have widened.

Both Tachibanaki's work and the claims made by critical economists are based on official statistics that mainly use the household as the unit of survey. In this respect, the SSM Survey data is advantageous in that it is a national sample that adopts individuals as the unit of survey, which is adequately representative of the total population in question, encompassing all occupations as well as the unemployed and students, at the time of the survey.

Figure 0.5 shows changes in the Gini coefficient for household income based on the SSM data. Individual incomes display a virtually similar change. From 1955 to 1975 during the period of rapid economic growth, overall individual and household income inequality declined amid the significant transformation of Japan's industrial structure. The Gini coefficient reached its lowest point of 0.293 in 1975 before rising again. However, it remained at a lower level than in 1955 and 1965. We basically recognise that this cannot be considered to be an extreme expansion of disparities.

*Figure 0.5: Trends in household income disparities*

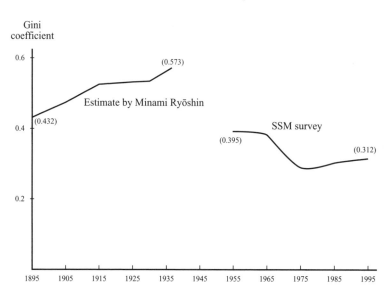

Source: Minani (2002) and SSM Survey data for males aged 20–69.

Figure 0.5 includes additional information about household disparities before World War II. This was estimated by Minami Ryōshin (2000) using large quantities of pre-war taxation records discovered at local tax offices. It is evident that Japan twice had the opportunity to reduce income disparities by a substantial amount: at the time of the collapse of the pre-war social and economic system in the latter half of the1940s and the period of high economic growth in the 1960s and 70s.

However, it is an undeniable fact that the Gini coefficient did rise again. What does this mean? Seiyama Kazuo (2001) notes that this rise was the result of an expansion of income disparities between different age groups. Among the structural factors brought about by differences in occupation, academic background and age group etc, the only element that has clearly become unequal since 1975 is income disparities based on age. Figure 0.6 shows the results of a comparison of median individual and household incomes between 25–34 year

*Figure 0.6:  Trends in income disparities between age groups*

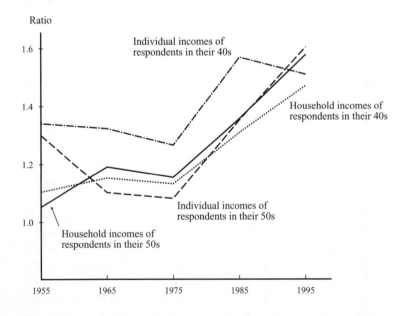

Note: The ratios of median values of the respondents in their 40s and 50s to those aged 25–34.
Source: Seiyama (2001: 20, Figure 2). The original source is SSM Survey data, but only for males.

olds and those in their forties and fifties. All have shown a tendency to increase from 1975.

Seiyama cites the following two points as reasons for the widening disparities between age groups. The first is the increasing popularisation of higher education and 'white-collar-isation.' These two trends mean that there has been an increase in the number of people who belong to organisations that have a seniority-based wage system such as large companies and government. Disparities between age groups on the whole will widen as a result.

The second is the spread of the seniority-based pay system to blue-collar workers in SMEs during the period known as 'low growth' and 'stable growth' following the rapid growth era. Because of this, disparities between age groups have widened from among highly educated white-collar workers to most combinations of academic background and occupation.

Aside from this, disparities within age groups have clearly remained unchanged or declined. In this manner, Japanese society following the period of high economic growth has experienced an increase in income disparities between age groups while restraining inequality within age groups.

## Opportunity Disparities

Satō Toshiki's *Japan as an Unequal Society: Farewell to the All Middle Society* (2000) played a role in relation to opportunity disparities in much the same manner as Tachibanaki did concerning income. Based on an analysis of the SSM Survey data, Satō claimed that the upper stratum of white-collar employees (upper W employees) located at the highest stratum has become increasingly closed and that Japan has made the transition from being a 'society where anything is possible with some effort' towards one in which 'nothing is possible no matter how hard you try.'

The starting point and very foundation of Satō's argument is figure 0.7. The vertical axis is a logarithmic odds ratio and compares the possibility of people from different strata reaching a particular stratum. The larger the value the more advantageous it is for members of a particular strata to enter. In other words, it shows that the stratum is closed (see chapter 3). While upper W employees were originally a highly closed stratum, it is clear from figure 0.7 that according to the 1995 data, it is certainly only this stratum that is becoming more closed. It shows that the logarithmic odds ratio is 2.07 and that it is

xxiv *Preface to the English edition*

*Figure 0.7:   Trends in the exclusiveness of strata (Father's occupation
– respondent's occupation at the age of 40)*

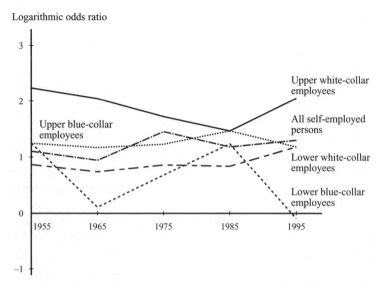

Source: Satō (2001: 58 Figure 2.4). The original source is SSM Survey data, but only
for males aged 40–59.

eight times more favourable for people from the upper W employee
stratum compared to those from other strata. In addition, the degree
to which the upper W employee stratum is closed is twice that of the
second-ranked self-employed.

However, among the analyses of social mobility using the SSM
Survey data, the claims made by Satō are extremely unique. Ishida
(2000), Kanomata (2001) and Kondō (2002) also analyse trends in social mobility using the same data but, unlike Satō, argue that mobility
opportunities have remained at virtually the same level since 1975. In
addition, Hara Junsuke (2002) concludes that the exclusiveness of the
upper W employee stratum reached its highpoint in 1965 and since
dropping substantially in 1975, is virtually unchanged.

In fact, in what is common knowledge among all specialists in
social mobility analysis is that there are an endless number of ways
in which the indicator of the 'openness' of mobility opportunities are
created. The results differ according to the indicator used. Therefore,
it is difficult to make a strong claim if similar results are not obtained
using different indicators. On this point, the results of Satō's analysis
are unique because he uses highly specific indicators.

*Figure 0.8: Trends in the exclusiveness of upper white-collar employees*

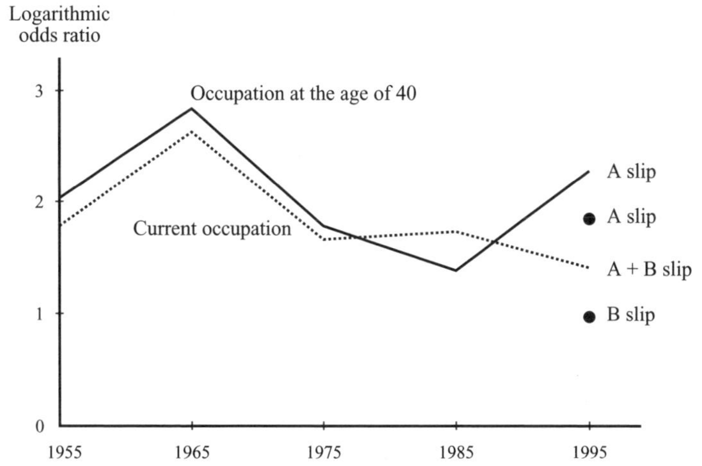

Source: Hara (2002: 46 Figure 1.9). The original source is SSM Survey data, but only for males aged 40–49.

First, Satō cites the occupations of respondents at the age of 40 as their attained strata. This differs significantly from most other analyses which use the 'respondent's current occupation.' Satō's 'upper W employee stratum' category comprises professional employees and management. Subtle differences arise according to the company and era when it comes to whether people reach 'management positions' before they turn 40.

Still, one cannot determine *apriori* whether it is best to choose 'occupation at the age of 40' or 'current occupation.' Figure 0.8 re-analyses the differences that arise due to these two for those aged between 40–49. When examining this, we see that at least until 1985, the graphs virtually overlapped and the indicator differences were not substantial.

However, the graphs differed significantly in 1995. This is because the data used in the analysis was not completely identical. In the 1995 SSM Survey the sample was split into two types of survey slips: an A slip and a B slip. In order to identify the respondents' occupation at the age of 40 like Satō, one needs to know their career history. However, this data is only included in the A slip. At the same time, since the necessary information regarding current occupations could be obtained from both the A and B slips, a logarithmic odds ratio of current occupations was calculated combining both slips. A logarithmic odds ratio calculated based on only the A and B slips is tentatively displayed in the form of • in figure 0.8. Both slips are quite different. Hypothetically, if the respondents' career history was also included in the B slip and the logarithmic odds ratio was calculated based on occupation at the age of 40, the value would be considerably lower than the results based on the A slip.

The main reason for such a difference, in fact, lies in the fairly low number of cases that were able to be employed in Satō's analysis. In other words, the results of the logarithmic odds ratio calculated based on the A slip only has a fairly low level of reproducibility. Instead, looking at trends until 1985, the value of the logarithmic odds ratio for the occupation of respondents at the age of 40 approximates that for current occupations. Therefore, one can only conclude that Satō's claim that the 'upper W employees' strata is rapidly becoming increasingly closed is hasty.

## Motivational Disparities

It was Kariya Takehiko's *Stratified Japan and the Educational Crisis: From Reproducing Inequality to a Society of Motivational Disparities* (2000) that tried to supplement Satō's claim that, in terms of consciousness, Japan has made the transition from a 'society where anything is possible with some effort' towards one in which 'nothing is possible no matter how hard you try.' Focusing on the generation younger than the SSM Survey respondents, Kariya surveyed high school students in 1979 and 1997 and noted that inter-strata disparities arose in scholastic motivation from their longitudinal analysis. The results of Kariya's research can be summarised below:

1. Comparing the results for 1979 and 1997, on the whole, there is a clear decline in scholastic motivation.
2. Examining the differences between strata (measured according to mother's academic background), there was no conspicuous difference in 1979. However, in 1997, it was evident that the higher a child's stratum, the greater the scholastic motivation.

The tendencies outlined above are clearly evident in figure 0.9. For instance, in response to the opinion that 'it is acceptable to achieve the grades necessary to avoid failing,' it shows the percentage of those who agree according to their mother's academic background. According to Kariya, Japan has become a 'society where they could

*Figure 0.9: Scholastic motivation of high school students by mother's academic background*

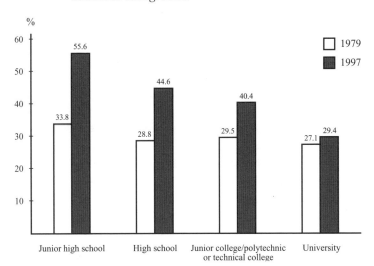

Note: Percentage of those who agree with the opinion that 'it is acceptable to achieve the grades necessary to avoid failing.'
Source: Kariya (2001: 182, Figure 6.1).

not be bothered trying' for a number of people. He calls this the 'motivation disparity society' (*iyoku kakusa shakai*).

However, Kariya's analysis only shows that 'there are strata disparities in scholastic motivation.' As expected, we must wait for future social conditions and data to ascertain whether this leads to widening disparities of academic achievement, strata and income.

## Background of the Theses of Expanding Disparities

In any event, the future of Japanese society depicted by the afore-mentioned theses of the expansion of disparities suggests, rather gloomily, that a clear, vertically differentiated and closed stratified society has developed in Japan. Is this really the case? In considering this problem, it is necessary to point out the following two similarities in these arguments.

First, they spread and reinforce the classic image that the 'lower strata = the poor' in a vertically differentiated future society. No matter how you think about it, this is not a realistic image. We should advance an argument premised on a 'basic equalisation' emphasised in the preface to the Japanese edition of this book.

For instance, when examining absolute income disparities, we represented the rather poor as a 25 percentile value and the rather wealthy as a 75 percentile value. If we convert the 1955 figure for real household income, which controlled for changes in consumer price levels, from 25 percentile value (approx. US$1,250) to 100, the 1995 figure is exactly 600 (approx. US$44,000). The 75 percentile value increases from 260 (approx. US$3,250) in 1955 to 1,302 (approx. US$94,000) in 1995. While the disparity in absolute values appears to be widening, the ratio of 75 percentile to 25 percentile declined from 2.6 to 2.17 (corresponding with changes in the Gini coefficient).

At 25 percentile, real incomes increased 6 times and at 75 percentile, 5 times. This applies to each occupational stratum. The lower stratum is no longer poor and poverty and hunger, which were a continual source of concern, are no longer an issue for most Japanese. The decline in children's scholastic motivation noted by Kariya is probably due to the fact that they have realised that a 'normal' or 'average' lifestyle has now become possible, even if one is a non-elite, rather than from a narrowing of the path to elite status through education.

Second, there is a tacit assumption that a career characterised by the link between a favourable academic background and a high occupational status makes people 'happy.' Takeuchi Yō (2001) referred to this as the 'desire for middle class through academic background' (*gakureki chūryū kaikyū ganbō*). He noted the importance of presenting a different lifestyle to that of the 'middle class with high academic background' (*gakureki chūryū kaikyū*) instead of lamenting the increase in the number of young people with a lack of scholastic motivation. The proportion of white-collar workers among those with a tertiary education is declining gradually and the different lifestyle is one which young people are forced to choice.

However, there is one more factor that, along with economic depression, offers plausibility to the theses of expanding disparities: the intensification of competition between companies and employees resulting from economic globalisation. It is white-collar workers in large companies, who previously enjoyed relatively high wages and stable employment, that is influenced the most by this phenomenon. This group provides the largest readership of Tachibanaki, Satō and Kariya's books. In other words, the theses of expanding disparities can be said to be an argument that responds to the concerns and anxieties of white-collar workers in large companies.

It is necessary to point out that researchers who predicted 'expanding disparities' and the 'second coming of a closed society,' journalists who propagated this argument and white-collar workers in large companies who read about it are relatively similar in terms of origins and circumstances. Therefore, it is easy for a situation to arise in which there is an 'intellectual community creating a discourse of inequality' among these people. One must be cautious about generalising this intellectual community's anxieties across society as a whole.

### Inter-generational inequality

In this manner, several doubts remain regarding the claims of expanding disparities. Of course, this does not mean that problems related to strata and inequality do not exist in Japan at present. If we were to focus on one of these doubts, it would be the problem of inter-generational inequality, in which a combined effect of time (depressed economic conditions) and age has directly impacted upon the young generation.

As Seiyama (2001) noted regarding figure 0.6, inter-age group disparities continued to rise since 1975. The income (median) of those in their 40s and 50s was 1.1 to 1.2 times that of those aged between 25 and 34 in 1975. However, in 1995, it grew to 1.5 to 1.6 times. The expansion of inter-age group income disparities undoubtedly increased the opportunity cost of young people becoming economically autonomous from their parents.

In addition, the younger generation struggles to gain employment and many are forced into part-time work. Freelance part-time workers (*furītā*) and young people not in education, employment and training (*nīto*) are becoming an object of public concern. If young people are anxious and lose motivation today as Kariya states, it is neither because of the anxiety to future 'poverty' nor the prospects of promotion, but because of being unable to find work during a long-term economic recession and not being able to see light at the end of the tunnel. According to Ōtake Fumio (2000), the wage disparity between part-time and full-time workers has continued to expand since the 1980s.

The wage disparity between part-time and full-time workers will be a serious issue for Japanese society. Seiyama (2001) also notes that since part-time work has continued to increase, if young people on low incomes such as freelance part-time workers continue in this type of work, it can only result in the emergence of a large middle-aged, low income stratum that will find it difficult to support a family.

Breaking free from these conditions requires a weakening of the seniority-based wage system and a legitimate evaluation of youth labour. In addition, by not only pushing ahead unilaterally with employment restructuring but also promoting worksharing within and between different age groups, increasing employment is also an effective countermeasure. At the same time, reducing wage disparities due to length of service, and cutting the special privileges enjoyed by university educated, elite, salaried workers that are protected by the practice of lifetime employment, it might be important to expand opportunities for people who are unable to become regular employees at a young age to find work that offers a certain level of wages that are tied to individual effort. These countermeasures may, conversely, lead to greater income disparities within age groups and produce results akin to the predictions of the adherents of the theses of expanding disparities. However, if expanding opportunities for young people only entails rising income disparities, this will be, to a certain extent, unavoidable. The reason is that even if this is the case, the 'basic equalisation' of Japanese society will not collapse easily.

Hara Junsuke
Seiyama Kazuo
September 2005

# 1995 Official SSM Survey Reports

*Nihon no Kaisō Shisutemu* (*Stratification System in Japan*), 6 volumes, Tōkyō Daigaku Shuppankai (Tokyo University Press), 2000.

Volume 1: Hara, Junsuke, (ed.), '*Kindaika to Shakai Kaisō* (*Modernisation and Social Stratification*).'

Volume 2: Umino, Michio, (ed.), '*Kōheikan to Seiji Ishiki* (*A Sense of Fairness and Political Consciousness*).'

Volume 3: Kondō, Hiroyuki, (ed.), '*Sengo Nihon no Kyōiku Shakai* (*Educational Credentials in the Postwar Stratification System*).'

Volume 4: Seiyama, Kazuo, (ed.), '*Jendā, Shijō, Kazoku* (*Gender, Markets, and Family*).'

Volume 5: Imada, Takatoshi, (ed.), '*Shakai Kaiso no Posutomodan (Postmodernity and Social Stratatification)*.'

Volume 6: Kōsaka, Kenji, (ed.), '*Kaisō Shakai kara Atarashii Shimin Shakai e (From Stratified Society to a New Civil Society)*.'

# Acknowledgements

The publication of this book was made possible by a grant offered by the CSSI and a Grant-in-Aid for Publication of Scientific Research Results (175213) from the Japan Society for the Promotion of Science. The authors and the publishers acknowledge their generous financial support.

# 1 How has Stratification Changed in Japan?

## Declining interest in class

The subject matter of this book is 'social strata' (*shakai kaisō*). The word 'class' (*kaikyū*) is used more frequently than 'stratum' in the English-language discourse. Both 'strata' and 'class' are not simply academic terms, but are embedded in everyday life. While the word 'class' derives from Latin, which is similar in meaning to the Japanese word *kaikyū*, in Japan and the West it usually refers to 'class' in a school environment (*gakkyū*). 'Class' is also used to designate the ranks among police officers, fire officers, defence force personnel and retired soldiers. 'Strata' is the plural of 'stratum,' which refers to a geological stratum (layer of earth). In a social context it has a relatively brief history of usage and is limited to academic research in the English-speaking world. In Japan, on the other hand, the word 'tier/stratum' (*sō*) is presently widely used even in everyday life in a sociological sense, for instance, when referring to 'white-collar stratum' (*sararimansō*), 'housewife stratum' (*shufusō*), 'peasant stratum' (*nōminsō*), 'high income stratum' (*kōshotokusō*) and 'stratum of impoverished people' (*hinkonsō*). It can be said that 'stratum' means a collective of people who are placed under similar socio-economic conditions. In the West, the word class is used in almost the same sense on a daily basis.

For a long time, class has been one of the major themes of modern society. In particular, during a seventy-year period of the twentieth century, which witnessed the emergence and subsequent collapse of the Soviet Union, class was considered to be an indispensable concept for understanding the social world around us. In Japan, with its own historical development of the social sciences, class came to denote, in particular, a Marxist perspective of society, while strata is often used in non-Marxian contexts. There is no such conspicuous dichotomy in the West at present. The question of which term we should use, class or stratum, is a core issue of the theory of stratification and we examine this aspect in the final chapter of this book. However, to give our conclusion in advance, we prefer to give priority to the term 'stratification' as a more comprehensive concept which can incorporate various specific meanings of the word 'class.'

## Changes in post-war Japan

Interest in class and stratification in Japan has declined rapidly among the general public, as well as in academic circles, since the 1960s. One of the causes of this decline is clearly the obvious reduction in absolute poverty and the overall rise in living standards in Japan as an advanced, industrialised society. In addition to access to food, clothing and shelter, escaping poverty in modern society means a guarantee of a stable income for the purpose of maintaining a decent lifestyle such as providing children with a basic education and attaining a basic sense of security for the family. Despite general economic development since the Industrial Revolution, until after the Second World War, no government anywhere in the world had been able to guarantee a basic standard of living for all people and eliminate the stratum of impoverished people within its territory. Of course, Japan was no exception with the overwhelmingly unmistakable reality of poverty, the concept of 'class' underpinned various forms of influential social thinking.

In the immediate aftermath of its defeat in the Second World War, Japan suffered from the destruction of its industrial base and its people sunk into abject poverty. America's dazzling culture and the affluent lifestyle of its people, which followed the Occupation Forces into Japan, captivated the Japanese. Post-war Japanese society concentrated all of its efforts into economic revival and development. As a result, until the end of the period of high economic growth in 1973, Japan advanced rapidly to become the world's biggest economy after the United States and the Japanese people began to experience for themselves the affluent American consumer lifestyle so many had dreamed of in the 1950s. Of course, this story of becoming affluent was not only limited to the Japanese. The global free-trading system and currency control regime, which were based on the lessons learnt from the pre-war period, coupled with the adoption of welfare policies and Keynesian economic management principles, led to the emergence of mass consumption society, which brought about unprecedented economic development in the advanced, industrialised countries during the 1950s and 1960s. Poverty was pushed into the recesses of people's minds.

People familiar with common Japanese scenery and lifestyles before the onset of high economic growth are limited today to those generations beyond their late 40s. Life in a Japanese country town around 1955 was led in much the following manner. Upon waking up in the morning, a person would haul water out of the well in order to wash his/her face. After putting firewood into the kitchen stove, he/she would transfer rice from the cooking pot to the rice tub and then eat breakfast at a *chabudai* (a low, round table). In the case of children brought up on a farm, before going to school, they would do chores such as taking care of the cows and cutting the grass. While the rice paddies were ploughed using a horse or cow, most of the work in the fields was done by hand. Planting, as well as clearing and cutting grass, were of course also done by hand. While gasoline-engine threshing machines were used, the most popular vehicle used to carry items was a large, ox-drawn wagon. Nearby would be a small general store, a draper's shop, a blacksmith, a watchmaker, and in some places electric appliance stores began to appear. While the town doctor's house would contain a washing machine, most people would wash using a washing board and a large tub. Nobody had a refrigerator. Because there was little vehicular traffic on the roads – only the occasional trishaw – they were the ideal place to play for children on their way to and from school. Fireflies would fly about near the river during summer and people would catch and release them into a mosquito net (*kaya*). In winter people would keep warm under a *kotatsu*[1] and charcoal brazier (*hibachi*). Farmhouses also had an open hearth. Houses were lit by incandescent light bulbs (with fitted light shades) at night and in the rare instance there was an upper class family with a high school student, the house would have a reading/desk lamp. Because there was no television, adults would do manual work while listening to radio programs from the national broadcaster NHK. Leisure consisted of occasional trips to the local cinema, which would play double features on weekends only, to watch movies amid the haze of cigarette smoke.

Between 60 to 70% of Japanese people lived in such an environment. Irrespective of its merits and demerits, this type of lifestyle no longer exists. It is no longer possible to live without a television, refrigerator or automobile. In fact, during the 50 years of the post-war era – or looking more narrowly, a 14-year period from 1960 to 1973 – Japan underwent enormous change. The changes taking place in Japanese society during this time are evident in several pieces of statistical data.

Figure 1.1 shows the changes in Japanese Gross National Product (GNP) from 1930. Looking at the changes in per capita GNP, this figure increased nominally from 97,000 yen in 1955 to 3,924,000 yen in 1995. This represented a 40-fold increase or a 10-fold rise in real terms. On the other hand, figures 1.2 and 1.3 illustrate the changes

*Figure 1.1: Trends in real GNP (1930 as a benchmark of 1)*

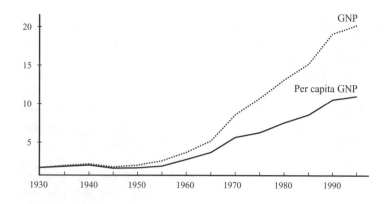

*Figure 1.2: Trends in the percentage of workers by industry*

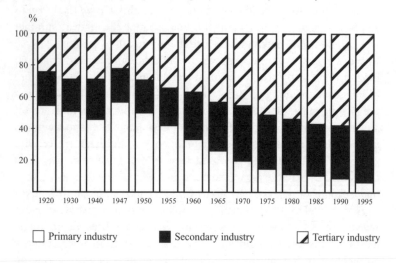

Source: National Census data. The data include both males and females.

in the percentage of workers according to industry and occupation, which underpinned this increase.

While half of the working population were employed in primary industry, mainly agriculture, in 1950, by 1995 this figure dropped to about 7%. On the other hand, the percentage of workers engaged in tertiary industries increased from about 30% in 1950 to about 60% in

*Figure 1.3: Trends in the percentage of workers by occupation*

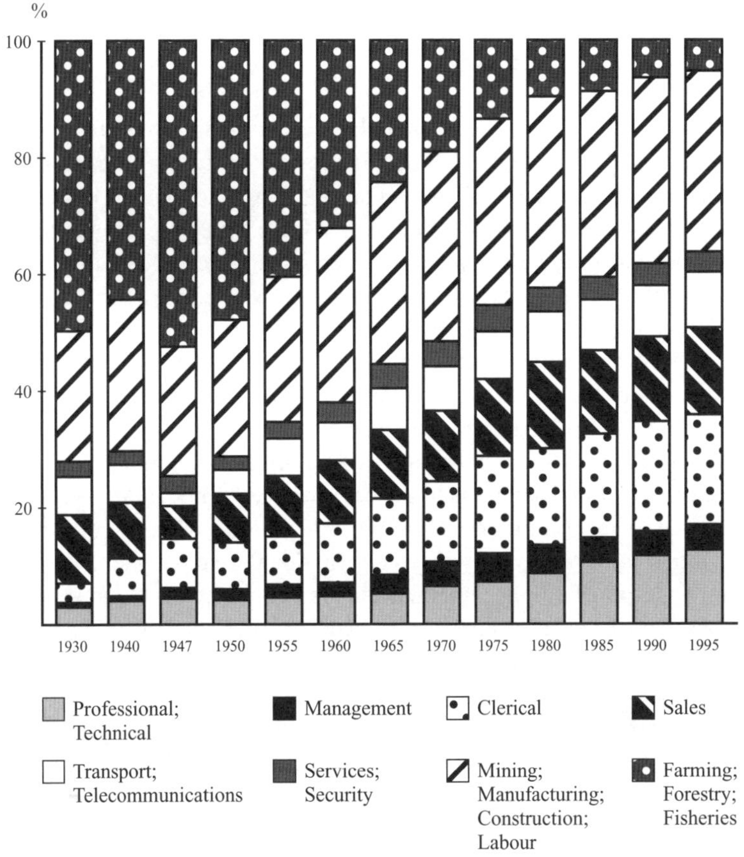

Source: National Census data. The data include both males and females.

1995. If we look closely, during the period of high economic growth in the 1960s and 1970s, the wholesale and retail industries experienced an increase, whereas from the 1980s, in what was a reflection of the expansion of the service economy, the service industry grew significantly. Secondary industry, centring on manufacturing, expanded slowly during the period of high economic growth, remaining fairly constant thereafter. Occupational changes were also a parallel to these shifts. That is, the percentage of white-collar workers engaged in professional jobs, management, clerical work, sales and the service industry rose fairly consistently. The percentage of blue-collar workers, centring on skilled workers, increased until the period of high economic growth. Those engaged in agriculture, forestry and fisheries declined rapidly.

## The aims of class theory

Does affluence really eradicate class and stratification? If it does, one can understand the declining interest in stratification caused by affluence. Because the phenomenon it attempts to explain has been eliminated, the theory would no longer serve a purpose. However, as will become gradually evident, this is not the case. Instead, this book argues that existing class and stratification theories have been unable to cope with the changing social reality.

Class was originally seen as a key concept in discussing modern societies for the following three reasons. First, class appeared to give an account of poverty and the various social problems that derived from it. Moreover, it was thought to be indispensable in considering the causes of and solutions to poverty from a theoretical perspective. Second, a large number of social movements, which centred on political movements, as well as international disputes and rivalries, were once understood, explained and created, based on the concept of class. Third, social history was narrated through the lens of class, by which even the future of human society was predicted at one time.

Historical research shows that the term 'middle class' was used in America from the mid-eighteenth century, while 'proletariat' and 'working class' were used since the time of the French Revolution. While Emmanuel Joseph Sieyès still used the word 'état' in 1789, Claude Henri de Saint Simon referred to what was almost the same stratum of society as 'classe industriels.' After this, 'class' was extolled by Marx and Engels as an instrument of historical transformation and occupied a key position in social theory, which resembled the notion of 'power' in Newtonian mechanics.[2] However, at the same time, class also raised questions regarding the meanings of these concepts. Marx's voluminous works featured various inconsistent perspectives of class. Moreover, his theoretical compilation *Das Kapital* was aborted at just the point where he began to develop his theory of class.

However, the theoretical sections of *Das Kapital* are, in fact, unambiguous, clearly conveying Marx's thoughts. Among these is the notion that social 'relations of production' determine an individual's class.

The relations of production hypothesis is based on the 'theory of labour value.' Because the theory of labour value itself derives from

the works of John Locke and was developed as an economic theory by Adam Smith and David Ricardo, it is not an inherently Marxist assumption. However, it can be argued that it was Marx's idea to base the theory of labour value on class theory. Marx basically posited that it was people's 'labour' that created economically valuable wealth and services. Administrative and managerial tasks were not components of this labour. The value of wealth and services originally belonged to working people. However, a truly capitalist society is divided into three main classes: the capitalists who receive a share of the value produced (or a major portion of it) by simply possessing the means of production; the workers who, because they do not own the means of production, only receive enough to maintain a minimum standard of living; and subsistence farmers and the self-employed who possess minor means of production and themselves work. The strength of this theory, above all, was its clarity. Moreover, it was highly compatible with actual social phenomena. Ranking people's incomes and living standards in order of capitalists, the self-employed and workers was an undeniable fact of all modern, capitalist societies.

However, the advancement of industrialisation in Europe gradually exposed several deficiencies in Marxist theories. First, many of Marx's confident predictions such as 'the absolute impoverishment of the working class,' 'declining profit rates,' 'the annihilation or downsizing of the self-employed' and 'the intensification of the class struggle' were off the mark. Second, Marx's theories cannot adequately explain the reality that capital and management break up and that the managerial and administrative strata constituted by highly educated employees take charge of giant industrial organizations. Third, the secondary industries this theory was premised upon, such as mining and manufacturing, have stopped expanding. In their place, tertiary industries such as finance, information and services constitute the core of modern economies. Even in secondary industries production equipment has become highly automated and the veracity of the classical notion of labour as 'labouring on nature' has faded.

Apart from Marxist accounts, there are three main arguments regarding the concepts of class and stratification, each with its own particular positive and negative aspects.

1. Weberian theory of class. In terms of placing an emphasis on economic activities, it is similar to Marxism. The Weberian theory of class attempts to analyse not only relations of production, but also diverse market, work and life situations.[3] Because Weberians do not put forward simple and powerful claims like Marxists, they

are not clearly bankrupt in a theoretical sense. At the same time, however, they do lack theoretical clarity and unity. Therefore, for instance, they are unable to answer the question 'Theoretically speaking, how and into how many categories is class divided?' While there is a body of research, such as that conducted by English sociologist John H. Goldthorpe (1980), which presents a class classification scheme in concrete terms, rather than being theoretically grounded, it is merely a summary of empirical knowledge from English society.

2. Theory of power elites. Power elite theorists believe class is a political rather than economic relationship. While Marxists claim that 'the state is a tool of domination used by the economically dominant class,' power elite theory turns this notion on its head, arguing that 'whoever dominates, political domination/being politically dominated is the first principle of class relations'.[4] This theory was highly geared towards explaining the existence of a 'new class' (Djilas 1957) in socialist society. However, by attempting to limit class to the political sphere, power elite theorists were unable to provide a perspective on the diverse status and differentiation of lifestyles among people engaged in various productive activities in modern industrial society.

3. Stratification theory. This theory does not centre on economic or political status, but rather on more generalised notions of 'social reputation' and 'prestige.' Social stratification is conceptualised in terms of a social hierarchy of ranked statuses, which is established on the space of reputation and prestige and other various 'social resources'. Stratification theory developed both from the energetic research of Pitirim Sorokin (1927) – an intellectual who was exiled from the Soviet Union – and as the basis of empirical research into the class composition of regional societies in America. It was Sorokin who replaced class with the concepts of strata and stratification as the core of this theory. He began researching social mobility, arguing that industrial society engenders a more open strata structure. However, in spite of the concept of continuous ranking on which this theory is constructed, a great deal of research into occupational stratification, in fact, employed a clear-cut strata categorisation.

There is a 'theory of the modernisation of stratification,' which was posited as a means of countering Marxism, in a manner more comprehensive than mere conceptual opposition. Known as the 'theory of industrialisation,' it argued that 'modernisation has led to the gradual levelling of class differences and the quelling of class conflict. In various spheres class disparities will either disappear or be alleviated.' This was not a claim made by only one theorist. Stratification theory was established in the context of the wide-ranging sociologically grounded modernisation theory. Apart from the aforementioned Sorokin, its proponents were Seymour Lipset and Reinhard Bendix (1959), Talcott Parsons (1951) and Daniel Bell (1960). Lipset and Bendix emphasised that European countries similarly share highly open class mobilities at the same level as America. Parsons systematised a conceptual scheme for the transition from the attribution-oriented to an achievement-oriented society. Bell spoke of the end of ideology. In an age where affluence spread throughout the post-war advanced, industrialised societies, this theory of the modernisation of stratification appeared to be extremely persuasive (Hara 1994b). In fact, as we will see in each of the following chapters, a not inconsiderable amount of empirical data on stratification accords with this claim. However, for a number of reasons, the theory of modernisation itself has suffered from declining credibility since the 1970s. We believe that apart from the issue of the Vietnam War and the civil rights movement in America, the continued existence of relative poverty in the advanced, industrialised countries, the emergence of problems associated with ethnic and gender 'identities,' various 'modernisation setbacks' in the developing countries and new social problems such as the environment and nuclear power have all contributed to this declining credibility.

Our task in this book is to present a vision for a new theory of stratification that can overcome the difficulties facing existing paradigms. It is understood that this task should proceed in parallel with addressing the conceptual problem of what stratification actually entails, and also must be based on empirically confirming the facts as they pertain to stratification.

Existing empirical research into stratification has focused on the following three issues:

1. Overall, has inequality among the various social strata grown or diminished?
2. Have the social strata exacerbated their mutual conflict of interests and deepened their political opposition and rifts or have their conflicting interests abated and political opposition quietened down?
3. Has inter- and intra-generational mobility between the various social strata heightened or has it declined with the boundaries between the strata undergoing consolidation?

The following section examines these issues in the context of post-war Japanese society. In presenting this data, we have adopted a specific method of classifying strata. While this classification method is designed to improve how we express the realities of strata in Japanese society, it is not necessarily exclusive. In the book's final chapter, we will explain the reason for our classification method.

## Trends in inter-strata disparities

### From the pre-war to the post-war era

Before discussing post-war Japan, we will briefly examine the circumstances surrounding strata in pre-war Japan. The Meiji government's abolishment of the pre-modern status system (*mibunsei*) and the principle of the equality of all people provided an opportunity for the Japanese people through the establishment of a modern education system and a system for the recruitment of government officials. However, it can be argued that socio-economic changes in Japan such as the modern industrial boom, the influx of people into the large cities and the development of the land-owning system, along with the introduction of an aristocracy system (*kazoku-sei*), led to the establishment of a new strata system in Meiji Japan.

Tominaga (1990) identified the following as the eight major classes in pre-war Japan: 1. the aristocracy; 2. the capitalists; 3. the new middle class; 4. the landowners; 5. the farmers/peasants; 6. the old urban middle class; 7. the workers; 8. and the urban lower class.

While the theoretical basis of Tominaga's classification is unclear, it serves as a fairly appropriate framework for an analysis of the circumstances surrounding strata in pre-war Japanese society. The primary reason behind our support for Tominaga's framework is that it easily conjures up specific images of each class by knowing and describing the lifestyles of particular individuals. Sôseki Natsume's novel *I am a Cat* (*Waga Hai wa Neko dearu*) portrays a teacher by the name of Kushami who belongs to the new middle class and loathes the capitalists. Gennosuke Yokoyama's *Japan's Lower Classes* (*Nihon no Kasô Shakai*) describes in detail the living conditions among the urban lower classes. The television drama *Oshin* and the movie *Jirō's Story* (*Jirō Monogatari*) provide a contrast, looking at Japan's lower peasant class and landowners, respectively.

Strictly speaking, this framework does not incorporate all elements of strata in pre-war Japan. One glaring omission is *buraku* communities. In what is linked with ethnicity, there was also discrimination against the Ainu and Okinawan peoples who were incorporated into the Meiji state, as well as those who came from the Korean Peninsula. Moreover, there existed various micro-class systems in all corners of society. For instance, industrial relations featured a comprehensive job-ranking system, comprising staff, machine operators/factory workers, apprentices, temporary workers and factory hands. Government officials were also divided into *Chokuninkan* (officials appointed by the Emperor), *Sōninkan* (officials appointed with the Emperor's approval) and *Hanninkan* (junior officials). Until the adoption of the Ordinary Election Law in 1925, suffrage was limited to the wealthy. It goes without saying that legal inequality existed between men and women.

Despite their small size, economic stratification permeated all life (including political) in Japan's farming villages. This was not simply a hierarchy of landowners and tenant farmers, but of upper class landowners, middle and lower class landowners, landed farmers, tenant farmers and day labourers. A hierarchy also existed among the head and branch families, as well as within the same family. During the Showa Depression of the late 1920s, tenant farmers rioted throughout the country.

It is well known that the situation surrounding strata in Japan changed radically in the post-war period. Tominaga (1990: 359) makes the following observation regarding this sweeping change:

> The destruction of [Japan's] cities caused by the [Allied] air raids and inflation brought about the ruin of the urban families of wealth. The new constitution stipulated the equality of all people under the law and abolished the aristocracy. Agricultural reforms swept away the last vestiges of the parasitic land-owning system. The dissolution of the *zaibatsu* made the closed ownership of large companies through blood ties impossible. Labour legislation raised the social status of workers. Civil law reforms abolished the Japanese traditional family system, leading to the dissolution of *dozoku* groups (kin groups of strongly and hierarchically tied families). Educational reforms promoted the popularisation of junior high and high school education....Compared to the pre-war period, post-war Japanese society is underpinned by a far more equalised strata structure.

From 1953 to 1985, three field surveys – led by Fukutake Tadashi – were conducted into the changes taking place in Japan's farming villages. The findings are summarised below:

By the time of the second survey (in 1968), the farming villages had changed significantly. The dismantling of the land-owning and class systems was clear for all to see. Family members enjoyed increased autonomy. People began to speak of the 'dismantling of villages' (*mura no kaitai*), which had maintained tight controls over the lives of their inhabitants (Takahashi, 1992: 5). In Akita the social structure in which the core, binding element was the hierarchical relations between the head and branch families was basically dismantled, and was rearranged as an agricultural community under the leadership [not the domination] of upper class, former landed farmers. While village leaders were more often from the head family strata rather than from the lower strata, this was not based on the former landing-owning and class-oriented authority, but was due to leadership as upper agricultural business leaders in the form of an association with other upper class, former landed farmers (*ibid*: 7)

The aforementioned transformation of stratification in Japan from the pre-war to post-war periods could appear to be congruent with modernisation theory, which posits that stratification will gradually level out/equalise as a society industrialises. Then, how has stratification changed in post-war Japan? The following sections will scrutinise quantitatively the shifts in inter-strata disparities in educational standards and incomes.

## Disparities in educational opportunities

The overall improvement in educational standards is one of the important changes that have affected Japanese society. In the pre-war period, Japan had a so-called double-track school system in which many students, after completing six years of compulsory education at a regular elementary school, advanced to a higher elementary school where they completed their education. Unless the household was fairly well-off, it was difficult for children to advance to industrial junior high school or a normal school for prospective teachers offering free tuition, let alone junior high school, which was the path to take for those wishing to advance beyond high school under the old education system. The total percentage of males advancing to this level was only about 20%. However, recognition that it was desirable for Japan's educational standards to improve further had spread under the wartime system. Amid the poverty of the immediate post-war period, wide-ranging educational reforms, which were intended to transform

Japan into a 'cultural state' (*bunka kokka*), were soon implemented. That is, the elevation of the former high schools and normal schools to university status, the opening of universities to women, the establishment of a new high school and junior high school system and the extension of the period of compulsory education created a new schooling system that continues today. This resulted in an overall increase in the number of children proceeding to high school and, subsequently from the 1960s, also the percentage of those advancing to university and junior college (see table 5.2 in ch. 5).

Is this overall expansion of educational opportunities in post-war Japan linked to an equalisation of other opportunities? First, looking at the figures of those proceeding to senior high school (secondary education), an overall increase in the advancement rate occurred immediately following the shift to a new system and, in what was essentially close to full admission, reached 95% by the end of the period of high economic growth. Figure 1.4 shows the percentage of people belonging to each stratum educated beyond high school (junior high school under the old system) as revealed in the various SSM Surveys of males aged between 25 and 34. This graph indicates that there was a sharp inter-strata disparity from 10% of the agricultural stratum to 80% of the professional specialist stratum for a period of time following the end of the Second World War. Then, the data from 1985 indicates that this disparity was virtually eliminated. The sample of this data comprises those who proceeded to senior high school in the years between 1966 and 1975, which means that the disparity was eliminated during the period of high economic growth in Japan.

What about the advancement rate of students wishing to receive tertiary education beyond high school? This advancement rate also rose rapidly for both males and females during Japan's high growth period. However, figure 1.5 indicates that there was a parallel movement in the gap in the advancement rate among the various strata of males. That is, while all strata benefited from expanded educational opportunities, inter-strata disparities continued in the sphere of tertiary education.

In this respect, there is an important point linked to the expansion of affluence and inter-strata disparities. This is that while equalisation in the distribution of 'basic goods' proceeds concomitantly with advancing affluence, the sharing of 'upper goods' remains unequal. Basic and upper goods are relative concepts. Basic goods refer to wealth that is initially diffused widely when affluence and opportunities expand.[5] Upper goods are goods that spread in the later

*Figure 1.4: The advancement rates to high-school by origin strata*

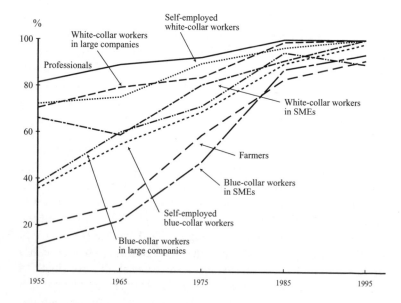

Note: This is the percentage of those possessing academic qualifications beyond or equal to secondary education from among the male respondents aged 25–34. For the occupations/strata categories refer to the terminology explanation at the end of this book.
Source: SSM Survey data.

stages gradually from those people from the upper strata of society. In terms of educational opportunities in pre-war Japanese society, education up to the higher elementary school level was mostly basic goods, while secondary education such as beyond normal school and junior high school was upper goods. During Japan's period of high economic growth, education up to the secondary level came to be seen as basic goods. However, it can be argued that to this day tertiary education continues to be a kind of upper goods.

**Income disparities**

Income is one of the most important indicators of stratified inequality. It forms the basis of purchasing power of a person's capacity to obtain an extremely diverse range of wealth and services, though not everything, and is a major determinant of living standards and lifestyles. All the same, it is not an easy task to measure income

*Figure 1.5:The advancement rates to junior college and university by origin strata*

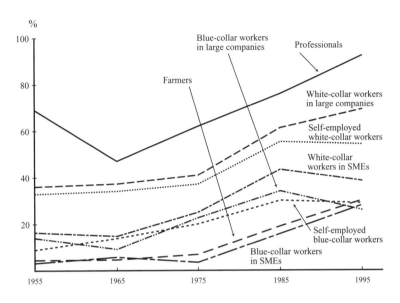

Note: This is the percentage of those possessing academic qualifications beyond or equal to junior college and university from among the male respondents aged 25–34. There were few cases of 'professionals' in 1955.
Source: SSM Survey data.

disparities correctly. For instance, as is commonly known, there is an ambiguity involved in the conceptual as well as operational definition of incomes. Even if levels of income are identical, income size and consumption levels do not strictly correspond with each other, because per capita consumption levels can differ greatly according to the number of people in and composition of a household, as well as loans and educational costs. Besides, there are problems associated with official government statistics. While the statistics of household budget surveys are calculated according to household units, the data is separately collected between employee and self-employed households, and it is difficult to get a grasp of the total picture. Because we cannot use sample data from official surveys, we are unable to analyse, for example, the income differences across strata and educational backgrounds.

Despite this problem, it was not impossible to trace the broad shifts in disparities using other macro-statistical data, such as our SSM survey data. While the SSM Survey data is derived from a smaller sample than government statistics, our data enable us to trace the long-term trends in the disparities among independent businesses and wage earners, which is superior to official government statistics.

There are a number of diverse indicators used in measuring income disparities. The most common indicator is the Gini index, which indicates the degree of deviation from the distribution of complete equality. However, for the purposes of comparison, it does require a fairly detailed spread of data. Among other indicators is the coefficient of variation or a comparison of the mean income among classes. One must exercise caution, however, that mean values are frequently affected by extreme values. As a comparatively simple indicator, we have decided to use median and a ratio of first and third quartiles.

Figure 1.6 is a graph indicating the accumulated relative frequency of annual individual incomes (including taxes) for males from the SSM data in 1995. Median refers to the amount of income of precisely the centrally ranked person when the entire sample is arranged in order of people with low incomes to those with high incomes. It is the amount of income that corresponds to 50 percent of the vertical axis. (In figure 1.6, it is 4.962 million yen.) The first quartile is the amount of income of the person who is located at the first quarter (25th per cent) from the bottom of the entire sample, while the third quartile value represents the amount of income of the person at the third quarter (75th per cent). Each one can be said to be a representative value of relatively low and high-income earners, respectively. The higher the degree of equality, the more the first and third quartiles approaches the median. Therefore, taking the ratio of each quartile to the median, the more the value of the ratio deviates from 1, the more it can be said that the level of inequality is high. Moreover, if we take the logarithm of this ratio, the size of the disparity can be expressed equally in a plus or minus direction centring on zero (for instance, twice and 0.5 times in the ratio becomes 0.693 and minus 0.693 on a natural logarithm).

Figure 1.7 shows the trends in the degree of total inequality for income distribution based on the responses of the entire male sample aged 20 to 69. The median of distribution for each year is located on the base line. Then, the ratio of the third quartile to the median is depicted in the upper area of the graph, and the ratio of the first quartile to the median in the lower area. According to the graph, the degrees of inequality both in individual and household incomes, on

*Figure 1.6:Individual annual income distribution in 1995*

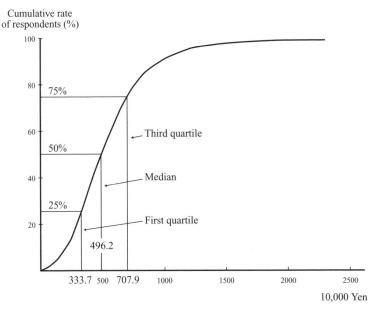

Source: SSM Survey data. Only for males aged 20–69.

the whole, declined considerably from 1955 to 1975. The ratios of the third quartile to the first quartile for individual and household incomes declined from 2.48 and 2.60 respectively in 1955 to 2.05 and 2.09 in 1975. However, from 1975 to 1995, despite some upward and downward movement, the overall trend seems to have remained at the same level. That is, although the total inequality in individual and household incomes declined from 1955 to 1975, amid the far-reaching changes to the industrial structure of Japanese society, it can be argued that equalisation did not proceed thereafter.[6]

Next, figure 1.8 shows the income disparities between occupational strata. This graph represents a logarithmic transformation of the ratio of the median income of each strata to the median of the entire sample. For instance, if the numeric value is 0.3, the median of a strata's income will be 1.35 times (= $e^{0.3}$) the median of the entire sample. Conversely, if the numeric value is minus 0.3, the median of a strata's income will be 1/1.35 times. First, regarding individual incomes, in 1955, there were four strata that received higher incomes than the entire sample: 1. self-employed white-collar workers; 2. white-collar workers in large companies; 3. professional; and 4. blue-

*Figure 1.7: Overall income disparities (20–69 years of age, male)*

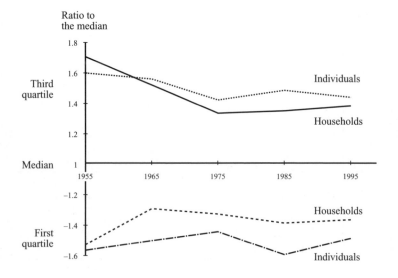

Note: The ratio of the third quartile value to the median and the ratio of the first quartile value to the median. (Minus signs indicate the inverse.)
Source: SSM Survey data.

collar workers in large companies. After 1955, the incomes of blue-collar workers in large companies declined somewhat to roughly the level of white-collar workers in small and medium-sized enterprises and self-employed blue-collar workers.

While a certain degree of equalisation is evident, it is not significant. The disparity between the incomes of white-collar workers in large companies, in particular, and those of the lower strata have been growing since 1975. On the other hand, household incomes have equalised significantly, especially through 1965 and 1975. In 1955, the median income of self-employed white-collar workers compared to the total median was 1.66 times and for professionals 1.59 times, whereas in 1975, the figures dropped to 1.27 and 1.18 times, respectively. However, the disparity between self-employed white-collar workers, in particular, and the other strata has continually grown since 1975. The household income of farmers had maintained, even in 1995, the level it had in 1955, avoiding a decline, unlike the case with individual incomes. This is

*Figure 1.8:Trends in inter-strata disparities of individual and house-
hold annual incomes*

**a. Individual incomes**

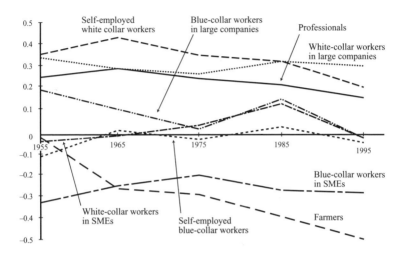

**b. Household incomes**

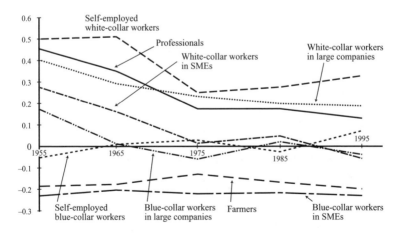

Note: 20–69 years of age. The logarithm of the median value of each stratum compared
to the median value of all cases.
Source: SSM Survey data. Only for males aged 20–69.

because income derived from non-agricultural sources, through the pursuit of a side-business, was used to provide household budgetary support for agricultural households.

It is evident from the preceding discussion of trends in the disparities of educational standards and incomes that while it can be claimed that equalisation progressed in certain spheres – especially those centring on basic goods – from 1955 to 1995, this was not necessarily the case in other areas.

## Political conflicts

Phenomena seen as the emergence of so-called class conflict such as the labour movement and the agrarian disturbances already existed in pre-war Japan. However, as a result of the ideological repression and mass mobilisation of the 1930s, class conflict was completely obscured during the war. Under the leadership of GHQ, initial hopes for 'democratisation' stimulated the labour movement and led to the formation and legalisation of socialist political parties in Japan. Following the (ultimately aborted) general strike of 1947, labour disputes resulting from worker layoffs under the deflationary 1949 Dodge Line had become a regular occurrence. Japan witnessed a series of bizarre events such as the Shimoyama, Mitaka and Matsukawa affairs and was swept up in a huge wave of labour protests. These protests, reached an apogee with the 1959–60 Miike dispute, which was played out against the backdrop of Japan's shift from coal to oil as a source of energy for industrial development. On a political level, the 1951 San Francisco Peace Treaty, the merging of the left and right factions of the Socialist Party and the formation of the Liberal Democratic Party (LDP) in 1955, and the turmoil of revising the security treaty with the US in 1960 were testimony to the fierce ideological conflicts, which continued to rage in post-war Japan (Kosaka 1994).

This was a period in which Japan was faced with a struggle between the two competing courses of 'capitalism or socialism.' Socialism was considered as one realistic alternative and had enormous appeal for youths, intellectuals and workers.

Following the controversy surrounding the revision of the security treaty, this appeal rapidly waned as the Japanese economy followed the path of heavy industrial development under the Ikeda cabinet's income doubling policy. Students who fought bitterly against the revision of the security treaty eventually graduated to become bureaucrats and company employees and it was in these positions that they worked towards constructing Japan as a highly industrialised society. The ideological conflict in Japan came to an end with the student rebellion led by the baby boomers on university campuses, as well as in streets, which began in 1968 and collapsed a few years later. Until the end of Japan's rapid economic growth, resulting from the first oil shock in 1973, the socialist dream faded for the majority of Japanese people.

Figure 1.9 shows, from SSM Survey, the trends in support for the LDP (conservative) and (so-called) reformist parties (the Japan Socialist Party and Communist Party) among the different occupational strata. We can highlight three aspects of the graph. First, support for the LDP was high from 1955 to 1985. Conversely, support for the reformist parties declined from the peak in 1955, during the same period. The data demonstrates that the ideological conflict in Japan was fiercest in 1955 and gradually declined in intensity thereafter. Second, while the difference in party support between the strata was pronounced from 1965 to 1985, it decreased remarkably in 1995. Therefore, strata-based political conflict also declined sharply by 1995. Third, nevertheless, even though the difference in political party support between the strata diminished, it basically maintained a similar pattern whereby support for the LDP was high among self-employed white-collar workers, farmers and large corporate executives, while support for the reformist parties was comparatively high among blue-collar workers in large companies. This indicates that while present-day strata differences may be less pronounced than before, they continue to be somehow significant politically.

## Social mobility

### Are strata in Japanese society rigid?

Social mobility refers to changes in people's status. It is referred to in this manner as if people physically move from one status to another.

Genuine data collection and debates regarding social mobility flourished as a result of a joint international research project beginning in 1951 entitled 'Comparative Research Project of International Social Strata and Social Mobility' under the auspices of the International Sociological Association. Participating in this project, the first SSM Survey was conducted in 1955 and data

*Figure 1.9: Trends in party support by strata (males aged 20–69)*

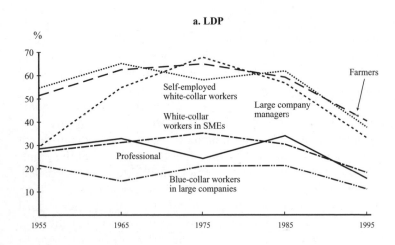

**a. LDP**

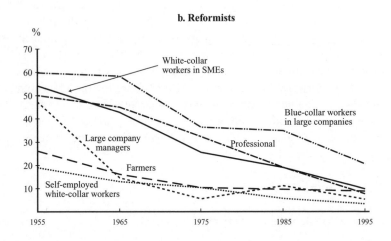

**b. Reformists**

Note: The 1955 figure for the 'LDP' is the combined total of the 'Liberal Party' and the 'Democratic Party', while the 'reformists' represents the total of the Japan Socialist Party (JSP) and the Japan Communist Party. This total includes the 'right faction of the JSP', the 'left faction of the JSP' and the 'Laborers and Peasants Party'. Among the strata, the intermediate groups namely white and blue collar workers in small companies, and self-employed blue collar workers are not listed. 'Large company managers' refers to the management strata among white-collar workers in large companies. 'White-collar workers in large companies' comprises the remainder apart from this stratum. Source: SSM Survey data.

Table 1.1: 1995 Intergenerational mobility table (males ages 20–69)

| Father's main occupation | Respondents current occupation | | | | | | | | | |
|---|---|---|---|---|---|---|---|---|---|---|
| | Professional | White-collar workers in large companies | White-collar workers in SMEs | Self-employed white-collar workers | Blue-collar workers in large companies | Blue-collar workers in SMEs | Self-employed blue-collar workers | Farmers | Total | % |
| Professional | 65 | 27 | 12 | 14 | 7 | 12 | 4 | 2 | 143 | 7.2 |
| White-collar workers in large companies | 47 | 70 | 34 | 30 | 20 | 29 | 7 | 3 | 240 | 12.1 |
| White-collar workers in SMEs | 14 | 22 | 19 | 10 | 9 | 15 | 4 | 1 | 94 | 4.7 |
| Self-employed white collar workers | 28 | 42 | 30 | 108 | 15 | 28 | 18 | 4 | 273 | 13.8 |
| Blue-collar workers in large companies | 14 | 25 | 19 | 8 | 18 | 31 | 4 | 1 | 120 | 6.1 |
| Blue-collar workers in SMEs | 26 | 37 | 37 | 11 | 37 | 73 | 21 | 2 | 244 | 12.3 |
| Self-employed blue-collar workers | 20 | 43 | 41 | 25 | 28 | 63 | 71 | 3 | 294 | 14.8 |
| Farmers | 25 | 78 | 62 | 51 | 45 | 133 | 75 | 108 | 577 | 29.1 |
| Total (column) | 239 | 344 | 254 | 257 | 179 | 384 | 204 | 124 | 1985 | |
| % (row) | 12.0 | 17.3 | 12.8 | 13.0 | 9.0 | 19.4 | 10.3 | 6.3 | | 100.0 |

Source: 1995 SSM Survey data.

concerning social mobility was collected on a national level for the first time in Japan.[7] The basic impression derived from the results of the analysis by Lipset and Bendix (1959), who collected and analysed comparatively the data from each country at the time, including Japan, was that all industrial societies are characterised by a high degree of inter-generational social mobility.

Table 1.1, which was created from the latest 1995 SSM data, shows inter-generational social mobility in Japan. The left-hand column comprises strata based on the main occupation of the respondents' fathers. At the top of the table appears the respondent's strata based on the occupation of the respondents themselves at the time of the survey. For instance, the number '65' in the upper left-hand corner indicates that among the sample there were 65 cases in which both the fathers' and respondents' strata are 'professionals.' The number '27' to the right of this reveals that there were 27 cases where the respondents' fathers were from the professional strata and the respondent moved to the category of 'white-collar workers in large companies.' This table refers to 1985 valid cases in total from male samples aged 20 to 69, excluding those respondents who either replied that they were unemployed at the time of the survey or did not give a response regarding their fathers' occupation. The diagonally positioned cells in this table refer to 'non-mobility' under this strata category and the non-diagonally positioned cells are cases of 'mobility.'

The percentage of people who have experienced strata mobility is called the 'gross mobility rate', which is the percentage of the total frequency of non-diagonal cells and amounts to 73.2%. This means that an overwhelming majority of people have experienced strata mobility.[8]

However, as the collection of data concerning inter-generational mobility flourished in many countries, extensive debates evolved surrounding the appropriate methods of analysis and concepts to employ for social mobility. First, scholars distinguished between the concepts of 'structural mobility' and 'circular' or 'relative mobility.'[9] Structural mobility refers to mobility resulting from differences in strata distribution between a father and son's generation brought about by changes in industrial structure. For instance, the percentage of Japan's agricultural population has declined consistently since the Meiji period (absolute decline, that is, a decline in absolute population occurred only after the Second World War), and, compared to the fathers' generation, there have been fewer children continuing in agriculture. This means that a portion of the population corresponding to the disparity between the number of fathers and sons engaged in agriculture must move from agriculture to other occupations. On the other hand, circular mobility refers to mobility caused, not by structural shifts, but by changes in people's strata affiliation.

Relating this to table 1.1, there were 577 cases in which the respondents' father was engaged in agriculture and only 124 incidents for the respondents themselves. Therefore, among the 577 cases, at least 453 (577 minus 124) must belong to strata other than agriculture. This is structural mobility. On the other hand, while the number 124 in the respondents' generation may be regarded as representing the capacity of agriculture, 108 of these cases were non-movers and 16 were those who moved to agriculture from non-agricultural strata. According to Yasuda's thinking, these 16 cases represent 'pure (circular) mobility.'

Expressed as a share of the entire sample, the volume of structural and circular mobility is called the structural and circular mobility rates. In the case of table 1.1, the structural mobility rate is 28.2% and the circular mobility rate 45.0%. Because the volume of gross mobility is the sum of the volumes of structural and circular mobility, structural and circular mobility are at a ratio of 4:6.

The scale of mobility differs according to strata. Among the various indicators, if we examine first the inflow rate (the percentage of people who have moved in from other strata), it amounts to 92.5% for white-collar workers in small- and medium-sized enterprises (SME) and 89.9% for blue-collar workers in large companies. About 90% of people comprising these two strata are originally from other strata. At 12.9%, agriculture has the lowest inflow rate, followed by self-employed white-collar workers and self-employed blue-collar workers at 58.0 and 65.2%, respectively. It is obvious that agriculture has relatively little appeal as an expansive industry. In a legal and customary practice, it is extremely difficult to obtain managerial capital (ie. farmland) anew in order to participate in agriculture.

Looking at the outflow rate (the percentage of people who have moved out to other strata), as expected, it is high for blue-collar workers in large companies and white-collar workers in SMEs at 85.0 and 79.8%, respectively. These two are the most highly fluid strata. The outflow rate is also high in agriculture (81.1%) and for self-employed blue-collar workers (75.9%). Agriculture experienced a large-scale outflow and overall contraction as a stratum. The situation surrounding self-employed blue-collar workers is somewhat similar. The outflow rate is low for professionals (54.5%) and self-employed white-collar workers (60.4%). In the sense that the next generation of professionals have a strong tendency to remain in this stratum once they reach it, the professionals strata may be regarded as 'destination strata'(*tōtatsu kaisō*) – to quote from Hara's study (1979) on intra-generational mobility – in intergenerational mobility. The fact that both inflow and outflow are relatively minor for self-employed white-collar workers suggests that it is a highly rigid stratum.

As a general indicator of each stratum's fluidity, we use an openness coefficient formulated by Yasuda and a logarithmic odds ratio. An openness coefficient is the ratio of actual to expected amount of circular mobility that is thought to occur when the son's stratum is distributed independently of the father's. The coefficient is 1 when actual and expected amount of circular mobility are congruent, but is usually smaller. The logarithmic odds ratio is a general indicator that measures the degree to which the distribution of the cell frequency on the cross table diverges from the independent distribution. It is zero when there is independent mobility, and the numeric value increases as a stratum experiences low fluidity and mobility.

After calculating these indices, we have ranked the strata in order of the highest openness coefficient (high fluidity) in table 1.2.

The ordering of the two indices is virtually congruent. The top four strata are highly fluid. These are the ordinary employees' strata. Conversely, agriculture has extremely low fluidity, followed by the professionals. As expected, the two self-employed strata also have low fluidity.

To be sure, in order to ascertain whether social mobility is increasing or decreasing in Japan, we must conduct a longitudinal analysis of not only data from 1995 but all past available data. This is discussed in greater detail in chapter three. However, what we can say at this point looking at the mobility table from 1995 is that intergenerational strata mobility in Japanese society has flourished greatly. In particular, the high fluidity of blue-collar workers in large companies – the stratum that is the main leader of the union move-ment and is a strong supporter of the reformist parties – deserves closer attention. This is because it is implied that this stratum has not constituted a consistent 'working class' beyond a generation.

If we were to point out the rigid stratum in Japanese society, then this would apply first and foremost to agriculture, which has experienced virtually no inflows from other strata. The next stratum is that of the professional. But, we should note that 72.8% of the respondents of this stratum are from other strata, and that over half of those from this origin stratum have moved to other strata.

*Table 1.2: The degree of openness for each occupational strata in the 1995 mobility table.*

| Occupational strata | Inflow rate | Outflow rate | Openness coefficient | Logarithmic odds ratio |
|---|---|---|---|---|
| Blue-collar workers in large companies | 89.9 | 85.0 | .934 | .625 |
| White-collar workers in SMEs | 92.5 | 79.8 | .915 | .560 |
| Blue-collar workers in SMEs | 81.0 | 70.1 | .869 | .674 |
| White-collar workers in large companies | 79.7 | 70.8 | .857 | .793 |
| Self-employed blue-collar workers | 65.2 | 75.9 | .765 | 1.316 |
| Self-employed white-collar workers | 58.0 | 60.4 | .672 | 1.927 |
| Professionals | 72.8 | 54.6 | .620 | 2.078 |
| Farmers | 12.9 | 81.3 | .182 | 2.997 |

Source: 1995 SSM Survey data. Only for males aged 20–69.

## Problems with mobility theory

The original intention of collecting data on mobility was to ascertain – in line with Marxist predictions regarding the intensification of class struggles – whether strata have become increasingly rigid or whether inter-strata mobility exists. It can be argued that most of the previous empirical research challenged this theory of strata rigidity. However, as researchers accumulated more data, an issue arose concerning long-term trends in mobility – a perspective different to that offered by Marxists. In particular, this relates to trends in the volume of circular mobility, which is distinguished from structural mobility. Empirical research into mobility has examined three main theses:

1. In any society that has achieved a certain level of industrialisation, total mobility between the white- and blue-collar strata commonly maintains a certain height. This is called the LZ thesis, which was devised by Lipset and Zetterberg (1959).

2. In any society that has achieved a certain level of industrialisation, the volume of circular mobility – not to mention the volume of structural mobility – is virtually common. This is known as the FJH thesis, which was developed by Featherman, Jones and Hauser (1975).

3. The volume of circular mobility increases the higher a society's level of industrialisation. Scholars such as Treiman (1970) and Tominaga made this claim, which is referred to as the industrialisation thesis.

These are theories that link strata mobility to the transformation in a society's economic structure known as 'industrialisation.' Unlike Marxism, they all share the common argument that a certain level of mobility accompanies industrial society. Among these, the LZ thesis does not distinguish between structural and circular mobility. Because a considerable amount of empirical research demonstrates that the volume of structural mobility differs among industrial societies, there is a consensus among most researchers that the LZ thesis cannot be supported.

There is also a concern with the FJH and industrialisation theses. Both of these focus on circular mobility. The industrialisation thesis adopts modernisation theory as a theoretical backdrop and posits that advances in industrialisation promote the 'achievement orientation' of personnel distribution. That is, it claims that since suitable personnel are efficiently allocated to suitable work independently of the strata to which they belong, this encourages changes in strata membership. It is called the 'achievement orientation theory.' While as a matter of fact there is a flaw in the logic of this theory, as will be discussed in chapter two, it appears, ostensibly at least, as a case of clear logic. On the other hand, the logic of the FJH thesis is unclear. Featherman and his co-authors, who first put forward this thesis, adopted the concepts of phenotype and genotype and explained that a pattern of circular mobility, in the form of a genotype, is common to industrial societies. However, unlike organisms, the mobility phenomenon does not contain genes. Therefore, this explanation merely changes the wording of a phenomenon (the commonality of circular mobility) that should be explained with a different concept (the commonality of genotypes) that also requires explanation. Erikson and Goldthorpe (1992), who later systematically analysed mobility data from 12 countries, believe that the entire pattern of circular mobility comprises several elemental patterns. However, they do not explain why a commonality exists between each country for the latter.

The common drawback of these three theses is, it should be noted, the ambiguity of concepts such as 'a certain level of industrialisation' and 'the degree of industrialisation.' None of the hypotheses attempt to specify these concepts. For instance, is it acceptable for the degree of industrialisation to indicate GDP per capita or should we use other barometers such as low agricultural population and widespread tertiary industry? Should the Japan of 1955, whose agricultural population still comprised nearly 50% of the working population, be considered a society that has attained a certain level of industrialisation or not? Which societies in the world today have attained a certain level of industrialisation? Both the FJH and industrialisation theses have not established any criteria for addressing these questions. It is impossible to examine empirically these propositions in a precise manner.

That said, as will be discussed in greater detail in chapter three, most of the previous empirical research, whether they be longitudinal analyses of Japan or comparative analyses of various countries – such as those conducted by Western scholars – have achieved similar results. In other words, generally speaking, while these studies have teased out some differences among the various countries, as a whole, their underlying tone is the commonality of circular mobility. While subtle differences lean towards the predictions made by the industrialisation thesis, they are not particularly worth emphasising. In short, researchers favour the FJH thesis over the industrialisation variant.

However, this was not necessarily a welcome result for mobility research. The FJH proposition only describes general characteristics and is not theoretically informed. While all research should be guided by theory, there are no guiding theories for mobility research. It can be argued that the disappearance of a theoretical underpinning for mobility research is, as a whole, representative of the problems faced by contemporary stratification research (Seiyama 1997).

## New challenges for stratification research

### Strata problems faced by females

Despite remarkable progress in empirical research since the 1970s, stratification research has reached an impasse. This is linked to the fact that the two grand theories of Marxism and modernisation theory, which traditionally guided stratification research, have both lost credibility in the social sciences. In addition, while this does not mean that there are no exceptions, the advanced industrialised countries have, for the most part, solved the problem of poverty as a result of overall economic growth during the 1960s. If we examine the issues of concern for the 'new social movements,' which developed in the advanced industrialised countries from the 1970s, it is easy to understand the extensive scale of this transition. These movements focused on 'the environment,' 'peace,' 'minorities' and 'females.' Stratification theory did not function sufficiently enough to understand these movements and the issues they presented. Certainly, some Marxists, as always, adhered to their method of explaining all issues through the lens of class. However, the lack of validity of the Marxist approach was clear in the eyes of the majority of those who became non-believers.

At about the same time, feminist scholars directly challenged stratification theory. It was an article by Joan Acker (1973) that launched the first salvo in this debate. She asserted that all traditional stratification theories, despite their clear opposition on ideological grounds, shared the following implicit assumptions and understandings:

1. The family (household) is the unit in the stratification system.
2. The social position of the family is determined by the status of the male head of the household.
3. The status of family members is equivalent to that of the family.

These assumptions are premised on the (presumed) fact that there is always a male household head who acts as the only breadwinner in each household. However, Acker noted that according to a census taken in America in 1960, two-fifths of all households did not have a male household head in the traditional sense of the term; there was either an absence of a male household head – the husband was unemployed or worked part-time. Moreover, many women increasingly became independent wage-earners. Acker (1973: 938) was particularly sceptical of the third assumption, arguing 'It is inconsistent to rank an unmarried woman on the basis of her education and occupation and then maintain that these factors are of no importance to her social status or class placement after she gets married the next day.'

Needless to say, such criticism was delivered against the backdrop of important social changes occurring since the 1960s whereby the number of women working independently of their husbands' or families' occupations increased. However, the question Acker raises is, in fact, far more problematic for stratification theory than she envisaged.

It is a fact that traditional stratification theory focused on the household. Scholars believed that the family or the household was the unit in the stratification system. The concept of 'origin strata' as it pertains to social mobility has been formulated on the premise that the stratum to which a child belongs is the same as that of his/her father. This premise is difficult to accept for independently working women. As a step towards resolving the issue she raised, Acker, though still placing an emphasis on women's work, thought that a stratification system for status in the form of individual identities, which can embrace the full-time housewife stratum, is conceivable by constructing some kind of stratification axis that does not rely only on occupational labour (cf: Hara and Hiwano 1990). If this is possible, then a stratification system embracing housewives who are not independently employed, as well as many other people, could be established. However, while such an individualistic stratification theory could be valid if limited to the market conditions of people involved in productive activities, it fails to capture consumption activities in a general sense. Almost half of the total population, including not only full-time housewives but also children and the elderly who do not work, live within the community known as the household.

It is not only the issue of individuals and households, but many other premises which stratification theory sees as axiomatic that have been called into question. This will be discussed in greater detail in the final chapter of this book. In any case, the problems posed by the challenge of feminism can be added to the list of difficult tasks faced by stratification theory – a theory that already appears to be in crisis.

## Challenges for stratification research

In this manner, stratification research faces many problems today. These are:

1. Marxism and modernisation theory – the grand theories that have guided previous stratification research – have lost their validity.
2. The problem of 'poverty,' which stratification theory has mainly tackled, has been essentially alleviated in the advanced, industrialised countries.
3. Concomitant with the advances made by women into society, it has become evident that problems exist regarding the concept of the household unit in the stratification system.
4. Theories no longer exist that can effectively answer the basic question of what is strata and class.
5. No theories have emerged that can suitably explain the vast quantities of accumulated data concerning social mobility.

Will stratification theory be able to move beyond these difficult circumstances? Will it perhaps share a similar fate to Marxism and modernisation theory and vanish like mist into a new era of postmodernism, becoming a relic of the past? Needless to say, the authors of this book believe the answer is NO. The following chapters represent our attempt to justify this claim.

# 2 A Society with an Enduring Emphasis on Education

## Credentialism

### In contrast to meritocracy

*[handwritten annotation: Doesn't mean determine Academic Background]*

Japan is said to be an education-conscious or credential (*Gakureki*) society. In most cases, this description of Japanese society carries negative connotations. There are not a few observers who claim that 'bullying,' 'school violence,' 'truancy' and 'classroom chaos' etc. are the result of this emphasis on academic background. Table 2.1 illustrates the notoriety of a 'credential society.' 'Inequity based on academic background' is always cited as the major contributing factor to feelings of overall inequity in Japan. In 1985, about two-thirds of males surveyed believed that 'inequity based on academic background exists.' In 1995, about half of Japanese males surveyed thought that 'inequity exists to a considerable degree,' and, if we include those who believed it exists 'to some degree,' this figure approaches 90 per cent. More males felt inequity based on academic background exists than that based on 'incomes,' 'assets' and between 'the rich and poor.'[1]

That there were greater feelings of inequity based on academic background than income is quite strange. As discussed in the previous chapter, income inequality increased somewhat after decreasing marginally during Japan's period of high economic growth. But, as for education, while the disparity between those possessing and those not possessing tertiary qualifications remains unchanged, inequality in secondary education has been eliminated, at least on the surface. Moreover, from a common-sense perspective, it is income and not academic background that determines how well people live. It is

Translator's note: *Gakureki shakai* has been translated variously as an education-conscious society, education-obsessed society, credential society, academic meritocracy and academic background-oriented society or a society which places disproportionate emphasis on educational background,. In this chapter, we use either 'education-conscious society' or 'credential society' more or less interchangeably to indicate the notion of *gakureki shakai*.

*Table 2.1: Percentage of those who feel that 'there is unfairness' in respective categories*

| Categories | 1985 Yes | 1995 Greatly | 1995 A little |
|---|---|---|---|
| Gender | 40.2 | 30.4 | 53.1 |
| Age | 28.2 | 23.0 | 52.1 |
| Educational background | 64.3 | 48.6 | 39.6 |
| Occupation | 50.8 | 33.8 | 48.2 |
| Rich and poor | 56.5 | - | - |
| Family lineage | 36.1 | 24.2 | 44.6 |
| Region | 35.0 | - | - |
| Ideology/credo | 24.3 | - | - |
| Income | - | 39.0 | 45.0 |
| Assets | - | 36.6 | 41.7 |
| Race/ethnicity | - | 37.8 | 38.7 |

Source: SSM Survey data, ages 20–69. The 1985 data include only males.

not uncommon to observe a situation in which a highly educated businessman struggles to pay off a large mortgage on a small house, while in his neighbourhood members of a farming household live luxuriously in a palatial mansion. Then, why is 'academic background' frequently raised as an issue of inequity?

In this chapter the term 'credentialism' (*gakurekishugi*) is used to refer to the large degree to which academic background determines the level of one's social status and amount of income. There are two contrasting views on credentialism: one positive and the other negative. The affirmative evaluation sees credentialism in contrast to the rank-estate (*mibun*) system, the hereditary system and closed academic opportunities. Under the rank-estate and the hereditary systems, a person's occupation and status was prescribed by the occupation and status of their father or household. This presently still occurs in the world of traditional show business and art, such as *kabuki*, tea ceremony and flower arrangement. Even in modern companies there are not a few cases in which the members of the founder's family are given priority when deciding the president and board members. In contrast, credentialism is understood as an open system in which status and occupation are at least not linked directly to a person's family situation or his/her father's status but rather to the type of education received.

Credentialism is often used interchangeably with similar concepts such as 'achievement' and 'meritocracy.' However, it should be clearly distinguished from these terms. Achievement (*gyōsekishugi*) is a concept that anthropologist Ralph Linton (1936: 115) originally defined in contrast to the term ascription (*zokuseishugi*). The word achievement means to achieve/accomplish something. However, as the term 'achievement test' suggests, it is considered to be inexorably linked to the (latent) ability to achieve/accomplish something. What Linton sought to emphasise in his use of the word achievement is the mechanism by which people's roles are apportioned only on the basis of their ability to actually accomplish tasks expected of them in their social roles. The term meritocracy is also very similar to achievement, since merit implies ability. However, by adding the suffix '- cracy', meritocracy was originally used to emphasise 'domination.' Credentialism, on the other hand, is based on the attainment of academic qualifications or academic background. Since academic background cannot be simply presupposed to mean ability accurately, we must consider achievement and meritocracy to be different concepts.[2]

## An encouragement of learning

Academic background has been an important means of attaining status in Japan since the Meiji period. At that time, it was understood as the fundamental building block of a modern society overflowing with wonderful opportunities. It is well known that the book entitled *An Encouragement of Learning* (*Gakumon no Susume*) by one of Japan's greatest ideologues of civilisation and enlightenment, Fukuzawa Yukichi, begins with the phrase 'Heaven never created a man above another...' (*ten wa hito no ue ni hito o tsukurazu*). Fukuzawa's main point is contained in the following passage:

> However, looking at this world of ours, we find wise men and ignorant men, rich men and poor men, men of importance and men of little consequence, their differences like the cloud and the slime. Why should all this be? The reason is apparent.... The distinction between the wise and the foolish is made from whether a person has studied or not.[3]

As early as in 1872, when the school system had yet to be established, Fukuzawa advocated a principle of stratification for Japan's approaching modern society. According to this principle, the division between the wealthy and poor, nobleman and commoner would be based on 'power by learning.' Fukuzawa's *An Encouragement of*

*Learning* was a bestseller at the time and laid the foundation for a large number of Japanese youths striving to obtain wealth, status and academic qualifications.

In terms of its strategic position as the basis for establishing a modern state, Japan's Meiji education system was perhaps the most advanced, even compared to the Western nations at that time. Foreign educators such as William S. Clark, Ernest Francisco Fenollosa, Edward S. Morse and Erwin von Bältz were provided large salaries to give modern, scientific higher education to Japanese youth and played an important part in the task of establishing the Imperial University, which was the pinnacle of higher education, emphasising the practical sciences such as medicine, engineering and law etc, and developing personnel who would become the driving force for the modern state. At the same time, this paved the way for ambitious, brilliant and resourceful young people to use their academic background as a lever to obtain 'success in life.'

Since this time, Japan has been an education-conscious or credential society. Of course, Japan is not the only society of this type; the same can also be said of the UK and America – in fact, all modern societies. However, in terms of living under a government that zealously promoted a national policy of transforming Japan into a credential society, Japanese people were fully conscious of the fact they 'live in a credential society.' We know from Takeuchi (1997) that as early as the beginnings of Taishō era, nervous breakdowns among students preparing to sit exams had been a frequent topic in preparatory magazines.

Amid Japan's advancing industrialisation, an education system was established as a recruiting path for civil servants, military personnel, doctors and teachers, as well as office workers, administrators and managers in modern companies. This led to a growing number of tertiary education aspirants and academic institutions. That said, from the pre-war period to the 1950s, the percentage of those who had received a tertiary education was extremely limited (see table 5.2 in chapter 5). Education was still the preserve of affluent households. As in the case of the rural village discussed in chapter 1, junior high school graduates who considered progressing to university was limited to a very small number of children from upper class merchant households and former land owners. Thereafter, the opportunity to advance to university rapidly opened up to people from a wide range of strata following Japan's period of high economic growth. Children from regular strata with scholastic ability also gradually began to seek a university education. On the one hand, this clearly represented the equalisation and opening up of academic opportunities in Japan. On the other hand, it also meant, with the high school advancement rate approaching 100 per cent, the extension of a competitive system of entrance examinations to incorporate children from all strata.

Japan as an education-conscious society has been discussed from various perspectives. First, from the perspective of stratification theory, the following six questions have been raised:

1. To what extent does the opportunity to obtain an academic qualification result in equalisation?
2. What factors determine academic background?
3. To what extent does academic background influence people's social and lifestyle opportunities?
4. Does the mechanism by which people attain status through their background promote or hinder social mobility?
5. Does an education-conscious society really possess a mechanism that develops people with ability and allocates status appropriately?
6. Is it not the case that an education-conscious society results in overheated exam competition, an overemphasis on the one-dimensional values of academic background, an advantage of those students who are merely skilful at exam taking, as well as bullying and truancy?

As a matter of fact, the debates on Japan as an education-conscious society are characterised not only by overly one-sided arguments but by a surprising number of unsubstantiated impressions and preoccupations, as well as contradictions. Since Japanese people are too accustomed to the notion of the education-conscious society, arguments are likely to gain currency by merely appealing to common feelings and images which would conform to the notion. Hence, the task of this chapter is twofold. First, it seeks to sweep away such erroneous images and arguments. Second, it attempts to understand correctly the real issues faced by credential society and education system in an affluent Japan.

## The actual situation surrounding disparity

As chapter 1 discussed the trends in the disparities involved in attaining an academic background based on strata membership, this chapter focuses on the differences in status attainment though academic background. From the Meiji period until today, have the wealthy and poor, and the commoners and nobles in Japanese society really been divided according to 'scholastic ability' and 'the strength of their academic background'? In fact, from the late 1970s to the early 1980s, there has been one dispute over this issue. First, Koike Kazuo and Watanabe Yukio (1979) claimed that disparities based on academic background are not significant in Japan – at least in comparison with the West – and that as a result, there exists 'a false image of Japan as a credential conscious society.' In particular, they raised the following points from data concerning large companies with over 1,000 employees:

1.  While highly educated people certainly occupy a large number of management positions, there are junior high school graduates under the old system who have attained the rank of department head or above. Hence, the difference in education level is not crucial.

2.  Comparing wage disparities based on education background in Japan and America, the disparity between high school and university graduates is greater in America.

3.  Comparing the disparity in white-collar and blue-collar wages in Japan and the (then) EC countries, it is generally greater in the latter.

4.  Based on the 1977 data, while the so-called brand universities were ranked at the top in terms of the number of graduates becoming section heads in companies listed on the Tokyo Stock Exchange, some no-brand universities and regionally-based national universities, which were newly-established after the war, also occupied the upper rank.

Takeuchi (1980) challenged this view when, using an indicator called the turn-out rate, he argued that 'an academic background disparity' exists in which it is easier for graduates from brand universities to enter top-ranking companies and gain promotion.

Unfortunately, after this controversy, no notable fieldwork for international comparison or longitudinal change was carried out on disparities in academic background. This is because the boom surrounding the theory of Japan as a credential society quickly receded after the mid-1970s. The rise and fall of this theory is itself a phenomenon that deserves further consideration, although we will not do so here. Instead, we would like to ascertain clearly the extent to which disparities in academic background actually exist.

Table 2.2 illustrates the relationship between academic background and occupation for males aged in their 40s from 1955 to 1995 (the unemployed and students are excluded). Because such a complicated table did not exist in the past, we will point out what we believe are the important changes from 1955 to 1995.

1. When reading this table, one must be aware of the fact that academic background composition has completely changed in the last 40 years. For instance, the percentage of those whose schooling ended at junior high school has decreased from 72% to 16%; the percentage of high school graduates with no further schooling has increased from 17% to 53%; and the percentage of university graduates has risen from a mere 11% to 31%.

2. Next, there have also been shifts in occupational distribution. In particular, the percentage of those employed in the agriculture, forestry and fisheries sectors has declined from 38% to a mere 3%. Conversely, the percentage of professionals, white-collar workers in large companies and SMEs, and blue-collar workers in SMEs has increased.

3. Meanwhile, the link between academic background and occupation has remained surprisingly stable. Let us consider the 'upper stratum white-collar' category – an amalgam of professionals and white-collar workers in large companies. In 1955, 63.8% of university graduates, 31.1% of high school graduates, and only 4.2% of junior high school graduates entered this stratum. 'Upper stratum white-collar' is an occupational category that is closely linked to higher academic backgrounds. The point is that this has virtually remained unchanged, even up to 1995. Likewise, taking into consideration 'the entire white-collar stratum,' which includes, in addition, those in SMEs and the self-employed, the link with academic background is most obvious. In 1955, 91.5% of university graduates, 58% of high school graduates and only 17.6% of junior high school graduates belonged to this stratum. This situation remained the same still in 1995.

In order to grasp the trend over time in the structure of the relationship between academic background and occupation, we will use an index known as the logarithmic odds ratio.[4] The occupational strata at the top of table 2.2 are divided into two categories: 'upper stratum white-collar' and 'other.' Then, if each two academic backgrounds among three are matched, we can create three types of 2x2 cross tables and calculate three kinds of logarithmic odds ratios based on them for each year. Figure 2.1 has plotted the longitudinal changes of the relationship between academic background and occupation that have been measured as logarithmic odds ratio according to this method.

Table 2.2: Respondent's present occupation by educational background (Males in their forties)

| Survey year | | Professionals | White-collar workers in large companies | White-collar workers in SMEs | Self-employed white-collar workers | Blue-collar workers in large companies | Blue-collar workers in SMEs | Self-employed blue-collar workers | Farmers | N | % |
|---|---|---|---|---|---|---|---|---|---|---|---|
| 1955 | University | 46.8 | 17.0 | 12.8 | 14.9 | 2.1 | 0.0 | 0.0 | 6.4 | 47 | 10.8 |
|  | High school | 8.1 | 23.0 | 8.1 | 18.9 | 10.8 | 1.4 | 13.5 | 16.2 | 74 | 17.0 |
|  | Junior high school | 1.3 | 2.9 | 3.2 | 10.2 | 10.5 | 8.9 | 15.6 | 47.6 | 315 | 72.3 |
|  | Total | 7.3 | 7.8 | 5.1 | 12.2 | 9.6 | 6.7 | 13.5 | 37.8 | 436 | 100.0 |
| 1965 | University | 46.2 | 23.1 | 3.9 | 21.2 | 0.0 | 3.9 | 1.9 | 0.0 | 52 | 12.8 |
|  | High school | 7.5 | 20.4 | 16.1 | 21.5 | 6.5 | 5.4 | 10.8 | 11.8 | 93 | 23.0 |
|  | Junior high school | 0.4 | 12.3 | 5.4 | 13.9 | 15.0 | 13.9 | 11.5 | 27.7 | 260 | 64.2 |
|  | Total | 7.9 | 15.6 | 7.7 | 16.5 | 11.1 | 10.6 | 10.1 | 20.5 | 405 | 100.0 |
| 1975 | University | 27.2 | 26.2 | 16.5 | 19.4 | 1.0 | 1.0 | 6.8 | 1.9 | 103 | 16.3 |
|  | High school | 9.1 | 19.7 | 13.6 | 19.7 | 7.1 | 11.1 | 8.1 | 11.6 | 198 | 31.3 |
|  | Junior high school | 1.5 | 4.8 | 4.5 | 9.1 | 13.9 | 25.7 | 14.2 | 26.3 | 331 | 52.4 |
|  | Total | 8.1 | 13.0 | 9.3 | 14.1 | 9.7 | 17.1 | 11.1 | 17.7 | 632 | 100.0 |
| 1985 | University | 30.2 | 31.8 | 14.7 | 17.8 | 0.8 | 3.1 | 1.6 | 0.0 | 129 | 22.3 |
|  | High school | 2.7 | 20.7 | 16.5 | 16.5 | 16.9 | 13.4 | 10.0 | 3.5 | 261 | 45.1 |
|  | Junior high school | 0.5 | 2.7 | 5.3 | 7.4 | 16.9 | 36.0 | 23.8 | 7.4 | 189 | 32.6 |
|  | Total | 8.1 | 17.3 | 12.4 | 13.8 | 13.3 | 18.5 | 12.6 | 4.0 | 579 | 100.0 |
| 1995 | University | 27.1 | 29.6 | 19.2 | 14.3 | 2.5 | 4.4 | 2.0 | 1.0 | 203 | 31.3 |
|  | High school | 6.7 | 22.5 | 14.3 | 13.5 | 11.1 | 17.3 | 10.2 | 4.4 | 342 | 52.7 |
|  | Junior high school | 1.0 | 1.9 | 6.7 | 4.8 | 10.6 | 52.9 | 19.2 | 2.9 | 104 | 16.0 |
|  | Total | 12.2 | 21.4 | 14.6 | 12.3 | 8.3 | 19.0 | 9.1 | 3.1 | 649 | 100.0 |

Source: SSM Survey data.

From this figure we find that, generally speaking, the academic background – occupation nexus is quite stable. After a closer examination, we can make the following assertions:

1. There are no indices which consistently reveal a declining tendency of disparity between the different academic backgrounds. Rather, when we consider the trends after 1965, it appears that the disparity in the chance of belonging to upper stratum white-collar has a tendency to rise between university and junior high school, and between high school and junior high school graduates.

2. The disparity between the university and the junior high school levels of education appears to have declined somewhat between 1965 and 1975. Returning to table 2.2, the main factor behind this is that in 1965 there were many cases of junior high school graduates landing upper stratum white-collar jobs. Moreover, there was a somewhat strong tendency in 1975 for university graduates to take up 'SME white-collar' jobs, which are not included in the upper stratum white-collar category. This means that during Japan's period of high economic growth, there was a temporary expansion of opportunities for those who had received only compulsory education to land high ranking jobs.

*Figure 2.1:Occupational disparity by educational background (Males in their forties)*

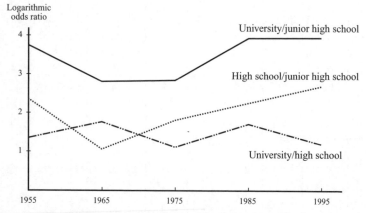

Note: The figures represent the logarithmic odds ratios between those from different educational backgrounds occupying upper white-collar positions. University/junior high school figures, for instance, indicate the logarithmic odds ratios for university graduates compared to those who have completed only junior high school education.. Source: SSM Survey data.

3. The opportunity for lowly educated people to gain promotion was short-lived and, since 1985, has again diminished for junior high school graduates compared to university graduates.

There will be probably not a few people for whom these represent unexpected findings. It is apt to assume that if the number of university graduates increases, a situation ought to arise in which not all university graduates should not simply be able to take those jobs previously considered to be suitable for university graduates, and more of them will be gradually forced to adopt occupations previously the preserve of non-university graduates.[5] In fact, this is, to a certain extent, a correct inference. The percentage of university graduates who landed jobs other than those associated with the 'upper stratum white-collar' category was 36.2% in 1955. This figure reached 46.6% in 1975, before dropping again to 43.3% in 1995 – still higher than in 1955.

However, we have only looked at half of the situation thus far. In fact, in the long-run after 1955, the percentage of high school and junior high school graduates who have landed 'upper stratum white-collar' jobs has declined more than the corresponding percentage of university graduates. This rendered the logarithmic odds ratio either the equivalent to or greater than the 1955 figure. In 1955, 4.1% of Japanese junior high school graduates were able to land 'upper stratum white-collar' jobs. This figure reached 12.7% in 1965, but declined rapidly thereafter and was only 2.9% in 1995.

Consequently, it should be understood, the academic background-occupation nexus certainly did not weaken, but rather strengthened, during the last four decades of the post-war period in Japan. Koike and Watanabe's theory of Japan as a false image of a credential society was correct in dismissing the popular assumptions such as 'Japan is far more credential-oriented than the West' and 'everything is determined by academic background.' But, it is equally erroneous to claim that 'Japan is not an education-conscious society' and 'Japan's level of credentialism is declining.'

## Why does the increase in university graduates not reduce disparities?

### The trend in income disparity

It is a fact of the post-war period in Japan that, while academic opportunities have expanded, the academic background-occupation nexus has strengthened during the last four decades. In a broad sense, this is a phenomenon referred as 'credentialisation.' In other words, the importance of academic background has risen as a means of screening job applicants and 'exclusion' based on academic background has become a matter of course in Japan.

Among the research conducted into Japan as a credential society, the argument that academic background disparities have diminished as a determinant of income disparities was popular for a short period of time. While the aforementioned research by Koike and Watanabe was representative, it was Ushiogi Morikazu's (1977) research that was particularly influential. Ushiogi argued that, as a result of the declining 'disparity in life-time wages according to academic background' and 'disparity in starting salaries according to academic background' – calculated based on the Ministry of Labour's Basic Survey on Wage Structure – during the 1960s to the 1970s, wage disparities based on academic background have decreased. Against the backdrop of Ushiogi's conclusion was the hypothetical theory that 'the more the percentage of university graduates increases among employees, university graduates' wages will approximate those from the other academic background strata.' In an international comparison, Ushiogi emphasised the pertinence of this hypothesis by demonstrating a correlation between the estimate of earning return of higher education and the percentage of those enrolled in higher education on a per capita basis.

Was Ushiogi correct in putting forward this hypothesis? Let us examine the trends in individual income disparities between those with different academic backgrounds based on the SSM Surveys. Because the distribution of both academic background and income differs greatly according to age, the sample for this analysis should be limited to those respondents aged between 40 and 59. While the time when those in this age bracket achieved their academic backgrounds is 20 to 30 years before the respective surveys were conducted, it is for this age bracket that the income disparity in academic background is the most pronounced. Figure 2.2, which divides the respondents according to age (40s and 50s), compares the trends in the average individual incomes of university, high school and junior high school graduates. Because average values are used here, we should note there is a danger that the disparities will appear to be exaggerated. Nevertheless, we can confirm the following points. Comparing the 1995 data with that from 1955, it is only the disparity between university and high school graduates aged in their 50s that has clearly

*Figure 2.2: Income disparity by educational background (Males in their forties and fifties)*

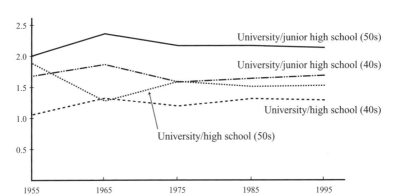

Note: 'University/junior high school (50s)' deals with males in their fifties and shows the trends in the ratios of the mean individual income of university graduates to that of those who have completed only junior high school education. The same measurement procedures apply to other categories. We excluded a few extreme values from the 1965 data because we dealt with the mean incomes.
Source: SSM survey data.

decreased and not the other three disparities. In particular, from 1975 to 1995, all four of the disparity indices were basically stable and, among those respondents in their 50s, the individual income for university graduates has been maintained at 2.1 and 1.5 times that of junior high school and high school graduates, respectively. This is strictly an 'average' disparity. One cannot forget that, on an individual level, there are junior high school graduates who are on higher salaries than what university graduates receive on average and, conversely, there are university graduates who are on lower salaries than what junior high graduates receive on average.[6] In any case, since 1955, one cannot argue that the disparity has a tendency to decline. Instead, the disparity between university and high school graduates in their 40s has a tendency to increase.

The data in this SSM Survey conflicts with Ushiogi's argument. Which of the two is correct? In fact, there are several problems with the data Ushiogi has used. First, the Basic Survey on Wage Structure only examines workers employed in businesses of more than 10 people, and does not include workers in small businesses, the self-employed, farmers and fishers. Next, as a matter of course, starting salaries based on academic background do not mean much when examining income

...es. What is important are the disparities among respondents in their 40s and 50s. Moreover, there are problems associated with .e period examined. For starting salaries, Ushiogi presents the data from 1960 to 1975, and for lifetime wage disparities he only displays the data from 1966 to 1974. It has been shown by the SSM Survey data that the period from 1965 to 1975 was one in which the income disparities between university and junior high school graduates in their 40s and 50s declined. The disparity between university and high school graduates also decreased in relation to obtaining a job and entering the upper stratum white-collar and entire white-collar categories. This raises two possibilities. First, a supply-demand gap in junior high school graduate labour led to a temporary and relative increase in the wages of junior high school graduates. Second, an expansion of corporate activities resulted in high school graduates landing high-ranking jobs. It is also suggested that there was somewhat of a tendency for the expanding number of university graduates to move into low-ranking jobs. However, this was only the case by 1975 and, since 1985, the disparity increased again, but certainly did not decrease.

## The disparity mechanism

The prediction that an increase in the percentage of university graduates will result in their wages approximating those with poor academic backgrounds, at a glance, appears to be correct. However, in order to ascertain whether this is really the case, we must examine wage disparities based on academic background from a solid theoretical perspective. At the present time, there are two main theories related to this question: the theory of human capital and the functional theory of stratification.

The theory of human capital (Becker 1975) posits that since education causes marginal labour productivity to increase, and wages are equally determined by marginal labour productivity, wage disparities based on academic background will result. While there are dubious aspects of the basic micro-economic thesis that wages equate to marginal productivity, if it is understood as merely an approximate model, this argument would not be entirely objectionable. However, there is a theory of screening that challenges the theory of human capital (see Spence 1974; Dore 1976; and Seiyama 1979). This theory claims that education does not increase people's marginal labour productivity – it simply serves to screen those who are highly productive. But, in the end, it agrees on the point that strong academic backgrounds equate to high marginal productivity.

The functional theory of stratification attempts to explain the high incomes of those with strong academic backgrounds by arguing that the enticement of a future high salary is important to make people undergo the psychologically and economically high cost process of tertiary education.[7] This theory is functionalist in the sense that it is premised on the assumption that producing a certain number of tertiary graduates is socially desirable. However, it is not necessarily functionalist if we only reinterpret it in a way that a fixed supply-demand function for tertiary graduates exists in the market.

However, both of these theories do not make any mention of the extent to which wage disparities are fixed between those with higher academic backgrounds and those with average/lower academic backgrounds, and how this changes according to various conditions. The following discussion considers these aspects in terms of a simple supply-demand function model without making assumptions that are overly speculative. Even without an unreasonable assumption, it is possible to hypothesise generally that, regarding identical wage levels, demand for those with strong academic backgrounds is higher than for those with poor academic backgrounds and, conversely, the supply of those with strong academic backgrounds is lower than those with poor academic backgrounds. The demand and supply functions for those with strong academic backgrounds and those with poor academic backgrounds are represented by the curved lines in figure 2.3. It can be seen that a H and L equilibrium wage disparity results from this mechanism.

Using this figure, it can be seen that Ushiogi's hypothesis is based on the conjecture that an increase in university graduates will cause the supply curve for those with strong academic backgrounds to shift to the right (downwards) and the supply curve for those with poor academic backgrounds to shift to the left (upwards). As a result, new wages will be determined at H* and L* and the disparity decreases. However, this conjecture is incomplete. That is, it is based on the assumption that the demand curve is immovable. A plausible forecast is that the demand curve also moves in relation to the increase in university graduates. First, if a major factor in the increase in the supply of university graduates was the strong advancement of the economic system in the background, this factor should also cause an increase in the demand for university graduates. Second, if the decrease in those with poor academic backgrounds accompanies a lowering in their average marginal productivity, it will bring about a shift in the demand curve for those with poor academic backgrounds to the left (downwards). Such a shift in the demand curve will offset the decrease

*Figure 2.3: Supply and demand curves and wage disparities by educational background*

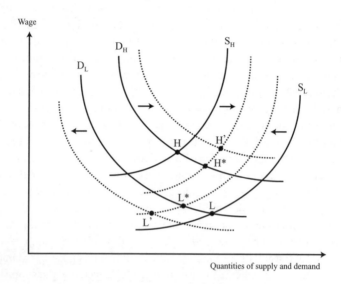

H: High educational background     D: Demand curve
L: Low educational background      S: Supply curve

in disparity caused by the shift in the supply curve. As a result, there will not be a significant change in the new wages, H' and L'.

This, of course, does not lead us to conclude that 'no matter how much variation there is in the percentage of university graduates, income disparities based on academic background necessarily remain fixed.' However, it should be certain that income disparities based on academic background do not correspond to the percentage of university graduates in a determinate way, and it is entirely possible for a decrease in wage disparities to occur while university graduate numbers increase.

## Examining the critical theories

The notion of Japan as an education-conscious society has been subject to various kinds of criticism. In this context, not only does the Japanese mass media bandy about such terrible expressions as 'cram education,' 'overemphasis on intellectual education,' 'examination hell' and 'people placing too much importance on Deviation Score[8]', but every time truancy, school violence, bullying and scandals such as that involving the Aum Supreme Truth sect and high-ranking civil servants occur, people see the Japanese overemphasis on credentialism as the cause. In response to such criticisms, the central and local governments have implemented various educational reforms. These include the school group system, which compels students to attend local schools, the general selection system, an emphasis on school reports, the uniform primary examination and the examination by the National Center for University Entrance Examination, entrance based on recommendations, the breaking up of exam schedules, 'leeway' education, and expulsion of the Deviation Score from course guidance in junior high school. Despite these initiatives, however, there has not been much change in the essence of what underpins Japan as a credential society.

There are four major ways of criticising the credentialism of Japan.

1.  The inhumanity of competition. This is the most general criticism among educators and is widely reported in the Japanese mass media. This criticism can be further divided into the following four categories:

    a.  Education in primary and junior high schools is distorted by examination competition. The original objective of education, i.e., to help students develop their own personality and various abilities is not carried out.

    b.  Because of this competition, education overemphasises scholastic ability and discrimination based on scholastic score is justified.

    c.  As a result of such discrimination, students fall behind and develop inferiority complexes, which are the background causes of delinquency and truancy.

    d.  Education that overemphasises ability and examination results prevents capable students from developing normal personalities and produces students who are highly skilled merely at sitting examinations and lack creativity, a sense of justice and sociability.

2.  Departure from meritocracy. There are many researchers of sociology of education who claim that credentialism is a deviation from the original principles of competency and achievement. In this manner, Shinbori (1977: 245) argues 'It cannot be said that [...] the ability demonstrated by a superior academic background

befits superior status,' while Tomoda (1977: 32) claims 'In order to put the principles of meritocracy and achievement into practice, it is necessary to establish a system that objectively evaluates one's merit and achievement.'

3. Creating and maintaining inequality. There are critics who claim that while credentialism, at a glance, appears to provide an equal opportunity for people to achieve status, it contributes to new forms of inequality and discrimination. Academic background becomes a form of rank-estate and those with strong academic backgrounds are guaranteed success in life and high salaries, whereas those with inferior academic backgrounds have to settle for low-ranking jobs.

4. Reproducing the existing social order. In response to the obvious question 'Why, despite these criticisms, has credentialism in Japan not diminished?' are the following arguments, which suggest that the very nature of credentialism has kept blocking criticisms and has developed a mechanism that makes it immune from them:

   a. Because a credential society infuses people through the education system with the belief that 'academic background is highly valued', disparities based on academic background and the divergence between academic background and ability are not criticised (Bowles and Gintis 1976).

   b. A credential society is premised upon the existing order characterised by a power and status hierarchy, and confers qualifications enabling promotion within that society. Not only are perspectives and capabilities that attempt to criticise and dismantle this order not cultivated, they also recede within the educational system.

   c. In a credential society people in the highly educated stratum are able to give their children a good education using cultural capital and various other resources. A credential society promotes the reproduction of status through academic background, and those with a high status find benefits in maintaining this system (Bourdieu et Passeron 1970; Bourdieu 1979).

It can probably be claimed that each of these criticisms is valid in part. However, behind these criticisms are particular beliefs regarding what an ideal society ought to be like, and are implicitly premised upon a special way of looking at actual society. These criticisms are, in fact, dubious.

1. The criticism of the pathological inhumanity of competition must inevitably imply a total rejection of competition. It ignores the human aspects such as creativity, dynamism, and emotional affection brought about by competition.
2. The criticism of the departure from meritocracy is based on the erroneous assumption that a meritocracy is realistically possible. In addition, it is not aware that the ideals that attempt to achieve a meritocracy contain a certain rationalistic anti-utopian character by design (Young 1958).
3. The criticism regarding the creation and perpetuation of inequality is based on an underlying egalitarianism. Certainly, legal and political equality in the form of human and civil rights and equality in basic life-standards are non-negotiable values. However, premised upon these rights, inequalities which exist in terms of social status, evaluation, economic affluence and lifestyle should be indispensable for freedom and creativity, which also are important modern values. Not only is it not necessary for us to perceive the existence of disparities in occupation and salary based on academic background as undesirable, but we should not actually do so. As will be discussed later, this is because the mechanism inherent in a credential society has a certain knack for making it possible to utilise individual capabilities and motivations to achieve for the greater social good.

The final issue concerning the reproduction of the existing social order will be dealt with in the following section.

## Reproduction or new entry?

### The meaning of the student riots

What caused the decline of the two great social theories of modernisation and Marxism was the simultaneous uprising by radical student movements in the advanced industrialised societies such as France, America, Germany and Japan in 1968. While Marxism was originally the students' theoretical pillar, the movements' increasing radicalisation led them to see actual revolutionaries such as Mao Zedong, Che Gueverra and Frantz Fanon as guiding stars. In addition to their scepticism regarding the system that had developed in the Soviet Union, the student movements gradually began to abandon and revolt against orthodox Marxism. For these students, modernisation theory naturally represented nothing more than colonialism and imperialism.

Marxism was not the original object of their protests. However, the student movements expanded their conflict with orthodox Marxists. It became obvious that the latter could not control the students. As a result, the trust and dreams the intelligentsia and workers had regarding Marxism crumbled.

This might have been simply an opportunity or an excuse for a break away from Marxism. From the 1960s, Marxism essentially lost its credibility in the advanced industrialised countries. Nevertheless, there was a climate in which it was accepted as a fact that the intellectuals should not speak of betraying Marxism. It may have been, then, that the fearless students shouted out 'the Emperor is naked' and the adults only jumped on the bandwagon.

In any case, the 1960s were a watershed in modern world history. The fact that universities were arenas for these ideological conflicts means that credentialism itself in modern societies also reached a turning point. Simply put, this represented the 'massification' of universities. In the case of Japan, after the number of universities increased as a result of post-war educational reforms, the university advancement rate still remained stable for 10 years (refer to figure 5.2 in chapter 5). However, from the 1960s, with the fanfare of high economic growth and human resource development, the advancement rate has risen in a rapid upward curve. New universities were established one after the other while existing universities significantly increased student intakes. University campuses and neighbouring communities were overflowing with students and conveyor-belt education was called into question. While not as far-reaching, a similar situation developed in the other advanced industrialised countries.

This undeniably created a severe identity crisis for students. Until that time, being a university student meant being a part of the elite who deserved special benefits from society. The black close-button collared school uniform was a form of identity and even in restaurants, bookstores and pawn shops 'students' were afforded a certain respect. This situation began to change in the mid-1960s. Students were no longer the elite and were forced to question who they were. What they encountered was a major turning point in the strata system in society. Various events in international politics such as the Vietnam War, Sino-Soviet dispute, Soviet invasion of Czechoslovakia and the Cultural Revolution cast doubts over the existing system and theories. Students perceived these doubts in terms of their own identity crisis. Slogans of the day such as 'self-denial' and 'university dissolution' were derived from these psychological reasons. Students discarded their uniforms and caps. The fact that long hair and jeans became fashionable on campus meant the end of special student privileges.

## The theory of reproduction

However, the expansion of tertiary education and Japan's development as an education-conscious society was in no way impeded by the student riots. The stratification of society based on academic background spread throughout the whole of Japan. It was the theory of reproduction, particularly Bourdieu's theory of cultural reproduction, which attempted to explain this stratification as a form of Marxist class theory without the revolutionary agent. Generally, reproduction theory, as it pertains to strata and class, emphasises two points:

1. Reproduction is carried out from parent to child in each stratum and class.
2. This strata system itself is reproduced.

Therefore, this theory does not provide for reform to the strata system itself as does traditional Marxism.

However, the concept of reproduction is a keyword Marxism employs to analyse capitalist economies. In this context, what is reproduced is 'capital' as a means of production. Bourdieu borrowed this terminology when he conceived the notion that class is reproduced through the agency of cultural capital. In addition to being premised on the structure of a credential society in which attaining an academic background prescribes the attainment of class, Bourdieu's theory of cultural reproduction posits that attaining an academic background does not derive from objective scholastic ability. Instead, it depends on the levels in cultural tastes that are adopted arbitrarily. In addition, these cultural tastes are inherited from parent to child through the agency of cultural capital. On the two points that academic background is basically unrelated to merit and that attaining an academic background and class are still prescribed by affiliation, Bourdieu's theory was diametrically opposed to the theory of achievement.

Bourdieu's theory began to be noticed in Japan in the 1980s and in America and the UK a little earlier. It instantly occupied a position as a major theory in sociology and educational sociology. The following reasons seem to have contributed to the rising influence of Bourdieu's theory:

1. Amid the declining credibility of orthodox Marxism, it presented, as a theory with Marxist tones, a new logic for critiquing the present strata system.

2.  Amid the progress towards an increasingly credential-oriented
    society, it seemed to have provided an explanation as to why
    strata equality and openness certainly did not proceed in a manner
    anticipated by the theory of achievement.
3.  Bourdieu's theory, as a whole, was thought to be an advanced
    theory that reconciled traditional aporia in social theory such as
    that between objectivism and subjectivism and macro and micro.

Frankly speaking, there has been no theory on class and strata with
such a broad perspective as Bourdieu's in recent years. Therefore,
there are sufficient reasons why Bourdieu's theory aroused interest
all over the world. Moreover, there were particular circumstances
surrounding Japanese society in which his theory appears pertinent.
The introduction of the school-group system in the municipality of
Tokyo in which students were forced to attend local schools and the
start of common primary examination for university entrance exams,
both in the 1970s, paradoxically led, as an unintended consequence,
to the increased prominence of the examination system. This also
resulted in an increase in 'early investment in exam coaching
education' (*sōki juken kyōiku tōshi*), in which the primarily urban
salaried worker stratum sends their children to cram schools and
subsequently to national and private combined junior high and high
schools, as well as hiring home tutors. These developments were
understood by Japanese scholars to be in line with the framework of
the theory of cultural reproduction.

Instead of providing an overall examination of Bourdieu's theory,
this section focuses on the theory of class, discussing its key components and empirical relevance. The first point of note when considering its core theoretical components is the concept of cultural capital.
While this concept is often expressed in such specialised terms as
linguistic capital and symbolic capital, it has basically been perceived
as a fundamental factor governing the generational reproduction of
class. It is clear that this concept is analogous to economic capital.
However, it differs from economic capital in that it has remained
ambiguous. The fact that it does not correspond clearly to empirical
referents has been long noted even by sympathetic observers (Osanai
1995). That said, this degree of ambiguity is not a crucial problem.
More important, however, is that most scholars have overlooked the
fact that 'class' itself, which is to be reproduced through the agency of
cultural capital, has not been clearly demonstrated and, as a result, it is
a theory that makes extremely vague claims about what is reproduced
and to what extent .

Bourdieu's theory of class is a hybrid-mix of the following four points:

1. 'Class' as it is used by traditional Marxists.
2. 'Class' in the sense of stratification theory without the special meaning of Marxist theory.
3. 'Cultural class' which is distinguished from economic class.
4. 'Constructed class' in the sense that it is distinguished from class as an entity.

For instance, Bourdieu distinguishes between 'upper class,' 'middle class' and 'the masses' in his books *La Reproduction* and *La Distinction*. However, as he includes 'free enterprise' – that is the self-employed stratum – in his concept of 'upper class,' this terminology is not Marxist but rather akin to stratification theory. Despite this, he uses 'upper class' interchangeably with 'ruling class.' The fact that Bourdieu speaks positively of 'class struggle' suggests he is appealing to a Marxist interpretation. In addition, in his claim that 'as artisans shift to the commercial and industrial management stratum, the volume of economic capital continually increases while the amount of cultural capital declines' (Bourdieu 1979: 180[9]), he does not refer to 'class.' He instead implies that the cultural dimension – as distinct from the economic dimension – forms one strata axis. Moreover, he states that 'As far as classes are concerned, I wanted to break away from the realist view that people commonly have of them and which leads to questions of the type "are intellectuals bourgeois or petty bourgeois?"' (Bourdieu 1990: 49–50). Not only is this a departure from Marxism, but is also a clear declaration of divergence from the concept of class/stratum as a 'natural existence' (Seiyama 1995), upon which most traditional theories of stratification are tacitly premised.

Then, what does Bourdieu's theory, which contains these contradictory concepts of class, attempt to explain; what kind of classes are reproduced and how? In fact, what Bourdieu attempts to demonstrate empirically at best is that, within a certain class hierarchy, in the sense of ordinary stratification studies, there is an increased possibility that the relevance of a father and child's class affiliation will strengthen as a result of the mediating effect of academic background. Hence, even if so-called cultural capital influences the attainment of an academic background – this cannot be empirically ascertained because cultural capital is not observable – the theory of cultural reproduction argues merely that a certain cultural style possessed by family affects the level of educational attainment to some extent. Cultural capital is nothing more than a collection of vague variables which may be called a 'household cultural environment.' This means that it cannot be said that 'cultural reproduction is carried out through an inheritance of cultural capital.'

## The actual situation surrounding generational reproduction

This section explores the actual extent of generational reproduction. For this exploration, we focus on the 'highly educated, upper stratum'. This is operationally defined in the following way. First, we combine 'professionals' and 'white-collar workers in large companies' from table 2.2 to form the category 'upper stratum white-collar.' Then, among those in this stratum we select 'highly educated' (junior college graduate and above) individuals and treat them as constituting the new stratum: the 'highly educated, upper stratum.' The reason why academic background is included in this categorisation is that the theory of cultural reproduction assumes a strong link between academic background and stratum attainment. If reproduction is to be carried out, it ought to be apparent in the reproduction of this 'highly educated, upper stratum'.

Table 2.3 is based on the SSM Survey data. It focuses on males aged between 30 and 59 and shows generational mobility based on this strata division over five survey years from 1955 to 1995. Looking at the table, the percentage of people in the 'highly educated, upper stratum' category is extremely low irrespective of the time period. This has continued to be a distinctive stratum. Several indicators are illustrated in table 2.4 for the purpose of examining the degree of reproduction. The '(pure) reproduction rate' is what is normally known as the 'same occupation rate' and refers to the percentage of respondents who are in the 'highly educated, upper stratum' from among fathers of the same stratum. The reproduction rate from 1955 to 1995 was a consistently high 60%. The 'occupancy rate' is what is commonly known as the 'inheritance rate' and refers to the per-centage, among sons in the 'highly educated, upper stratum,' of those whose fathers are in the same stratum. This percentage rose somewhat from 19.3% in 1955 to 25.2% in 1995. However, it is important to note that among those sons in the 'highly educated, upper stratum' category, an overwhelming number (75%–80%) consistently come from other strata origins. Therefore, while we may say that 'reproduction' occurs in the sense that as about 60% of the children of the extra-high stratum origin remain in the same stratum, the term 'reproduction' is inappropriate in a strict sense, not only because access is not closed to newcomers from the lower strata, but also because a large volume of newcomers continuously exist.

The rise in the occupancy rate in 1995, at a glance, might be interpreted as an increase in the reproduction rate over time. However, the occupancy rate has a natural tendency to increase in accordance with the increase in the percentage of those from the 'highly educated, upper stratum' category in the fathers' generation. In order to control for changes in the strata distribution of the fathers' generation, we can

*Table 2.3: Intergenerational mobility table of highly educated, upper white-collar workers (absolute numbers) covering males in their thirties, forties and fifties*

| | | Respondent's status | |
|---|---|---|---|
| Year | Father's status | Highly educated, upper | Other |
| 1955 | Highly educated, upper | 17 | 12 |
| | Other | 71 | 1159 |
| 1965 | Highly educated, upper | 23 | 14 |
| | Other | 72 | 1278 |
| 1975 | Highly educated, upper | 36 | 22 |
| | Other | 138 | 1529 |
| 1985 | Highly educated, upper | 41 | 31 |
| | Other | 192 | 1366 |
| 1995 | Highly educated, upper | 65 | 45 |
| | Other | 193 | 1138 |

Source: SSM Survey data.

*Table 2.4: Reproduction index of highly educated, upper white-collar workers*

| Year | Reproduction rate | Occupancy rate | Relative reproduction rate | Relative occupancy rate |
|---|---|---|---|---|
| 1955 | 58.6 | 19.3 | 10.16 | 18.85 |
| 1965 | 62.2 | 24.2 | 11.66 | 22.34 |
| 1975 | 62.1 | 20.7 | 7.50 | 14.59 |
| 1985 | 56.9 | 17.6 | 4.62 | 7.93 |
| 1995 | 59.1 | 25.2 | 4.08 | 6.62 |

Note: Derived from Table 2.3.

use two indicators: 'the relative reproduction rate' and 'the relative occupancy rate.' These are defined below:

$$\text{Relative reproduction rate} = \frac{\text{reproduction rate for the highly educated, upper stratum}}{\begin{array}{c}\text{outflow mobility rate from other strata to the}\\ \text{highly educated, upper stratum}\end{array}}$$

$$\text{Relative occupancy rate} = \frac{\text{occupancy rate for the highly educated, upper stratum}}{\begin{array}{c}\text{inflow mobility rate from the highly educated, upper}\\ \text{stratum to other strata}\end{array}}$$

In table 2.4, each of these rates has a tendency to decline significantly. In other words, if we take marginal distribution into consideration, both the reproduction and occupancy rates continue to fall significantly.

In fact, the parallel rise in the university advancement rate according to strata revealed in figure 1.5 in chapter 1 can be shown to imply logically a 'weakening' of the relative reproduction rate.[10] Moreover, as Seiyama (1993) has demonstrated, given the observed relationship between strata affiliation and academic background attainment, if the relationship between the father's strata and the son's strata had been completely mediated through academic background, the relationship between father and son would have been much weaker than what it actually was. This means that even if cultural capital intervenes, the mediation of academic background will work to weaken reproduction. Kondō also notes that 'More people are becoming highly educated without even slightly eliminating the disparity in strata affiliation' while at the same time 'intergenerational mobility has risen' (1997: 32, 35).

At a glance, the reality demonstrated by the data might seem contradictory to the claim that Japan has become an increasingly education-conscious society characterised by rising investment in exam coaching classes, which is believed to predict a strengthening of reproduction. In fact, the importance of academic background as a means of landing upper stratum-type jobs has not declined, but rather increased. As a result, people with high aspirations of achieving a high status have come to invest heavily in their children's education. This forms the basis of the presumption that reproduction is advancing.[11] However, the fact that people are becoming highly educated means namely that the children of those who were not highly educated are also increasingly becoming so and that these children are using academic background as a springboard to the upper occupational strata. Becoming an increasingly education-conscious society means that educational opportunities have expanded, which is contrary to reproduction.

'Reproduction' today is a kind of illusion. While the brothers Takanohana and Wakanohana (who both won the grand championship in *sumo* and whose father was a famous *sumo* wrestler) are conspicuous examples, they are the exception even among *sumo* wrestlers. As is popularly known, a famous professional baseball manager was not successful at reproduction. While the number of cases of university students at Tokyo University and other institutions whose 'fathers are also graduates of prestigious universities' has increased, this only reflects the fact that an increasing number of the fathers' generation were also becoming, on the whole, highly educated. Although it is well known that a large number of second- and third-generation politicians occupy seats in the Diet, it is just abnormal, and special factors are at work here, which do not extend to society as a whole. Because some incidents of reproduction stand out, they make a strong impression upon people. However, if we look at it the other way around, the fact these cases are conspicuous means that there are far more examples of new entrants in general than reproduction.

## The paradox of an education-conscious society

Another issue associated with the theory of reproduction is that the existing order – that is an education-conscious society – reproduces itself through school education. However, whether it be school education, home education or employee education, since passing on the culture and lifestyle of the society in question to new generations is one of the principal aims of education, this represents an obvious truth. It would be terrible if we failed at reproducing social order to a certain extent. Therefore, for this criticism to be valid, it must have a new vista critical of what society ought to be apart from the phenomenon of order reproduction. However, as we have already discussed, there have been no satisfactory criticisms of Japan as a credential society.

Despite the various criticisms and self-styled educational reforms, not only has an education-conscious society obstinately persisted, but it has also increasingly strengthened. Perhaps, we need to revise our thinking. Not only will an education-conscious society not easily collapse, it is actually not a bad thing for people. This is because, in addition to being one of the fundamental mechanisms that support an advanced industrial society and lifestyle affluence, it is closely linked to people's desires and dreams.

Needless to say, occupations and careers are apportioned according to academic background in a credential society. Of course, because academic background is not the same as merit, this apportionment cannot be called a meritocracy. However, it is an undeniable fact that academic background is not unrelated to merit. For instance, in the case of university lectureships, in order to be able to enhance academic research, it essentially requires four years of undergraduate education and more than five years of training at the postgraduate level. It is extremely rare to become a university lecturer without such an academic background. Even salaried workers in large companies do not perform simple clerical tasks. Carrying out corporate activities in an internationally competitive market requires a wide range of skills including language skills and economic knowledge, as well as creative capabilities and education in the fields of planning, business, personnel management and finance. A university education is certainly not a waste of time for those wishing to attain these skills. Needless to say a university diploma is neither sufficient nor necessary in a strict sense for these skills. But, a statistical correlation clearly exists here. Criticisms such as that a culture valued in school education is arbitrary and that academic background has become detached from actual ability are fundamentally flawed.

As long as we approve of contemporary industrial society and civilisation, subject matters and values that are taught in the Japanese education system today should be basically appraised. This is a mechanism that fosters various skills and knowledge, by an education system based on each individual's desire to achieve, before sending students out into society. Modern civilisation relies on people's creative abilities. This opportunity is open to individuals, in principle.

However, this does not mean that Japan's development as an education-conscious society has not been without its problems. On the contrary, there have been many problems. Despite the fact that there has been absolute equality in educational opportunities, Japan as an education-conscious society has clearly functioned as a stratified type of 'ranking.' While higher education does not necessarily guarantee a high income and status, it is accompanied by honour and values. This is perhaps the reason why feelings of inequity towards academic background are strong in Japan. That is, a characteristic of academic background is the fusing together of the two opposing principles of equality and the rank system.

The maturing of modern society has further complicated the issue. In the early period the most serious problem was, despite Fukuzawa's *An Encouragement of Learning*, the inequality in educational opportunities that actually existed. It is concerning this point that criticism by stratification theory, including present-day reproduction theory, of Japan as a credential society, in general, consistently sought to problematise. In the second stage, then, competition over education was called into question. This was the focus of criticisms of Japan as an education-conscious society from the late 1960s to the present day. What is more a new problem has arisen today. The 'truancy' and 'classroom chaos' phenomena are revealing that the individual sense of striving towards occupational attainment through educational attainment has diminished (Morita 1991; Tanaka 1999). These problems are not caused by competition in school education. The fundamental problem is that individuals are no longer as strongly aware of the significance of school education as before. Even though competition has been relaxed, the situation will not improve. The significance of education will become increasingly lost on the Japanese people.

Against the backdrop of this is, of course, nothing other than the affluence of Japanese society overall. This is the paradox of Japan as an education-conscious society. When Japan was mired in poverty, schools were a window on the modern and the progressive, and the path to affluence and honour. Schools were places full of excitement, fun and stimulation. However, the education system, which is a basic mechanism that uses individual attainment as a lever to promote industrialisation at the societal level, has been gradually losing its *raison d'être* as a result of the fruit of affluence brought about by industrialisation.

Japan as an education-conscious society today is saddled with the two mutually conflicting problems associated with the old and the new. While reinforcing academic background disparities or strengthening competition is a quick means of resolving education's loss of meaning, a danger exists that this will aggravate the problem of inequality and competitiveness. On the contrary, eliminating unequal opportunities by educational background and competitiveness will probably magnify the loss of meaning in education. There is no simple prescription for this dilemma.

Amid the increase in affluence and the saturation, as it were, of education levels today, the education-conscious and credential-oriented system will be forced to undergo a transformation as society develops anew. This may be towards an emphasis on more human values, or a new form of elite education centred on graduate schools or neither of these. Whatever changes may occur, it should be towards an education system that continues to encourage dreams and hope in the future for the young generation.

# 3 Occupational Career Structure

Occupation in modern society is something 'one should hope for and acquire' and has become the most important basis for strata differentiation. The process by which people undertake various careers and acquire occupations can be said to be nothing other than the tangible formation of strata. It is self-evident that this freely competitive aspect of occupational attainment has been behind the problems associated with 'the cult of success' that has developed since the Meiji period, as well as contemporary 'education-conscious society.' This chapter explores the structure of such occupational careers and its contributing factors. According to research on stratification, changes in occupational status that accompany career formation are conceptualised as 'social mobility.' The terms 'occupational career' and 'social mobility' introduced in the following discussion will be used interchangeably.

## Occupational careers of the Japanese

### Three strata destinations

First, we will examine broadly the situation surrounding the occupational careers of contemporary Japanese. Figure 3.1, which is based on the results of the 1975 SSM Survey, highlights the major trends in the occupational careers of males – referred to as intra-generational mobility (Hara 1986). It has added 'management' to the eight categories used in table 1.1 and further divided white- and blue-collar according to job description, giving us 12 gross categories.[1] The data upon which this chart is based features detailed information concerning respondents' occupational backgrounds from their first job to current occupation. While SSM Survey data provides full information about respondents' occupational careers, this chart shows the link between first and current occupations alone. Twenty years have already passed since this survey was conducted and while it is possible to explore the trends using the latest data, data from 1975 – immediately following the end of Japan's period of high

*Figure 3.1: Major flows of occupational careers*

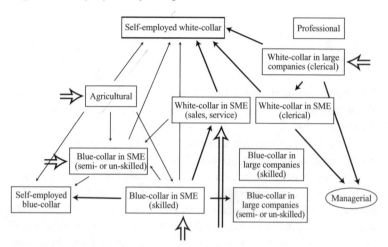

Note: Unshaded arrows (⇐) indicate major paths of entry into first occupations. Those in rectangular boxes are those occupations in which many people remained when these were a first occupation.
Source: Hara (1986: 219, Figure 2). The original source is 1975 SSM Survey data, only for males aged 20–69.

economic growth – is better suited for gaining an understanding of typical occupational careers in post-war Japanese society.

The arrows in the chart indicate the direction in which many people move from one occupation to another. However, as the number of movers is greatly influenced by occupational distribution, the fact that there are merely a large number of movers does not mean there is a particularly strong structural link between two occupations. The thick arrows (←) show that a strong structural links exist, controlling for the various influences exerted by occupational distribution.

Occupational careers begin with either of the occupations featured in the above diagram. The unshaded arrows (⇐) point to five occupations that represent the main paths to entering an occupation (first job). A relatively large number of people begin with these occupations, although a not inconsiderable number also begin with other occupations. However, there are virtually no people whose first jobs were in management. In addition, the number of those whose first job was in agriculture rapidly declined to the point that it can no longer be said to be a major occupational path at present.

isn't spec of
C reciprocality

The number of people who remain in their first job or a similar occupation is quite large. According to the 1975 data, half of the respondents did so. The other respondents moved to different occupations according to paths indicated by the arrows. Here we may note that, among the arrows linking two occupations, there is none that is multi-directional – even in an indirect sense. In other words, it can be said that in Japanese society, as a whole, there is a tendency for occupational careers to flow in particular directions. There are three main directions.

The first is the movement towards self-employed white-collar workers. There are various occupations from which flows of people into this category are observed, where the content of the work performed is different. Those moving from office workers (white-collar workers in large as well as small- and medium-sized enterprises – hereafter cited as SMEs) tend to be engaged mainly in managerial and clerical duties as self-employed. On the other hand, in cases from 'sales and servicing' white-collar workers or from blue-collar workers, they are, as self-employed, mainly engaged in sales or servicing.

The second is the flow towards self-employed blue-collar workers from blue-collar workers in SMEs ('skilled,' unskilled' and 'semi-skilled' blue-collar workers in SMEs) and agriculture. The third is the movement towards management from office workers ('clerical workers' in large companies and SMEs).

There are no arrows pointing to other occupations from these three occupations. In other words, they can be said to be career 'occupational destinations' (*tōtatsu shokugyō*). In contrast to this, the flow of workers in SMEs (white-collar 'clerical' workers, white-collar 'sales and service' workers, as well as 'unskilled, semi-skilled and skilled' workers) are directed towards these occupational destinations, while there are non-negligible flows to SMEs workers from other occupations. That is, SMEs constitute a kind of transit point for occupational careers in Japan.

There are also occupations from which people do not move to occupational destinations. Included among these are professionals and blue-collar ('unskilled, semi-skilled and skilled') workers in large companies. Professionals, in particular, represent an isolated occupation, which experiences very little outflow or inflow. This is not only because it is possible for such workers to enjoy relatively high prestige and incomes without having to move to other occupations, but also because it requires special education and training before working, as well as being difficult to enter from other occupations. 'Semi-skilled and unskilled' blue-collar workers in large companies differ from professionals in that there is an inward flow from 'skilled' blue-collar workers in SMEs. They are in a relatively privileged position compared to other blue-collar workers and represent another occupational destination for those who start their working lives as blue-collar.

What figure 3.1 indicates is nothing but the change in occupational categories from first job to current occupation. Actually, various types of occupational mobility occur during this transition. Particularly important among these movements is inter-firm mobility (including a change of business for the self-employed), which is what 'mobility' or 'a change in occupation' usually implies. According to the 1975 SSM Survey data, about 65% of all respondents had experienced inter-firm mobility on one or more occasions, while the average frequency was 1.34 times.

When does inter-firm mobility occur? In the case of regular employees, the mobility rate is fairly high until the age of 25. It drops a little after that and reaches its lowest point between the ages of 40 and 50, before rising again thereafter. The mobility rate does not differ according to job type or birth cohort (Seiyama and Tsuzuki et al., 1990). The high mobility rate among the younger generation reflects a great deal of trial and error on their part in searching for a suitable occupation, while the rise in the mobility rate among workers over 50 years of age can be attributed to the influence of retirement.

It is important to consider the influence of the period in question when analysing mobility rates. For instance, it was considered that during the period of high economic growth, when significant changes occurred in the demand for labour, the mobility rate generally rose. However, this rise was influenced by a person's age and the period in which they encountered it, which affected the birth cohort. It is difficult to separate the three effects of age, birth cohort and time. However, the influence of age only becomes apparent when we make an estimation based on Nakamura Takashi's (Nakamura 1988) Basian model cohort analysis (Seiyama and Tsuzuki et al., 1990: 86–88). While the influence of time, seen as a reflection of extreme mobility during the post-war period of chaos from 1946 to 1950, was evident, this was not the case with the other periods.

**How are careers determined?**

By what factors are the occupational careers determined, following this pattern? Indeed, an individual's ability and enthusiasm are significant factors, but when considering how these are efficiently utilised, it is important to focus on factors that are influential before one enters the workforce such as parents' status and academic background, as well as the labour market and structure after commencing work.

For instance, it is often said that contemporary modern Japanese society is characterised by a 'second-generation era.' Surely, second generation people cut conspicuous figures even today in the worlds of traditional entertainment and politics. Arguing that Japan is a 'second-generation' society suggests that parents' status basically determines occupational careers. Obviously, this does not mean that the children of heads of a school (*Iemoto*) and members of parliament are necessarily able to follow in their parents' footsteps, but their careers until this stage will be determined by their parents' status.

Even though second-generation entertainers and politicians are conspicuous in Japan, it cannot be argued that throughout the whole of Japanese society the family to which one belongs determines occupational careers. In fact, while the household to which one belongs greatly influences academic achievement and occupations for those beginning work for the first time, it does not necessarily continue to be a direct influence on occupational careers after this time. Rather, as illustrated in figure 3.2, the structure of labour markets is critically important.

Figure 3.2 indicates the results of a path analysis of occupational careers using the same 1975 SSM Survey data as figure 3.1. A path analysis is a statistical method of analysis used to make estimations regarding the extent of the causal relationship among variables (refer to the terminology explanation at the back of this book). The arrows indicate the direction of the causal relationship among the variables while the numbers show the scale. A positive number means a positive relationship. For instance, since the number between academic background and first occupation is positive, we know that the stronger one's academic background, the higher one's occupational status.[2] A path analysis is used to analyse quantitative data. The data for occupational status is taken from a SSM occupational prestige score, which indicates how people grade their occupations in terms of status. For academic background, the number of years one attends school is used. The occupational prestige score was calculated based on a SSM occupational prestige survey carried out at the same time as this survey (refer to the terminology explanation at the back of this book). The curved arrow on the left-hand side of the chart shows a correlation, and not a causal relationship, among the variables, in which the

*Figure 3.2: Determining factors of occupational career*

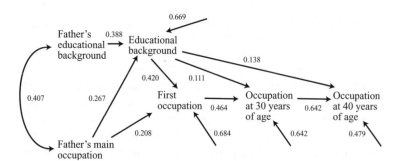

Note: The analysis is based on the sample at 40–69 years of age at the time of survey (1975).
Source: Hara (1979: 226, Table 6-11). The original source is SSM Survey data, only for males.

number is the correlation coefficient. The arrows from the outside and their numbers show exterior influences, which are considered as random and unrelated to the preceding variables.

Let us examine the influence on occupational careers from the respondents' first job to occupations held at the age of 40. The chart only indicates a statistically significant relationship among the variables. To start with, we notice that no arrow points from the respondents' fathers' academic background or occupation – which equates to parents' status – to occupation held at the ages of 30 or 40. In other words, the direct influence of parents' status is limited to the one from respondents' first occupation. Only the occupations respondents hold beforehand exert a significant influence on their occupations between the ages of 30 and 40. As for the direct influence of academic background, it is certainly significant, but far weaker compared to the influence of earlier occupations. In addition, the direct influence of academic background increases slightly more for occupations held at the age of 40 than for those held at the age of 30. This possibly indicates the emergence of disparities based on academic background when respondents seek promotion to managerial positions. We may be reminded here that, in contrast, an analysis of the situation in America revealed that academic background continued to have a strong influence over people's entire working careers (Hara 1979; Blau and Duncan 1967).[3]

# Labour markets and career intentions

## The dual structure of labour markets

Examining the trends in occupational careers, it is revealed that white- and blue-collar occupations in SMEs serve as a kind of entrepot, whereas blue-collar jobs in large companies are isolated or occupational destinations. These features are related to the dual structure of labour markets.

The theory of the dual structure of labour markets differs from the teachings of classical economics in that it posits that labour markets are not homogenous, but are divided into core and peripheral components. It was also agued that this tendency was also found in Western society mainly from the 1970s. But in the case of Japan, it has been noticed that a dual labour market combined with a dual industrial structure comprising large, modern companies and subcontractors, as well as traditional SMEs, has existed from a much earlier time. It was argued that the large corporate sector was favourable in various ways and that, in relation to occupational careers (labour mobility), there exists a 'corporate closeness' (*kigyōteki fūsasei*) in which workers in large companies have a strong tendency to remain in the same company. It is also difficult for workers from SMEs to flow in, and a 'stratified character' in which movement from SMEs to large companies is difficult in comparison to mobility in the opposite direction (Ujihara 1966).

This argument has been explored through various data analyses, and not a few of them have cast doubts over it, however. Many of these analyses were derived from macroscopic data compiled from the Employment Status Survey (*Shūgyō Kōzō Kihon Chōsa*) and, as such, there are limits, as indicated by Ojima Fumiaki (1994), in that one cannot gain an understanding of mobility in an individual's occupational career. An analysis based on SSM Survey data, which is able to trace detailed occupational careers such as the name of the business in which an individual works, a description of the business (industry) and its size, employees' status, job description (occupation) and appointment, can clarify the situation more precisely.

Based on SSM Survey data, 'corporate closeness' is still found to exist to some extent. It is related to the degree of development of the internal labour market. According to an analysis conducted by Seiyama and Tsuzuki et al., the degree is prescribed by the two factors

of company scale and job description. In large companies and in white-
collar occupations the internal labour market is more developed and
there is a strong tendency for occupational mobility to occur within
companies rather than between them. This only means that inter-firm
mobility is, from the beginning, infrequent among large companies,
which does not necessarily mean that inflows from SMEs are more
difficult than between large companies (Seiyama 1994b).

At the same time, the studies by Seiyama et al. and Ojima (1994)
have refuted the notion of 'stratified character.' Focusing on Ojima's
analysis, table 3.1 aggregates the volume of inter-firm mobility on
a company scale that occurs among respondents (ages 20 to 69)
between 1946 and 1985 based on the occupational career data from
the 1985 SSM Survey (excluding movement to and from agriculture).
If the stratified character of labour markets does exist, the volume
of movement from large-scale companies to small firms ought to be
greater than vice versa. Surely, self-employed occupations, which are,
for the most part, small-scale operations, experience excess inflows
vis-à-vis any sized company, and conversely, large companies with
over 1,000 employees experience excess outflows.

But this does not necessarily mean that the same tendency is
evident for companies of all-scales. In addition, it is unreasonable
to use the actual volume of movement as an indicator of the strength
of the linkages between companies. Because there are differences
among sectors in their scale, that is, each sector's number of people

*Table 3.1: Inter-company job-switchers by firm size (number of
employees)*

| From | To | | | | | | | | |
|------|------------------|-----|-------|-------|---------|---------|-------|---------------------|-------|
| | Self-employed | 1–9 | 10–29 | 30–99 | 100–299 | 300–999 | 1000– | Government office | Total |
| Self-employed | 73 | 28 | 28 | 24 | 21 | 10 | 19 | 6 | 209 |
| 1–9 | 94 | 110 | 71 | 48 | 19 | 15 | 15 | 6 | 378 |
| 10–29 | 60 | 66 | 95 | 50 | 34 | 15 | 16 | 11 | 347 |
| 30–99 | 55 | 34 | 64 | 76 | 31 | 15 | 20 | 12 | 307 |
| 100–299 | 36 | 24 | 35 | 25 | 33 | 12 | 19 | 9 | 193 |
| 300–999 | 27 | 17 | 19 | 24 | 13 | 17 | 23 | 5 | 145 |
| 1000– | 61 | 25 | 23 | 37 | 30 | 41 | 67 | 25 | 309 |
| Government office | 23 | 7 | 7 | 11 | 11 | 8 | 22 | 61 | 150 |
| Total | 429 | 311 | 342 | 295 | 192 | 133 | 201 | 135 | 2038 |

Source: Ojima (1994: 46, Table 2). The original source is 1985 SSM Survey data, but
only for males aged 20–69.

(reflected in the aggregates at the bottom of the table), which is referred to as the market size of career mobility, it is necessary to control for the influence of this. Ojima employed what is called a log-linear analysis to explore the presence or absence of stratified character more precisely.

A log-linear analysis is used to evaluate statistically the fitness of specific frequency distribution models in the table (refer to the terminology explanation at the back of this book). According to Ojima, when we control the differences in market scale according to size in the case of table 3.1, the distribution model (the semi-symmetrical model), which posits that there are no differences in the volume of movement based on the direction of mobility between companies of different scales, is an extremely good fit. Examining each mobility pattern separately based on period and industry reveals that 'the stratified character of the labour market' holds only within the manufacturing industry between 1946 and 1960. In this manner, one can argue that the dual labour market in Japanese society is extremely limited.

## The truth and falsehood of permanent employment

It is commonly accepted that 'permanent employment' (*shūshin koyō*) is an employment practice adopted by mainly large companies in Japan. According to Nomura Masami (1994), the following two points are important in the definition of permanent employment:

1. Companies hire people upon their graduation and guarantee employment until retirement.
2. School graduates enter a company immediately after graduation and continue to work at that company until retirement.

As a matter of fact, the Japanese word '*shūshin koyō*' was the translation from 'permanent employment' in the book entitled *The Japanese Factory: Aspects of its Social Organization* written by James C. Abbeglen (1958) and was rapidly popularised thereafter.

However, according to Nomura, this popular notion is extremely questionable. This definition only applies strictly to an elite minority of highly-educated white-collar workers in large companies after the Meiji period. In contemporary Japanese society regular male employees in large companies may approximate this. However, because of mass personnel transfers to subsidiary companies and the like, only a small minority of employees, in fact, remain in the one company for their entire working lives.

Two factors during Japan's period of high economic growth, in particular, contributed to the popular notion of permanent employment:

1. A scarcity of young workers.
2. To cope with technological innovation, large companies hired large numbers of new graduates as blue-collar workers and strived to keep them at the company (long-term employment).

However, the reality was that, along with economic fluctuations, large-scale mid-career recruiting and mass layoffs were common.

Nomura's argument, for the most part, completely contradicts the popular view. However, it should be noted that the arguments by Nomura and other economists were based mainly on administrative employment policy and on subjective aspects such as work expectations among employees in large companies, which are insufficient to gain a true understanding of working conditions. Inada Masaya (1998) carried out a fascinating analysis of working conditions in Japan, using occupational career data from SSM Surveys.

Inada seeks to answer two questions concerning the practice of long-term employment connected to permanent employment:

1. Does this practice exist in Japanese companies?
2. If it does, when was it established?

He conducts two types of analysis in order to answer these questions. The first is a retrospective analysis, which focuses on how the rate of long-term employees ('long-term' according to Inada, refers to 20 years or more) changed through the different survey years. The second is an event history analysis, which applies a stochastic process model to the occupational career data and analyses how the average number of expected years people have been working at the same company has changed (refer to the terminology explanation at the back of this book).[4]

Inada notes that according to the first analysis, in post-war Japanese society there has been a tendency for employees of any type of job to stay longer in the same company. For instance, table 3.2 shows, among people with between 20 to 30 years work experience, the percentage of employees whose continuing employment in the same company exceeds 20 years, for each survey data. The sorting of employees into white-collar and blue-collar workers is based on the job description when entering the company. The highest percentage of long-term employment is shown by white-collar workers in large companies. The percentage rose sharply among those entering companies between 1946 and 1955 and continued to increase thereafter. While the percentage is somewhat low for blue-collar workers in large

*Table 3.2: Long-term employees with 20 or more years service (%)*

| Occupation at the time of company entry | Year of entry | | | |
|---|---|---|---|---|
| | 1936–45 | 1946–55 | 1956–65 | 1966–75 |
| Professional | 57.1 (7) | 75.0 (12) | 13.3 (15) | 37.5 (8) |
| White-collar in LC | 22.9 (35) | 64.6 (65) | 66.7 (96) | 83.1 (59) |
| White-collar in SME | 53.1 (49) | 40.8 (49) | 46.8 (62) | 50.0 (34) |
| Blue-collar in LC | 17.5 (40) | 48.8 (84) | 67.7 (96) | 71.9 (32) |
| Blue-collar in SME | 34.9 (63) | 20.6 (126) | 40.9 (127) | 46.8 (47) |

Note: The numbers in the brackets show the sample sizes.
Source: Inada (1998: 70, Table 3). The original source is 1995 SSM Survey data, but only for males aged 20–69.

companies, a similar trend is evident. Combining these findings with the results from other data, Inada suggested that white-collar workers increasingly became long-term company employees during the twenty-year period from 1936 to 1955, while for blue-collar workers, this occurred over a thirty-year period from 1946 to 1975.

In the case of workers in SMEs, the long-term employment percentage for those who entered companies between 1946 and 1955 dropped temporarily, but continued to rise thereafter. In addition, the percentage consistently rose even for self-employed workers and professionals not appearing in table 3.2.

According to the event history analysis, the average number of expected years people worked at the same company increased for all job descriptions in the late 1960s. Combining this with the aforementioned retrospective analysis, Inada notes that it was during this period that 'long-term employment' among companies and 'long-term continual service' for workers was established as a social norm. This is fairly consistent with Nomura's claims regarding the establishment of permanent employment as a socially common notion. However, according to Inada, this is not due to the introduction of a any particular institution, but to an accumulation of coincidental events such as high economic growth and the chaotic economic situation during the war and early post-war years – 'historic and coincidental events' so to speak.

## The shift in career orientations

Apart from Inada's claims, the aforementioned argument is mainly based on analyses of the data of SSM Surveys in 1975 and 1985. This is because the data of these years is considered to best reflect the

*Table 3.3: Trends in inter-company mobility*

(a) Number of companies employed by

| Age bracket | Year of survey | | | | |
|---|---|---|---|---|---|
| | 1955 | 1965 | 1975 | 1985 | 1995 |
| 20s | 1.81 | 1.72 | 1.74 | 1.58 | 1.74 |
| 30s | 2.51 | 2.15 | 2.14 | 1.99 | 1.98 |
| 40s | 2.74 | 2.85 | 2.34 | 2.23 | 2.29 |
| 50s | 2.46 | 2.78 | 2.59 | 2.36 | 2.45 |
| 60s | 2.25 | 2.95 | 2.87 | 2.93 | 2.64 |
| Total | 2.35 | 2.37 | 2.23 | 2.16 | 2.24 |

(b) Frequency of inter-company movements per year

| Age bracket | Year of survey | | | | |
|---|---|---|---|---|---|
| | 1955 | 1965 | 1975 | 1985 | 1995 |
| 20s | 0.102 | 0.095 | 0.104 | 0.099 | 0.153 |
| 30s | 0.089 | 0.067 | 0.070 | 0.062 | 0.069 |
| 40s | 0.064 | 0.068 | 0.051 | 0.048 | 0.051 |
| 50s | 0.039 | 0.047 | 0.044 | 0.038 | 0.040 |
| 60s | 0.027 | 0.042 | 0.040 | 0.042 | 0.036 |
| Total | 0.058 | 0.060 | 0.055 | 0.048 | 0.048 |

Source: SSM Survey data. Only for males.

characteristics of 'post-war' Japanese society, focusing on the period
of high economic growth. Then, the question will arise: how have
people's occupational careers changed through the levelling-off of
growth rates following this, the emergence of the bubble economy
and its subsequent collapse? Moreover, how will this change in the
future?

The most noticeable recent change is the clear emergence of an
increasing fluidity of occupational careers centring on the young
generations of society, which had only formerly been spoken of in
a notional sense. Table 3.3 shows respondents' mean number of
companies employed by, as well as average yearly frequency of
corporate mobility according to age-group, based on data collected
from five SSM Surveys between 1955 and 1995. According to this
table, until 1985 there was either no discernible change or a decrease
for any age-group. However, from 1985 to 1995, not only was there no

decrease evident (apart from those in their 60s), but for those in their 20s, both values clearly increased.

Does this trend towards fluidity between 1985 and 1995 indicate a change in orientations towards occupational careers in which people have developed positive views in regard to job changes (inter-firm mobility)? Or does it reflect an increase in layoffs and corporate restructuring as a result of the recession following the collapse of Japan's bubble economy?

Figure 3.3 is based on the results of the 1975 SSM Survey and The National Character Survey conducted in 1993. The Figure shows the ratio of people who have a positive attitude towards inter-firm mobility to those with negative feelings according to age-group. Because the questionnaires in the two surveys are different, a straightforward comparison is impossible. Nevertheless, changes are obvious. In 1975, the number of people with a positive attitude was only half (0.48) of those with negative feelings. No matter what age-group, negative attitudes were preponderant. On the other hand, according to the 1993 results, though the negative attitudes were still superior

*Figure 3.3: Changes in the views on job-changes*

Ratio (Positive/negative)

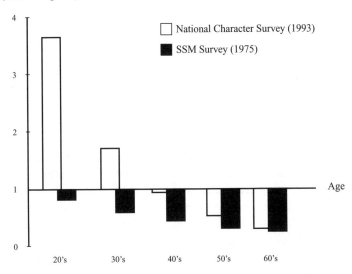

Note: The National Character Survey data was provided by Yoshiyuki Sakamoto at the Institute of Statistical Mathematics.

as a whole (0.92), both were roughly even. In particular, there was an overwhelming majority of people with positive attitudes among 20 and 30 year olds.

However, while the change in orientations is obvious, it is important to notice that the increase in mobility (trend towards fluidity) shown in table 3.3 does not necessarily indicate an increase in favourable or upward mobility. Based on the results of the 1973 National Survey of Occupational Mobility, Hara (1986) once demonstrated that the ratio between the volume of induced mobility – finding a better company or job – and the volume of forced mobility – arising from dissatisfaction with the company and the job, or from dismissal or bankruptcy – was roughly 1:2, and that inter-firm mobility is not always beneficial for workers. Unfortunately, as there is no data for comparison, we may not ascertain whether any change occurred in this favourable/unfavourable mobility composition.

Whatever the determining factors, however, it seems, the practice among large companies of 'permanent employment' established during the period of high economic growth has been gradually waning. It is too early to conclude whether this is a temporary phenomenon linked to the recession or is a new trend impossible to turn back. Opinion is divided in Japan as to whether 'permanent employment' is an advantage or disadvantage for Japanese corporate competitiveness. However, there is no doubt that the current recession has shaken the foundations of this practice and that Japan's employment system has reached a turning point.

## Fluidity and openness

### Status inheritance from parent to child

Among the myriad of sociological factors, it is undeniable that academic background (education) and family background (parent's status) are of importance. Family and relatives are claimed to be the most significant determinants of individual's occupational career and other status. In societies characterised by the class and caste systems children are almost entirely forced to adopt the same class and caste as their families (parents).

Modern society has basically dismissed this principle of status determination. It is claimed that the freedom to select an occupation is an individual's basic right. That is, equal opportunities to choose an occupation must be guaranteed irrespective of the status and class of one's parent so that an individual is able to obtain an occupation in accordance with his/her abilities and desires. This is congruent with societal demands to mobilise people's energies in order to promote industrial modernisation (industrialisation).

However, the extent of openness in societies is believed to be insufficient. Even in contemporary industrial societies family influences an individual's occupational career in various ways and it cannot be denied that the higher a parent's occupational status, the higher the child's will be. In other words, social resources such as wealth, privileges and information etc. are directly passed from parent to child and, at the same time, a parent's occupational status determines a child's means of obtaining an occupation in terms of school education and occupational information. In addition, a parent's lifestyle and social consciousness influence a child's motives to achieve status or enter an occupation and the necessary basic abilities to adapt in school and work life.

In this manner, while it is not an institutional (*mibun*) constraint, it seems that parents' occupational status continues to exert a significant influence on occupational careers for various reasons and that, because of this, equal opportunities to choose an occupation are impeded. Consequently, stratification research has payed considerable attention to the influence of parents' status on occupational careers, in other words, social openness.

## Mobility indicators that capture fluidity and openness

It is 'industrialisation theory' that has guided stratification study as a kind of basic academic assumption regarding this issue. This theory perceives industrialisation as a process of long-term comprehensive social changes. But in particular it means first of all the change in industrial composition, which causes mass social mobility (occupational mobility) and social fluidity. The noticeable point of this change is the move from farming and self-employment to various kinds of employment. In this case, education (academic background) becomes an important means of acquiring occupational status in place of a parent's occupation and assets. This leads to progress towards the opening up of society. The second change is the increase in the size of organisations accompanied by industrialisation, which promotes role and status differentiation. Managing diversely differentiated organisations requires one to be objectively rational and bureaucratic. As a result, relocating personnel within the organisation must rely on so-called achievement principles, which also lead towards an opening up of society.

Based on the argument above, many researchers of stratification considered that even if the influence of a parent's occupational status will not entirely disappear, the opening up of society basically progresses in accordance with advances in industrialisation. In order to ascertain whether this is in fact true, this section examines the relationship between a parent's and children's occupational status and the changes to this.

While the most recent (1995) inter-generational mobility table (table 1.1) and mobility indicators (table 1.2) were discussed in chapter one, table 3.4 shows the main mobility indicators using the mobility tables between 1955 and 1985, including indicators in 1995.

Here we explain each of the mobility indicators based on the simplest two strata mobility tables (table 3.5).

*Table 3.4: Trends in mobility indices (1955–95)*

| Index | Year of survey | | | | |
|---|---|---|---|---|---|
| | 1955 | 1965 | 1975 | 1985 | 1995 |
| Gross mobility rate | 0.494 | 0.655 | 0.686 | 0.711 | 0.732 |
| Structural mobility rate | 0.188 | 0.320 | 0.342 | 0.334 | 0.282 |
| Circular mobility rate | 0.306 | 0.335 | 0.343 | 0.378 | 0.450 |
| Coefficient of individual openness | | | | | |
| Professional | 0.530 | 0.666 | 0.676 | 0.701 | 0.620 |
| White-collar in LC | 0.853 | 0.803 | 0.748 | 0.742 | 0.857 |
| White-collar in SME | 0.888 | 0.828 | 0.879 | 0.845 | 0.915 |
| Self-employed white-collar | 0.700 | 0.663 | 0.713 | 0.651 | 0.672 |
| Blue-collar in LC | 0.729 | 0.833 | 0.846 | 0.822 | 0.934 |
| Blue-collar in SME | 0.780 | 0.813 | 0.747 | 0.821 | 0.869 |
| Self-employed blue-collar | 0.708 | 0.713 | 0.717 | 0.667 | 0.765 |
| Farming | 0.256 | 0.256 | 0.243 | 0.195 | 0.182 |
| Coefficient of overall openness | 0.570 | 0.646 | 0.661 | 0.685 | 0.748 |
| Logarithmic odds ratio | | | | | |
| Professional | 3.00 | 2.37 | 2.29 | 1.88 | 2.08 |
| White-collar in LC | 1.21 | 1.11 | 1.38 | 1.30 | 0.79 |
| White-collar in SME | 1.30 | 1.31 | 0.83 | 0.97 | 0.58 |
| Self-employed white-collar | 1.93 | 2.09 | 1.64 | 1.99 | 1.93 |
| Blue-collar in LC | 1.88 | 1.09 | 1.09 | 1.29 | 0.62 |
| Blue-collar in SME | 1.54 | 0.96 | 1.11 | 0.81 | 0.67 |
| Self-employed blue-collar | 1.77 | 1.70 | 1.78 | 1.84 | 1.32 |
| Farming | 2.68 | 2.31 | 2.37 | 2.73 | 3.00 |

Source: SSM Survey data. Only for males aged 20–69.

*Table 3.5: Intergenerational mobility table*

| | Child's stratum | | |
|---|---|---|---|
| **Father's stratum** | **Stratum A** | **Stratum B** | **Total** |
| Stratum A | $n_{11}$ | $n_{12}$ | $n_{1.}$ |
| Stratum B | $n_{21}$ | $n_{22}$ | $n_{2.}$ |
| Total | $n_{.1}$ | $n_{.2}$ | $n_{..}$ |

The gross, structural and circular mobility rates are the proportions of each volume of mobility among the sample aggregate $n...$ The volume of gross mobility refers to the number of people who have experienced movement and is represented by $n.. - (n_{11} + n_{22})$. When the number of strata is $I$, it is generally shown as:

$$\text{Volume of gross mobility} = n.. - \sum_{i=1}^{I} n_{ii}$$

Structural mobility conceptualises a type of mobility that inevitably arises due to the differences in strata distribution between fathers' and child's generations. If stratum A is an expanded stratum (a stratum in which distribution is greater in the child's generation than that of the father), $n_{.1} - n_{1.}$ becomes the volume of structural inflow mobility. Conversely, stratum B is a contracted stratum, and $n_{2.} - n_{.2}$ becomes the volume of structural outflow mobility of B. This accords, in fact, with the volume of structural inflow mobility in stratum A. Whichever, stratum A or B, is expanded, the volume of structural mobility in society as a whole can be computed as $( | n_{.1} - n_{1.} | + | n_{2.} - n_{.2} | ) / 2$. In a general equation it becomes:

$$\text{Volume of structural mobility} = \sum_{i=1}^{I} | n_{i.} - n_{.i} | / 2.$$

The volume of circular mobility is the difference between the volume of gross mobility and the volume of structural mobility. If stratum A is an expanded stratum, the volume of gross inflow mobility is $n_{.1} - n_{11}$ while the volume of structural inflow mobility is $n_{.1} - n_{1.}$. As a result, the volume of circular inflow mobility becomes $n_{1.} - n_{11}$. If we look at the volume of outflows, the volume of gross outflow mobility is $n_{1.} - n_{11}$ and, because structural outflow mobility is impossible in the case of an expanded stratum, its volume is zero. Consequently, the volume of circular outflow mobility $n_{.1} - n_{11}$, is equivalent to the volume of circular inflow mobility. The volume of circular mobility in society as a whole is $(n_{1.} - n_{11}) + (n_{.2} - n_{22})$. In terms of a general equation, it becomes:

$$\text{The volume of circular mobility} = \sum_{i=1}^{I} \{\min (n_{i.}, n_{.i}) - n_{ii}\}$$

The coefficient of individual (i. e., for each stratum) openness and the logarithmic odds ratio are suited to examining the fluidity of each stratum. The expected volume of mobility when mobility is assumed to occur independently of a father's stratum is called the volume of independent mobility. The coefficient of individual stratum openness is the value of the volume of independent circular mobility divided by the actual volume of circular mobility for each stratum. The value is 1 when both volumes are the same. But normally, because there is a tendency for status to be passed between father and child (in other words, the actual volume of non-mobility is greater than independent non-mobility), it is less than one. If stratum A is an expanded stratum, the volume of independent structural mobility is $n_{1.} - n_{1.} \cdot n_{.1}/n_{..}$. The volume of (individual) independent structural mobility and the (actual) volume of structural mobility per stratum are generally shown as:

$$\begin{array}{l}\text{The volume of individual} \\ \text{independent circular mobility}\end{array} = \min (n_{i.}, n_{.i}) - n_{i.} \cdot n_{.i}/n_{..}$$

$$\text{The volume of actual individual circular mobility} = \min (n_{i.}, n_{.i}) - n_{ii}$$

The coefficient of overall openness can be derived from the ratio of the total sums of the above two kinds of individual mobility (Yasuda 1971).

In the case of a logarithmic odds ratio, if movement towards stratum A is unrelated to the father's stratum, it is expected that there is no difference between non-mobility in stratum A $(n_{11}/n_{12})$ and movement from stratum B to stratum A $(n_{21}/n_{22})$. The ratio between the two is:

$$\text{Odds ratio} = (n_{11}/n_{12})/(n_{21}/n_{22}) = n_{11}n_{22}/n_{12}n_{21}$$

Moreover, it is the logarithmic odds ratio that is transformed in a logarithmic sense. This is zero when there is independent mobility, and the lower the strata fluidity and the smaller the mobility, the greater the numeric value moves in a positive direction. In the event the number of strata is greater than two, it is acceptable to substitute stratum B in table 3.5 with all strata, apart from stratum A (Seiyama 1986).

**Trends in fluidity and openness**

As table 3.4 highlights, what was discussed for the mobility table from 1995 in chapter one seems still basically applicable to the earlier surveys. At a first glance, the change in the numeric value might appear to accord, as a whole, with the claims made by industrialisation theory.

For instance, if we examine the gross mobility rate, which may be the basic indicator of fluidity, it has consistently tended to increase. On the other hand, the structural mobility rate peaked in 1975 and declined thereafter. This reflects Japan's transition from high to low economic growth. Nevertheless, the indicators of openness, namely the circular mobility rate and the coefficient of overall openness, have consistently risen.

One may expect that the overall changes in fluidity and openness indicators are based on similar changes in individual strata. However, there is no stratum that shows a constant rise similar to the overall changes. Let us relax the comparison level and examine the changes from 1955 to 1985 and from 1965 to 1995, those within one generation (about thirty years). The strata which show changes that are congruent with industrialisation theory are, according to the coefficient of individual openness, blue-collar workers in large companies and SMEs and, according to the logarithmic odds ratio, professionals and white-collar workers in SMEs besides the above two strata. In other words, strictly speaking, among the eight individual strata, there is none that evinces changes congruent with industrialisation theory, and barely four that do so if we relax the comparison level.

In order to evaluate the trends more in detail, it is necessary to shed light on the data from different angles. One of the problems associated with table 3.4 is that the mobility table used to obtain these numeric values encompasses a total sample, that is, from people aged between 20 and 69. If people generally enter an occupation between the ages of 15 and shortly after 20, it was 50–55 years before for 69 year olds, and their current occupations is the result of an accumulation of occupational careers since then. On the other hand, 20 year olds are those who are starting work. Hence, it is impossible to identify the time of occupational structure that each mobility table reflects.

Figure 3.4 demonstrates the changes in the mobility indicators for only those people aged between 25 and 34 based on each SSM Survey data.[5] Utilising occupational career data from the 1955 survey, this figure reconstructs a social mobility table, which would have possibly been equivalent to that of surveys conducted in 1935 and 1945 had we done them, as well as the mobility indicators for that table.[6] Because the target age group is limited, each piece of data reflects the mobility structure of the 10 to 15 year period before the survey was conducted. In other words, figure 3.4 highlights the changes in the mobility structure of Japanese society from the early Shōwa period until the 1980s. However, because the size of the sample is small, as a result of concentrating on a limited age group, we have made calculations based on the four strata categories of white-collar ( professionals, management and clerical), grey-collar (sales and services), blue-collar and agriculture. Of course, the numeric value of the mobility indicators is low when compared to the eight categories.

Because we have changed the age group and strata categories, the trends other than structural mobility rate differ from those in Table 3.4, and after the long-term upward trend, these declined from 1985 or 1995 in Figure 3.4. Here, the decline in 1955 and subsequent rapid rise in the four indicators seems to be a reflection of two exceptional

*Figure 3.4: Trends in mobility indices (1935–95)*

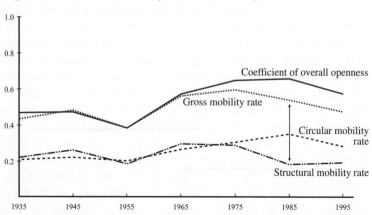

Source: SSM Survey data. Only for males aged 25–34. Values in 1935 and 1945 were estimated from the 1955 data. The circular mobility rate is the difference between the gross and structural mobility rates.

and anomalous phenomena: the mass return to farming (to home villages) resulting from Japan's wartime defeat and the subsequent mass abandonment of agriculture due to the period of high economic growth. In order to understand long-term trends, one should take these phenomena into consideration.

### The log-linear model and FJH thesis

The second problem associated with an analysis based on mobility indicators is that even if there is a change in numeric values, it is unclear whether this is statistically significant or not. In other words, no method has been developed for carrying out a direct statistical test on these indicators. One of the methodologies designed to resolve this issue is to use a log-linear model, which has been adopted in an analysis by Ojima Fumiaki, as well as Featherman, Jones and Hauser's (1975) FJH thesis, which employs this method (see chapter one).

This section employs a similar method of analysis. If we express the FJH thesis in terms of a frequency distribution model, it is represented by a model in which the frequency is determined by the effect of the marginal distributions of the father's and son's strata at the time each survey was conducted, as well as the invariant strength of the linkage between the father's and son's strata. We will call this the 'invariant opportunity model' (*kikai fuhen moderu* – refer to the terminology section at the back of this book). Table 3.6 displays the results of a chi-square test of the distribution of the anticipated mobility tables from 1935 to 1995 based on the invariant opportunity model and its degree of fitness to the actual mobility tables.

The upper level displays the results of the mobility table over seven points in time and the risk ratio ($p$) of the hypothesis that the data does not accord with the invariant opportunity model is at the tenuous level of 8%. Hence, if we set the significance level (i.e., the criterion value of risk ratio below which the model is rejected) at 10%, then we may conclude that the invariant model does not hold. If we set it at 5%,

*Table 3.6: Fitness of fixed opportunity model*

| Comparison | $x_G^2$ | df | p |
|---|---|---|---|
| 7 time points from 1935 to 1995 | 69.08 | 54 | 0.079 |
| 6 time points excluding 1955 | 44.92 | 45 | 0.484 |

Note: The same data as Figure 3.4 were used.

the model does hold. (Lower the risk ratio, higher the probability that the model does not hold). However, if we exclude the 1955 data from these mobility tables, the risk ratio is about 48% and the degree of conformity rises dramatically. Thus, if we consider the results of the analysis that was conducted after changing the strata categories and exclude the 1955 data, which reflects the anomalies of the wartime and immediate post-war periods, it is appropriate to conclude that the invariant opportunity model is applicable not only to post-war Japanese society, but to the period from the beginning of the Shōwa era to the present.[7] That is, apart from the effect of the changes in occupational distribution among the parents' and children's genera- tion, the strength of the link among strata, namely, inter-generational mobility between strata, has remained constant since the early Shōwa period. Therefore, social openness has certainly not increased during this time.

In addition to this analysis, many other scholars have also analysed the trends in inter-generational mobility in Japan. Even though these scholars all use the same SSM Survey data, they adopt different strata categories and methods of analysis, and their results differ slightly. Generally, while there is a tendency among those analyses based on the coefficient of overall openness to claim a basic increase in openness, there is also an inclination to argue that, when based on the log-linear model analysis, openness has not changed significantly.[8]

At least part of the difference between the two analyses is due to the fact that the total volume of circular mobility is prescribed to a cer- tain extent by the ratio of agricultural workers. This occurs because of the conspicuous differences in the openness of agriculture and the other strata. Because agriculture is a contracting stratum, new entry into it becomes circular mobility. However, not only because there are external factors such as the legal difficulty of purchasing agricultural land, but because agriculture has had very little appeal during Japan's industrialisation, entry has been extremely limited. Because of the inherently low levels of openness in agriculture, the greater the pro- portion of farmers among the fathers' stratum, the smaller the ratio of total circular mobility (Seiyama et al., 1988: 46–47). One of the rea- sons why the coefficient of overall openness is beginning to decline among 25–34 year olds in figure 3.4, whereas in table 3.4 it has still risen for total respondents, is the small proportion of farmers among the fathers' stratum for the young cohort.

In this manner, because the coefficient of overall openness is influenced by the proportion of people who belong to the agricultural stratum, which has extremely low levels of openness, it is necessary to examine precisely the trends in the coefficient of individual stratum openness. By doing this, it will be recalled that among the eight strata in table 3.4, only two were congruent with industrialisation theory.

What kind of conclusion can we derive based on the above results of the various analyses of the mobility table? First, based on figure 3.4, it can be said that the gross and structural mobility rates rose consistently from the early Shōwa period until the 1970s, and they declined thereafter. This can be explained by Japan's industrialisation process, which centred on heavy industry, during the period of high economic growth and the ensuing period of low growth. While the expression 'rose consistently' may be too strong, there was clearly a difference between pre-war and post-war levels of gross and structural mobility. This is very much a change made applicable by 'industrialisation theory.'

The coefficient of overall openness and circular mobility rate (the difference between gross and structural mobility rates), which are the indicators of openness, also reveal a similar change. However, this should not be taken at face value. As the coefficients of individual stratum openness did not reveal a consistent rise, it can be surmised that the effect of the decline of the atypical stratum that is agriculture was significant. In addition, that the results of the log-linear analysis did not indicate a trend towards openness means that, even if there was a slight rise in openness, it was neither as strong nor consistent as claimed by industrialisation theory. Industrialisation is certainly a process of long-term social change, but what had decisive effect on strata mobility seems to be just the transformation in core industrial structure from primary (agriculture) to secondary and tertiary industries. Industrialisation theory may explain satisfactorily the change in social openness entailed by this transformation but not necessarily what happens thereafter.

This is where the FJH thesis is beneficial. Although this thesis does not contain any obvious theoretical elements, it can be understood in the following manner. For instance, even if a shift in emphasis from secondary to tertiary industry takes place, there will be no concomitant change regarding the importance of education (academic background). The same can also be said of the relationship between the principle of modern organisation and openness (becoming achievement-oriented). In this manner, the argument put forward by Featherman et al. can be interpreted in the following manner: during the modernisation and industrialisation process, social openness does not continually increase. Instead, once the basic mechanism of an industrial society is established, the structure of social mobility does not fundamentally change.

Thus, making a general assessment, we must at least dismiss the image of a Japanese society that has continued to gradually open up (equalisation of opportunities). Even if openness in Japanese society has increased, it has only been piecemeal in nature. On the other hand, the argument in recent years that strata are rapidly becoming rigid is an over-exaggeration. Irrespective of the indicators of the four categories in figure 3.4, the coefficient of overall openness shows a value of close to 0.6. In addition, because the gross mobility and structural mobility rates are approximately 0.5 and the 0.3, respectively, up to about 60% of gross mobility comprises circular mobility. The conclusion drawn from this is that, apart from for a short period during the war and its immediate aftermath, inter-generational mobility in Japanese society has not fundamentally changed.[9]

**International comparison**

International comparisons of inter-generational strata mobility are extremely popular among the various international research projects that have employed quantitative methodologies. Robert Erikson and John Goldthorpe (1992) analysed mobility data from 11 countries in the 1970s, including the UK, Europe, the US and Japan. They claimed that these societies basically followed a similar pattern of circular mobility, which supported the FJH thesis. However, if we look closely, there is a slight difference in the level of circular mobility between these societies. Moreover, there are considerable disparities in structural mobility.

Before examining the distinctive features of strata mobility in Japan, it is important to note that the composition of occupational strata differs greatly between Japan and other advanced industrialised societies. Using the same data as Erikson and Goldthorpe, Ishida (1998: 153) shows the distribution of the fathers' and respondents' strata in Japan and eight European countries based on six strata categories. From this, it is evident that in Japan the proportion of the 'self-employed stratum' is extremely large and that conversely, among the nine countries, it also has the smallest proportions of 'skilled' and 'unskilled workers.' And, while the proportion of 'agricultural workers' is not the largest, it still belongs to a large family.

Of course, the distinctive features of this type of strata composition exert an influence on the patterns of mobility. First, at 34.7%, Japan has the second highest structural mobility rate of the countries researched after Hungary, which has 44.6%. Second, conversely, at 30.8%, Japan has the third lowest circular mobility rate after Hungary and Poland.

In fact, a decline in the number of agricultural workers from the fathers' to the respondents' strata engenders most structural mobility. Therefore, if a society with a large original proportion of agriculture is rapidly industrialised, it tends to show a high structural mobility rate. Since the data was taken from the mid-1970s, this corresponds mostly with the 30-year industrialisation process that began in each country following the end of the Second World War.

There may be many people for whom Japan's relatively low volume of circular mobility is quite unexpected. There is a widespread belief that Japanese society is open and therefore is strata-less. However, that openness is surprisingly low in Japan has already been noted previously in Morishima Michio's (1978) *England and Japan (Zoku Igirisu to Nihon)*. Morishima's study compares the 1955 SSM Survey data (Survey Committee of the Japan Sociological Society 1958) with English data from 1970. While he points out that there is greater mobility in England, looking closely, we can easily find out that the higher agricultural proportion in the Japanese data is the main cause of this. Seiyama (1994a) conducted an analysis of America (1975) and England (1972) using SSM Survey data from 1985,[10] noting that Japan had greater structural mobility and lesser circular mobility. Moreover, in terms of an important structural difference apart from the agricultural proportion, the Japanese data corresponds with a period of rapid expansion of the blue-collar stratum rather than that of the white-collar stratum during the period of high economic growth, whereas the English and American data indicates that the blue-collar stratum was expanding slowly or rather contracted. As a result, particularly in comparison with America, in terms of an elevation from the blue-collar to white-collar stratum, there is less circular mobility in Japan.

In this manner, concerning the openness of strata mobility in post-war Japan, structural mobility due to rapid industrialisation is greater, while circular mobility arising from a high agricultural proportion is somewhat smaller than in other advanced industrialised societies such as England and America.

## Change and underlying trends

Examining how occupational careers are determined was one of the foci of stratification theory. This is because occupational strata have been the focus of stratification in modern societies. This is prescribed by three main sociological factors:
1. Family background centring on the father's strata.
2. Academic background.
3. First occupation and career thereafter.

Various theories have made claims regarding how these factors operate, as well their longitudinal changes. Among these, Marxism, as well as reproduction theory which it has influenced, has tended to emphasise the salience of family background. However, as we have observed, there is greater mobility than reproduction of occupational strata and this trend has remained consistent over the long-term. Conversely, while industrialisation theory predicts a decline in the influence of family background, this also does not strictly accord with actual experience. In fact, due to the decline in the proportion of the extremely closed agricultural stratum, openness measured in terms of the coefficient of overall openness has slightly expanded. While the so-called FJH thesis emphasises the invariance of circular mobility and tends to conform basically to the data, a closer examination reveals that there have been fluctuations in circular mobility between different periods and societies, which it cannot explain. In addition, the so-called theory of meritocracy, like the theory of human capital, predicts that the influence of academic background will increase. However, this is also incorrect. As Seiyama (1993) demonstrates, the direct influence of the father's stratum, which is not mediated by academic background, on current occupation is undeniable, although somewhat limited. Moreover, while dual structure theory emphasises the importance of first occupation for employees, one of its premises regarding the stratified nature of occupational mobility does not hold true. In addition, that occupational mobility exhibits Markovian features means that first occupation does not continually have a direct influence (refer to note 3).

In this manner, many of the existing theories concerning strata mobility do not accord with reality. This is one of the major reasons why stratification theory has stagnated. We must formulate a new theoretical framework. However, this chapter only provides some preliminary considerations. We present the following six points which are considered to be universally underlying features in industrial societies. An industrial society, irrespective of having a market economy or not, is one which abolishes the feudal estate system, continually promotes the development of new industries, possesses a modern education system that cultivates human resources for these tasks.

1. Although influenced by a person's ability, qualifications, capital and career, choosing an occupation is basically free.

2. The opportunity to engage in professional occupations or become government officials is quickly linked with tertiary education.

3. The opportunity to gain employment in the managerial stratum of large private companies (in some cases, public corporations) is also gradually linked with higher education.

4. The opportunity to receive a higher level of education is influenced by a person's ability, the economic situation in their household and aspirations etc., which in their turn are inevitably prescribed to a certain extent by the family to which they are born.

5. Regarding the opportunity to be self-employed, academic qualifications may or may not relevant. However, 'capital' is an important common element, which is clearly advantaged by inheritance.[11]

Instead of affiliation with the family in which one is born, employment and relocation are based on the standardised qualifications and careers of a person's academic background etc. We believe that modern organisations had already established such a mechanism in industrial societies at least by the beginning of the early twentieth century. It does not appear that a much more achievement-oriented mechanism developed thereafter. In addition, while families' economic conditions had an overwhelming effect on households' attempts to attain academic qualifications in the early period, it gradually diminished as a factor as Japan became more affluent (although not completely). In its place, the influence of parents' academic background increased as that generation became more highly educated. Generally, this will not necessarily decline as a factor.

This section finally highlights the underlying trends in occupational careers.

6. The hierarchy of socially preferable occupations in modern industrial society is relatively stable. Besides the superior positions in the hierarchy of organisations and the political system, professional occupations are linked to high educational backgrounds.

There are several pieces of evidence supporting the last argument. Figure 3.5 shows the relationship between occupational prestige scores surveyed at 20-year intervals in 1955, 1975 and 1995. An occupational prestige score indicates a person's general evaluation of occupations (Naoi 1979). As the figure clearly demonstrates, while the level of the total scores has changed, there has been virtually no change in the relative positions of the various occupations. Although not shown here, even over a 40-year period from 1955 to 1995, the value of the correlation coefficient has remained extremely high at 0.932.

In addition, figure 1.8 in chapter one shows the trends in average individual incomes according to occupational strata. While there has been some variation in terms of relative disparities, the ranking of occupations has remained fairly stable over this 40-year period.

Next, we will raise five points concerning changes in trends and short-term fluctuations.
1. Changes in the proportion of people who are self-employed in agriculture, commerce or industry. There is a particular mechanism (ownership of capital) at work in these areas that differs to the employee sector.
2. The speed of industrialisation. This prescribes the volume of structural mobility.
3. Relative disparities in the incitant strength of demand between occupations.

*Figure 3.5: Changes in occupational prestige scores*

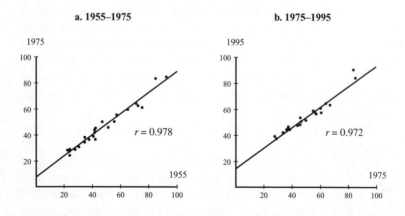

Source: Hara (1998b: 34, Figure 2). The original source is SSM Survey data, only for males aged 20–69.

These three points have already been addressed in this chapter and chapter two. In addition, the following two points seem to be linked to the small fluctuations:

4. The relational structure of each occupation and academic qualifications.
5. The relative disparities in economic resources and academic background that members of each occupational stratum present to their children.

These influence the relative disparities associated with mobility opportunities for those born in each strata. For instance, compared to the 1955 data, the 1995 data indicated that the relative opportunities for sons of agricultural fathers to enter the strata of professionals or white-collar workers in large companies have declined. This seems to be related to the relative delay in sons of farmers becoming highly educated, while academic qualifications required to enter these strata have been enhanced generally.

Among the factors of change, (1) the decline in agriculture as a change in the proportion of the self-employed sector and (2) the speed of industrialisation have caused an increase in openness such that it conforms with the claims made by industrialisation theory. However, the influence of the other factors has either brought about very minimal or non-directional and short-term fluctuations. One would be correct in thinking that, as a whole, after the speed of industrialisation levelled off in Japan, despite continuing industrialisation, the universal underlying structural feature of occupational careers would remain unchanged.

# 4 Changing Political and Strata Consciousness

Strata consciousness originally derives from the Marxist concept of 'class consciousness.' It is considered that people's knowledge, values and interests vis-à-vis their social world maintain a distinctive character based on the peculiar perspectives and interests inherent in 'class,' which, in particular, results in differences in political attitudes and awareness of one's historical mission. This is premised on the existence of definite 'objective class.'

In Japan, however, 'strata consciousness' has been developed into a broader concept. According to Hara (1990), it contains two different meanings: the first is a basic extension of the notion of class consciousness and points to the unique social consciousness of each 'objective class,' and the second is 'strata-related consciousness,' which includes the following broad elements:

1. Consciousness of one's hierarchical status such as strata identification, as well as consciousness related to overall strata distribution such as occupational ranking (prestige evaluation).
2. Consciousness of one's level of importance of hierarchical status manifested in upward orientation and educational aspirations.
3. Consciousness that is closely linked to social strata differentiation such as feelings of social satisfaction and a sense of fairness.

In the sense of 'strata-related consciousness,' strata consciousness does not need to be necessarily premised upon 'objective strata.' In a sense, 'subjective strata' arise in one's consciousness.

Although Marxism once stated that the modern state was an instrument of rule for the bourgeoisie, it is no longer valid to consider the actual relationship between strata and politics based on this assumption. The subject that ought to be pursued is that pertaining to the type of politics to which certain strata are inclined and support. This cannot be determined in advance. Since there are no definite criteria of strata, the question pertaining to the types of strata divisions that are linked to the phenomenon of politics and the manner in which they are related will be elucidated heuristically. It is for this reason that the relationships between strata consciousness (meaning strata-related consciousness) and politics are explored through the medium of political consciousness.

# Politics and strata

## The 1955 regime and its dissolution

Excluding the chaotic period shortly following its wartime defeat, post-war Japanese politics can be divided into two periods: the first, under the '1955 regime,' which continued from 1955 to 1993, and the second, a period of frequent political realignment following its collapse. 1955 was the year the left and right factions of the Socialist Party united. It was also the year in which the Liberal Party and the Democratic Party merged to create the Liberal Democratic Party (LDP).

The most salient feature of the 1955 regime was the continued one-party dominance of the LDP. At the same time, the regime was characterised by a rivalry between the conservatives (LDP) and reformists (Japan Socialist Party, or JSP, and the Japan Communist Party, or JCP, which was ideologically aligned with the JSP's left faction), which constituted a major political faultline. This rift was essentially one between capitalism and socialism in relation to objective economic and political systems, as well as foreign alliances. In terms of increasing affluence, the LDP sought to expand the overall pie while the reformist parties promoted redistributive policies.

The 1955 regime underwent a gradual transformation, reaching its apogee around 1965. A significant feature of this transformation was the steady loss of popular support for the reformist parties. In 1955, the young generation, the highly educated, white- and blue-collar workers and professionals[1] constituted the major support base for the reformist parities. During the course of social change in Japan, which is characterized by the 'popularisation of higher education,' 'increase in employee numbers' and 'urbanisation,' the supporter categories rapidly expanded. Therefore, it was expected that the power of the reformist parties, which enjoyed the support of these groups, would also rapidly rise. But the result was contrary to expectation. The LDP maintained a support rate of about 40%, whereas support for the reformist parties, especially the JSP, not only failed to increase thereafter, but actually declined rapidly from the 1970s. This period also witnessed a concomitant increase in the number of so-called 'unaffiliated voters.' Therefore, it is appropriate to consider the period until the late 1960s, during which more people supported the reformist parties than 'no party', as the 'early 1955 regime,' and the period thereafter as the 'late 1955 regime.'

The dissolution of the Soviet Union and the collapse of the socialist regimes in Eastern Europe significantly altered the world political map. The 1955 regime in Japan responded to these changes and soon came to an end. New parties were established, while existing parties underwent a frequent realignment, which continued until this day. In addition, the results of the 1993 general election heralded the birth of a non-LDP coalition government. This was soon followed by a coalition government that included the LDP, a minority LDP government and finally a LDP government that commanded a majority in the House of Representatives.

By 1993, the decline of the reformist parties had continued unabated. The reasons for this have been discussed in various ways. The fundamental cause lies in the reformist parties' failure to adapt to the development of an 'affluent' society in Japan (Hara 1993). The demise of the idea of 'socialism' also played a crucial role as well. In addition, what is important is that the LDP also suffered from a significant decline in its public support rates following the collapse of the 1955 regime. From 1955 to 1991, the LDP consistently received a support rate of 40%, but according to the 1995 survey, this ratio was reduced to 25%. Even if we include the support rates for the New Frontier Party, which drew from a similar support base to the LDP, this does not add up to the corresponding numbers for 1991 (see table 4.1).

*Table 4.1: Trends in support for political parties (%)*

| Political parties | 1955 | 1965 | 1975 | 1985 | 1991 | 1995 |
|---|---|---|---|---|---|---|
| Liberal Democratic Party | 40.0 | 40.5 | 38.7 | 40.6 | 38.7 | 24.5 |
| New Frontier Party | - | - | - | - | - | 8.8 |
| Japan Socialist Party | 32.5 | 31.0 | 16.6 | 12.1 | 14.1 | 7.1 |
| Komeito | - | 2.5 | 2.7 | 2.9 | 3.0 | - |
| Democratic Socialist Party | - | 4.0 | 4.3 | 4.4 | 3.1 | - |
| Japan Communist Party | 1.0 | 1.8 | 4.7 | 2.7 | 2.5 | 2.4 |
| Other | 0.5 | 0.2 | 0.2 | 2.0 | 0.6 | 2.6 |
| None | 21.0 | 16.1 | 29.5 | 32.6 | 35.9 | 52.3 |
| Unknown | 5.0 | 3.9 | 3.3 | 2.7 | 2.2 | 2.3 |

Note: The 1991 data are based on the 1995 SSM Survey question about the political party that the respondents supported 'about five years ago, before the formation of the New Frontier Party.'
Source: SSM Survey data. Only for males aged 20–69.

During this time, it was the unaffiliated voters (those who do not support a particular political party) who advanced rapidly. In 1955, about 20% of voters did not support a particular political party, but by 1985 this figure increased to about 30%. In 1995, the number of unaffiliated voters had already exceeded 50%, making 'no party', in essence, the party of choice. A voter backlash against the changing nature of the existing political parties resulting from the advent of coalition governments is probably a major contributing factor to the rapid rise in the number of unaffiliated voters in 1995. That said, since the number of unaffiliated voters had already reached 36% by the time new parties were established, most of which remained fairly constant in 1995, this should be seen as a continuation of the previous upward trend.

This rapid advance in the number of unaffiliated voters was attributed to, of course, the decline of the reformist parties. Most of those who stopped supporting the reformists did not jump on the LDP bandwagon, instead preferring to become unaffiliated voters. In fact, if we compare the 1955 and 1985 data, the support base for the reformist parties was completely transformed into a band of 'no party' (unaffiliated) voters, which indicates the LDP was unable to take in disaffected reformist voters. It is well known that from the 1960s to the 1970s, the LDP created a powerful vote-gathering machine in the form of various corporations, industry groups and the supporters' groups of each parliamentarian that were based on these organisations, as well as regional communities. This vote-gathering machine was based on a simple *quid pro quo*: in return for mobilizing votes during an election, these organisations and communities received various subsidies and public works projects etc. This is referred to as so-called 'interest (guided) politics' (*rieki/yūdō seiji*). While interest politics succeeded in creating a solid political base for the LDP, it prevented the party from incorporating into its support base those who did not benefit from or were critical of the style of politics that was interest politics. Among these were the urban white- and blue-collar workers, the young generation and others who were the main support base for the reformist parties in 1955.[2]

## Class politics and status politics

Although there are some scholars who claim that Japan's political transformation under the 1955 regime represents a transition from 'class politics' to 'status politics' (Imada 1989; Hara 1993 and 1994a), there is a certain degree of conceptual confusion inherent in this argument.

According to the notion of class politics, objective class prescribes people's political attitudes and politics evolves as a result of the clash of interests between classes. The concept of 'class' in this context is mostly used in a Marxist sense. Under the 1955 regime, there existed a clear differentiation in the support bases between the conservative (LDP) and reformist (JSP and JCP) parties in accordance with occupation, academic background and age etc. Among these factors, it was occupation that most forcibly and consistently contributed to this differentiation (Miyake 1985). How can this be interpreted from the perspective of class politics?

Figure 4.1 shows the level of support among the different occupational strata for the LDP and the reformist parties in 1955 (the early 1955 regime), 1985 (the late 1955 regime) and 1995 (after the collapse of the 1955 regime). Looking at the 1955 survey, the level of support for the LDP among the managerial strata, which comprises the capitalist and old middle class (this also includes corporate executives), and the self-employed and farmers is certainly high. At the same time, the reformist parties enjoy strong support from white- and blue-collar workers who belong to the working and new middle class. Moreover, not only is the support rate for the LDP relatively high among the managerial strata, the self-employed and farmers compared to white- and blue-collar workers, but also the actual percentage is higher than it is for the reformist parties. In addition, the support rate for the reformist parties among white- and blue-collar workers is higher than that for the LDP.

Table 4.2 shows the support rates for the LDP and the reformist parties according to strata and class identification in the 1955 and 1985 (Hara 1993 and 1994a). Surely, looking at the 1955 survey, a clear differentiation in support based on 'class' identification is obvious. If we compare the capitalists and middle class with the working class, support for the LDP is higher among the former, while support for the reformist parties is higher among the latter. There is a difference of about 20% in the support rates for the parties between the classes. In addition, the support rate for the LDP is higher than it is for the reformist parties among the capitalists and middle class, while the reverse is true for the working class. For the most part, 'strata' identification is unrelated to political party support.

This data demonstrates that in 1955 political rifts mainly revolved around the notion of 'class.' However, it is unreasonable to refer

Figure 4.1: *Changes in support for political parties by occupation*

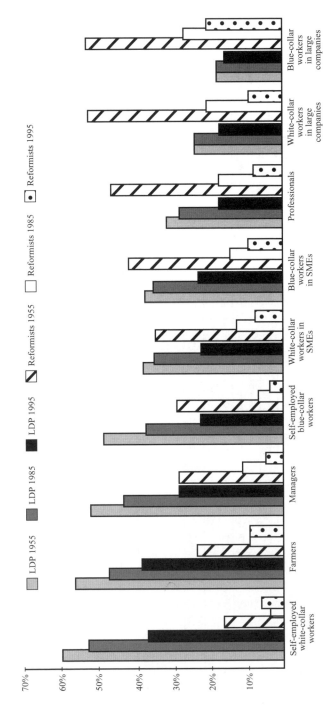

Source: SSM Survey data. Only for males aged 20–69.

Table 4.2: Support for political parties by class and stratum identification (%)

**(a) 1955**

| | LDP | | | | | Reformist parties | | | | |
| | Stratum | | | | | Stratum | | | | |
| Class | Upper and upper-middle | Lower middle | Upper lower | Lower lower | Total | Upper and upper-middle | Lower middle | Upper lower | Lower lower | Total |
|---|---|---|---|---|---|---|---|---|---|---|
| Capitalist and middle | 57.7 | 55.5 | 54.7 | - | 55.5 | 25.6 | 19.6 | 18.0 | - | 20.7 |
| Working | 33.3 | 35.1 | 34.6 | 36.8 | 35.2 | 43.5 | 41.7 | 39.5 | 31.6 | 38.5 |
| Total | 46.2 | 43.0 | 38.0 | 37.7 | 40.3 | 34.0 | 33.7 | 35.8 | 31.7 | 34.0 |
| | | | | | (N=787) | | | | | (N=664) |

**(b) 1985**

| | LDP | | | | | Reformist parties | | | | |
| | Stratum | | | | | Stratum | | | | |
| Class | Upper and upper-middle | Lower middle | Upper lower | Lower lower | Total | Upper and upper-middle | Lower middle | Upper lower | Lower lower | Total |
|---|---|---|---|---|---|---|---|---|---|---|
| Capitalist and middle | 53.8 | 43.5 | 41.1 | - | 48.0 | 7.3 | 12.5 | 16.1 | - | 10.3 |
| Working | 43.0 | 38.5 | 33.5 | 32.3 | 37.5 | 17.4 | 17.1 | 18.3 | 19.5 | 17.6 |
| Total | 49.1 | 40.0 | 34.5 | 32.4 | 41.0 | 11.6 | 15.7 | 18.0 | 19.5 | 17.6 |
| | | | | | (N=981) | | | | | (N=354) |

Note: '-' indicates that the number of cases in the cell was too small for computation.

Source: Hara (1993: 106, Table 1). The original sources are 1995 and 1985 SSM Survey data, but only for males aged 20–69.

to 'class' as something to which people are objectively located. For instance, the support rate for the reformist parties among professionals and white-collar workers in large companies, who correspond to the new middle class, is higher than it is among blue- and white-collar workers in SMEs belonging to the working class. One might assume that they would have the most irreconcilable interests in relation to the capitalist class. In addition, that many self-employed workers and professionals even identify themselves as working class will be discussed later (see table 4.3).

What this data reflects should instead be referred to as an ideological rift between the capitalist and socialist systems. It is not incorrect to call it 'class politics' in this context. However, that it does not necessarily overlap with the notion of being located within an objective class is due to the intervening influence of cultural and ideological conflict over traditional morals, norms and the new constitutional system,[3] as well as what may be deemed 'Japanese' political networks in regional organisations, industry groups and enterprise unions centred on large companies (Watanuki 1976; Flanagan and Richardson 1977).[4]

The data from 1985 and 1995 – during the periods when Japan's high economic growth had come to an end and the country had, for the most part, achieved overall affluence – do not evince a clear rupture in the parties' support bases, such as the case in 1955. Support for the LDP according to occupation exceeds that of the reformist parties for virtually every strata (see figure 4.1). The support rate for the LDP, regardless of class identification, also eclipses that of the reformist parties (see table 4.2b). This is referred to as 'status politics.' However, the term status politics contains two different meanings. One of these is the aforementioned 'interest politics,' which refers, in particular, to a political base of the LDP as the government party, based on a sense of people's realistic interests. As many political scientists have observed, it was Tanaka Kakuei – a post-war Japanese politician who was representative of a particular era in Japanese politics – who, in particular, created interest politics. It is also referred to as 'special-interest politics' (*riken seiji*). The other is the phenomenon known as 'satisfaction politics' (*manzoku seiji*). As people grew increasingly affluent as a result of the success of Japan's high economic growth, they became satisfied with their present state of affairs and did not desire any significant changes, preferring instead to give support to the ruling party's management of national politics. This is evident in the tendency for people to support the LDP, the higher their strata and status.

Therefore, Japan's political transformation under the 1955 regime can be summarised as follows: while the early period can be characterised as 'ideology politics' centred on the selection of ideological systems, it was closely linked to strata; the concept of 'class' denoted the pertinent parts of strata. The power of ideology gradually weakened during the late period of the 1955 regime, which featured 'interest politics' and 'satisfaction politics,'[5] to which two aspects of 'strata' are related in this context. The first is through the mediation of the business world within the context of interest politics while the second pertains to the height of the strata on the vertical axis within the realm of satisfaction politics.[6]

With the collapse of the 1955 regime and the current economic recession, satisfaction politics has perhaps weakened in Japan, while interest politics, although persistent, has come under considerable criticism and is gradually on the decline. While it is unclear how 'strata' will relate to politics in the future, based on this analysis, it cannot be surmised that it will come to be unrelated.

## Affluent society and unaffiliated voters

### Drifting voters

What attributes and consciousness did the unaffiliated voters, who grew rapidly under the late 1955 regime, possess? As discussed previously, the number of unaffiliated voters exceeded half of Japan's registered voters by 1995. Regardless of their attributes, the percentage of unaffiliated voters is high, yet, this does not mean they are uniform. The clearest difference to emerge is associated with age. Following on from Figure 4.1, Figure 4.2 shows the percentage of unaffiliated voters according to age in 1955, 1985 and 1995. While differences based on age were minimal in 1955, the percentages in 1985 and 1995 increased the lower the age group to reveal a 30% difference among those in their twenties and sixties.

While not shown in figure 4.2, the percentages according to age categories in 1985 are mostly congruent with the support rate for the reformist parties in 1955. The percentages according to age in 1955 also correspond mostly with the support rates for the reformist parties in 1985. As discussed previously, reformist parties and 'no party affiliation' have ostensibly exchanged their support bases.

Why have the young generation, who were once the main pillar of support for the reformist parties, become unaffiliated voters?

*Figure 4.2: Trends in the ratio of those who do not support any political party by age*

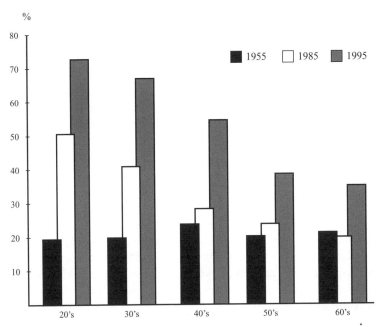

Source: SSM Survey data. Only for males.

There are various schools of thought regarding this trend among the young generation. For instance, scholars argue that it is attributed to increasing conservatism, a retreat into their own private spheres (Kojima 1978) or an increasing disinterest in politics (Akiyama 1985). However, the authors would suggest that the following two points are valid. The first is the declining appeal of ideology. This does not only apply to socialism. Among the former young generation, there are those who are critical of the current situation and who have been attracted to various ideologies that speak of an ideal future. However, as people become more affluent, these ideologies lose their appeal. The second factor is that in comparison to middle-aged and elderly people from the same period, there are few people who have maintained political attitudes formed under the previous 1955 regime or have been incorporated into political networks. This is the main factor behind the fall in the percentage of those supporting the LDP and is also manifested in low levels of support for the reformist parties to which labour unions serve as a vehicle.

It is during elections that unaffiliated voters play a leading role in politics. It is believed that their decision as to whether to vote or not, together with voting patterns, exerts an enormous influence on election results. However, their political orientations are not constant and the tendency towards incertitude is growing further. They could be described as being in a 'drifting state' (hyōryū jōtai).

There are two aspects to this drifting state. First, the Japanese sense of loyalty to one particular party is not as strong as it is in Britain and the US. This is due to the rapid pace of industrialisation in Japan, which resulted in parents and children seldom belonging to the same strata and, therefore, supporting different political parties. It is also because, compared to Britain and the US, political parties in Japan were in a constant state of flux. On this point, Miyake Ichirō distinguishes three different types of attitudes: 'I will support this party;' 'I do not particularly support this party, but neither do I particularly loathe it;' and 'this is the only party I am unwilling to support.' Miyake dubbed the reach of parties contained in his first two categories 'the scope of attitudes towards support for political parties' (seitō shiji taido no haba). However, in a more positive sense, are there not in reality many people who are also of the view that 'both this and that party are OK'? If this is the case, that voting trends among unaffiliated voters are not constant is not necessarily a bizarre phenomenon (Hara 1988).

Second, as Japanese society became 'affluent' and reached a dead-end in many ways, parties and voters no longer had positive goals to strive for. Contemporary Japanese society is certainly faced with many problems, including stimulating economic growth, environmental issues and problems concerning the elderly etc. However, one would venture to say these are passive problems (goals), which do not arouse long-standing political passions in people. Under these conditions, 'drifting,' in a way, engenders an attitude towards voting among people that emphasises performance evaluation and is not tied to a rigid ideology.[7] Conversely, there is also a danger which may lead to political populism.[8]

## A new core element of political rifts

It goes without saying that the growth of unaffiliated voters is linked to the increasingly ambiguous nature of political rifts (conflict) in Japan. Due to the collapse of the socialist regimes in Eastern Europe from the late 1980s, the Japanese reformist parties abandoned their socialist orientations in both form and substance. As a result, the differences in each party's policies became less obvious and the conservative and reformist camps were no longer so openly in conflict with each other.

It cannot be denied that this dampened people's passion for politics and elections. In addition, an arbitrary realignment of political parties and their policy inconsistencies accelerated people's abandoning and distrust of politics.

It is difficult to anticipate whether a distinct and persistent conflict, such as that played out between the conservatives and reformists, will emerge in future. However, it is the common-sense supposition that some political fissures will emerge and accordingly parties will realign themselves since the phenomenon of politics is, in a way, games of power seizure in which symbols are held aloft. It can be argued that one of the axes of conflict following the collapse of the 1955 regime is the issue surrounding interest politics. The 'destroying of the structure of vested interests' is something the 'anti-LDP' parties commonly advocate. However, this conflict is one of 'method' and not 'ideals' and it is difficult to consider that it will hold long-term significance as an axis of conflict.

What types of philosophical fissures are likely to occur in the future? There are three possibilities. The first axis can be expressed as a conflict between micro- and macro-elements. The conflict over political goals and concrete policy between the conservatives and reformists will not remain unchanged as it was in the past. Rather, it may emerge as a difference of perspectives between macro, which focuses on the state and the world, and micro, which looks toward the individual and citizen. If we think about it, these two elements were also intermingled within the former LDP and JSP. In terms of the LDP, these take the form of reactionism and 'ditch plank politics,'[9] which lead to statism, and for the JSP, they represent Marxism as the lofty cause, as well as an affinity toward citizens and residents' movements.

The second axis is the conflict over freedom or regulation. Presently, under the influence of the United States, there are increasing calls for economic and other 'deregulation' in Japan. Its proponents believe that by removing regulations on economic activities, the economy will be revitalised, as well as the administrative organizations will be slimmed down. However, there is the danger that deregulatory policies may lead to further disparities in incomes and wealth. Where acute problems concerning the quality of life in areas such as the environment and welfare (for the elderly and disabled) become an issue, there are strident calls for greater regulation (political and administrative intervention) than there is at present, which may lead to serious conflict.

Third, one cannot deny the possibility of resurging conflict between the conservatives and reformists. While this was the core element of political conflict under the 1955 regime, its substance was not necessarily constant. By the 1970s, for instance, the LDP essentially abandoned its reactionary ideology. In addition, social claims concerning human rights, environmental and women's issues were made in a way that overlapped with the conflict between conservatives and reformists. The scope of the reformists' interests expanded, so to speak. However, by continuing to adhere to their traditional ideology, the reformist parties failed to redefine what it meant to be 'reformist' (Seiyama 1998a). The current political map features a conflict between the LDP, on the one hand, and opposition parties of various persuasions, on the other. If the opposition parties converge upon the 'reformist' banner, there is another possibility that the new conservatives and reformists will become a central axis that engenders political rifts.

While there is merit in the fact that the increase in the number of unaffiliated voters forces political parties to be more cognizant of the interests of the broader electorate since they can not rely on the stable supporters no longer, there is also a negative aspect that the political parties will increasingly advocate political populism, which will result in inconsistent policies. This heightens people's distrust in politics and leads to further increases in the number of unaffiliated voters. When parties emerge that regularly present a consistent political vision without resorting to populist measures, some unaffiliated voters may return to the fold.

Nevertheless, present-day Japanese society has realised the long-term goal set in the Meiji period of achieving affluence in line with Europe and the United States. While in a state of conceited absent-mindedness, Japanese society has been hit by an economic recession and is in a state of confusion. As a result, Japan is presently at an important turning point in its modernity while politics has lost sight of its directionality and has been thrown into confusion. It can be argued that the issue concerning what kind of social ideals will emerge in future and, based on this, what new type of axis of political opposition will develop depends not on outside models but Japanese people's own present and future activities.

# Strata location and strata identification

## Strata identification and class identification

Among the various forms of strata consciousness, the most significant are strata and class identification. These are both forms of consciousness that are linked to how people position themselves in a stratified society. This chapter has already considered the relationship with political party support based on table 4.2. Strata identification is a form of consciousness that refers to how people position themselves hierarchically in society. The SSM Surveys are based on the following strata classification: 'upper,' 'upper middle,' 'lower middle,' 'upper lower' and 'lower lower.'

On the other hand, class identification is a form of consciousness linked to the kind of social groups or categories to which people belong. It is considered that the various social groups and categories in this context experience different socio-economic conditions and, to a certain degree, interests. The SSM Surveys are also based on the following class classification: 'capitalist class,' middle class' and 'working class.' Figures 4.3 and 4.4 show the distribution of the survey responses from 1955 to 1995.

First, we would like to confirm some of the facts highlighted by now regarding strata and class identification:

1. Examining the trends in the total distribution of strata identification reveals that from 1955 to 1965 and 1975, the percentage of people who claimed that they belonged to the 'upper middle' and 'lower middle' (the so-called 'middle') strata increased to 70% or 75%.[10] However, virtually no change is evident thereafter.

   Unlike strata identification, there are no easily discernible trends in class identification. While there are some upward and downward shifts evident in the percentage of those claiming to be 'working class' (1955 and 1975 – about 70%; 1965, 1985 and 1995 – about 63%), it can be said to be basically stable. The percentage of those who identify with the 'working class' has consistently exceeded 60%, while the percentage for 'capitalist class' has always been in single-digits. These are the main characteristics of Japanese class identification.

2. While these charts have been abridged, a fairly clear correlation exists between these forms of consciousness and objective attributes. For instance, if we look at the distribution of strata identification according to income ranking, the higher the rank,

*Figure 4.3:   Trends in strata identification*

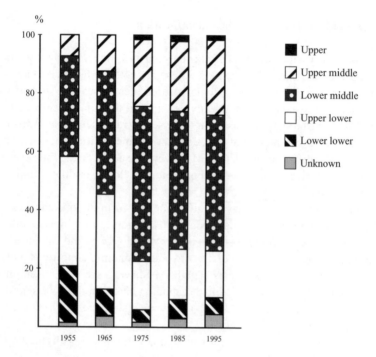

Source: SSM Survey data. Only for males aged 20–69.

the greater the percentage of those claiming to have 'middle' consciousness and the smaller the percentage of those asserting 'lower' consciousness. In addition, based on a Marxist definition, if we divide class into the four categories of capitalists, old middle, new middle and workers, and examine the distribution of class identification, the percentage of new middle and working class employees, who claim to be 'working class,' is high, while the corresponding percentage of capitalists and the old middle class is low. In addition, over 40% of the capitalist class claimed to possess 'capitalist' consciousness, which only constituted a single-digit percentage of total respondents.

3. Strata and class identification are correlated. For instance, if we examine the distribution of strata identification according to class identification, the percentage of those who claim to have 'middle' strata consciousness is highest among the 'capitalist class' and lowest among the 'working class.' In addition, the opposite pattern emerges for 'lower' consciousness.

*Figure 4.4: Trends in class identification*

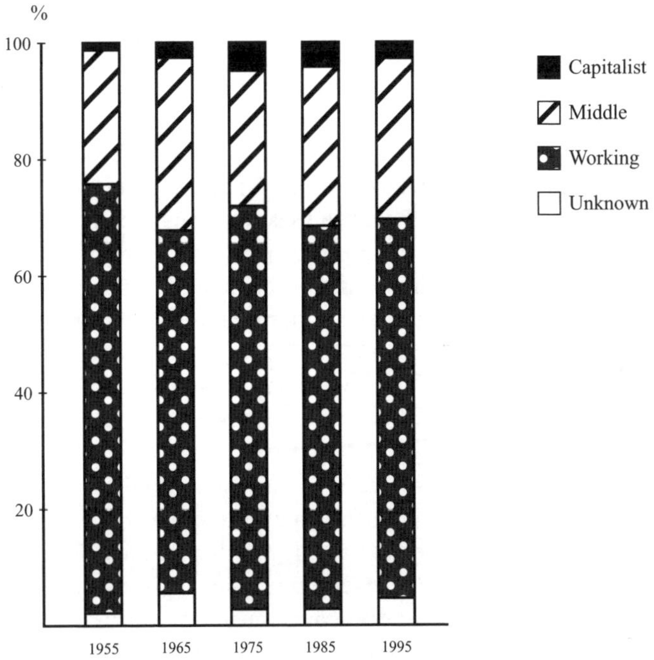

Source: SSM Survey data. Only for males aged 20–69.

## Bloated and stagnant 'middle' consciousness

Among the various forms of consciousness, not only researchers, but also society as a whole has payed attention to strata identification. As figure 4.3 highlights, it was precisely during Japan's period of high economic growth that the percentage of those claiming to have 'middle' consciousness rapidly increased. It was felt that changes in strata identification were a response to the increasing affluence of Japanese society and people's economic circumstances. According to these phenomena, Hara (1997) referred to strata identification as the 'focal point of strata consciousness' (*kaisō ishiki no shōten*).

However, if we examine more closely the relationship between people's socio-economic circumstances and strata identification, several questions arise that require answering. For instance, does the increase in the number of people who claimed to have 'middle' consciousness from 1955 to 1965 and 1975 suggest a rise in the number of those leading a similarly moderate lifestyle? In other words, does it mean that Japanese society has become increasingly egalitarian?[11] In addition, the period after 1975 was marked by the end of Japan's high economic growth and the ushering in of so-called stable growth. As we saw from figures 1.6 to 1.8 in chapter one, in addition to a continuing and moderate increase in incomes, there were also widening disparities. What influence did these changes have on the distribution of strata identification?

Various studies have attempted to answer these questions. What was commonly recognised in these analyses was that strata identification is an awareness of how people evaluate the extent of their own 'circumstances' – or put simply, their economic affluence (Naoi 1979). It was also recognised that, as highlighted by the extremely small number of those claiming to possess 'upper' consciousness,' 'middle' consciousness is akin to 'affluent' consciousness, which places an emphasis on what is not 'lower' rather than on what is located directly between 'upper' and 'lower.'

Taking this into consideration, Seiyama (1990) provides the following answer to the aforementioned question. A common mistake the previous analyses have made is that they hypothesize that people's circumstances are simply reflected in their consciousness. Even people with the same 'middle' consciousness experience diverse circumstances. Instead, people have their own minimum standards (image) for what moderate/middle circumstances entail and if they judge that their own livelihoods have exceeded that standard, they reply that they are in the 'middle.'

Since strata identification is an evaluative awareness of economic affluence, it is appropriate to assume that the 'middle' standard (image) is basically determined by income and asset levels. Of course, although standards change, reflecting societal standards as a whole, it is necessary to consider the time lag between people's real circumstances and changing perceptions of these. According to Seiyama, Japan's period of high economic growth from 1955 to 1975 was one in which income and asset levels rose rapidly, by which the 'middle' standard lagged behind. 'Middle' consciousness expanded through this process. If we survey society in general following the end of Japan's high economic growth, the majority of people had reached the former 'middle' standard, but people noticed that this did not necessarily mean they were leading 'affluent' lifestyles. Consequently, the 'middle' standard has gradually become more exacting (higher) than before and, as a result, the 'middle' consciousness has ceased to expand.

Is it possible to anticipate how the distribution of strata identification will change? Of course, if economic disparities among people rise sharply and an economic depression occurs, causing a rapid decline in living standards, the distribution will probably change. What is anticipated apart from this situation is that the transformation of the meaning of 'affluence' will give rise to the possibility that standards other than those relating to economic conditions will assume importance. For instance, Kikkawa Tōru (1998a) reports that, according to the 1995 SSM Survey, the correlation between strata identification, on the one hand, and income and assets, on the other, has weakened, while the correlation between strata identification and academic background has strengthened. In addition, according to Sudo Naoki (1998), even if income and asset standards are identical, differences emerge in the percentage of those claiming to have 'middle' consciousness based on academic background. Sudo claims this is because lifestyle aspiration levels differ according to academic background. However, academic background, income and assets are not unrelated. Even if academic background has become an important element of 'middle' standards, it is not expected to significantly change the distribution of strata identification.[12]

Seiyama does not discuss specifically the kinds of standards (images) associated with the 'middle' circumstances under which Japanese people are placed. However, it is a fact that in contemporary Japanese society the overwhelming majority of people have 'middle' consciousness. This view is widely disseminated through the Japanese mass media. This might also be the reason why people continue to reply that they are in the 'middle' when asked about the strata to which they belong. At any rate, strata identification at present has permeated remarkably among people and remains tenaciously resistant to change.

However, even if many Japanese at present possess a kind of affluent consciousness that is manifested as being in the 'middle,' this does not mean that they are not dissatisfied or uneasy about their own status. In addition, there is data suggesting that people's sensitivity towards status and strata has definitely not declined. For instance, SSM Surveys from 1975 and 1985 explore the extent to which people are concerned with strata and status – a so-called sense of status. According to the results, during at least a 10-year period until 1985, there was absolutely no discernible weakening of people's sense of status (Hara 1990). However, this type of consciousness and sense can no longer be grasped based on 'strata identification.' Therefore, it can be stated that strata identification has lost its status as a focal point of strata consciousness.

## What is 'working class consciousness'?

Class and strata identification are related. As discussed previously, the percentage of those claiming to have 'middle' consciousness is the highest among the 'capitalist class,' while it is the lowest among the 'working class.' For 'lower' consciousness, it is reversed. In addition, the lower the identified strata, the higher the percentage of those asserting 'working class' consciousness. However, the relationship between these two elements is quite loose and can be considered a different type of consciousness.

The major feature of class identification as seen in the SSM Surveys is that 'working class' consciousness has consistently exceeded 60% in Japan. In order to examine the elements of this 'working class' consciousness, table 4.3 displays the distribution of class identification according to occupational strata. The following four points can be cited as features of the Japanese data:

1. The percentage of those asserting 'working class' consciousness is high in all occupational categories. Even in the case of the managerial strata, which are believed to be the most capitalistic, 'working class' consciousness is 40%. This demonstrates that there are quite a few people who consider the term 'worker' to be synonymous with 'working person' (Misumi 1990).
2. What the table shows is that the percentage of those asserting 'working class' consciousness is high (over 70%) among blue-collar workers in large companies and SMEs. In addition, the percentage is higher among blue-collar workers than the white-collar strata, including professionals. This indicates that there are those who perceive 'workers' to be 'physical workers.'
3. 'Working class' consciousness is relatively low among managers and self-employed white-collar workers. This indicates that 'workers' are perceived as 'employees/managed workers and, conversely, administrators, managers and capital ownership are viewed as being 'bourgeois' or 'capitalists.' In fact, it is known that among managers, the higher the position and the greater the management scale among self-employed blue-collar workers, the lower the 'working class' percentage. If the management scale increases, there is a heightened tendency for people to focus on

*Table 4.3: Working class identification by occupational strata*

**(a) Japan (1985)**

| Stratum | Working class identification | Sample |
|---|---|---|
| Professional | 57% | 217 |
| Managerial | 41 | 236 |
| White-collar in large companies | 69 | 215 |
| White-collar in SME | 67 | 278 |
| Self-employed white-collar | 49 | 168 |
| Blue-collar in large companies | 75 | 176 |
| Blue-collar in SME | 79 | 532 |
| Self-employed blue-collar | 69 | 225 |
| Farming | 66 | 167 |
| Total | 66 | 2214 |

**(b) UK (1984)**

| Stratum | Working class identification | Sample |
|---|---|---|
| Upper professional managerial | 22% | 123 |
| Middle professional managerial | 36 | 235 |
| Clerical sales service | 50 | 256 |
| Self-employed/agricultural | 48 | 115 |
| Lower technical/supervisory | 74 | 107 |
| Skilled | 76 | 165 |
| Semi- or unskilled | 75 | 314 |
| Total | 56 | 1315 |

Note: Percentage figures for Japan were calculated after excluding the 'unknown' category.
Source: 1985 SSM Survey data. Only for males aged 20–69. Data on the UK are based on Marshall et al. (1988: 22, Table 2.2 and 180, Table 7.8).

administration and management and not involve themselves in direct labour (Jeong 1998).
4. Irrespective of whether they are white-collar or blue-collar, it certainly cannot be claimed that the percentage of those asserting 'working class' consciousness is low even among employees in large companies, who are thought to have benefited from favourable working conditions, compared with employees in SMEs. It is considered that this is linked to the fact that a high percentage of employees in large companies are union members. Even though there is a degree of variation, labour unions commonly place workers within the framework of capitalist-worker conflict. This is evident in the union-influenced notion of being 'anti-capitalist.' In fact, according to the SSM Survey data

from 1985, if we look at the relationship between union presence and class identification, the percentage of those asserting 'working class' consciousness is noticeably high among people working in companies where unions are present.

Table 4.3 (b) shows the English data in virtually the same period. Comparing the Japanese and English data reveals a clearer picture of the characteristics of 'working class' consciousness among Japanese. While the Japanese percentage (66%) is higher than the English one (56%), there is no extraordinary difference between the two. Instead, the more significant difference lies in the disparities among strata. In England it is among low-level engineers, supervisors, skilled, semi- and unskilled workers that the percentage of those asserting 'working class' consciousness is high, while in Japan it applies to blue-collar workers in large companies and SMEs, where the percentage is virtually the same. However, the percentage is clearly higher in Japan among the other occupations. For instance, combining upper- and middle-level professionals and managers in England, it is 33%, whereas in Japan the combined percentage of professionals and managers is 48%.

In other words, Japanese 'working class' consciousness might be a mixture of the preceding four elements, but it is not Marxist working class consciousness per se. Nevertheless, the exploration of the relationship between this and the other various forms of consciousness seems to reveal that, when a person places himself/ herself as a 'worker,' he/she includes not only one class or category but the kind of conflicting emotions (antipathy) he/she has toward the 'capitalist class' and the 'middle class.' It appears that even in Japan people have a strong sense of hierarchy in relation to the concept of 'worker (class).'

## Strata consciousness amid affluence

### A new focal point in strata consciousness

As discussed previously, class identification, especially 'middle' consciousness, was the previous 'focal point of strata identification' for two reasons. First, it can be said that the desire to become 'affluent' was at the core of many Japanese hopes and dreams. Second, strata identification was a general evaluative consciousness of this affluence. However, strata identification is mainly concerned with a sense of 'material' affluence. This feeling had already reached a certain 'saturated' state as a result of Japan's developing into an 'affluent' society (Hara 1990; Seiyama 1990).

What kinds of consciousness will become the foci of the various forms of strata consciousness in place of strata identification? It is difficult to answer this question immediately. Nevertheless, this section will examine the types of hopes and aspirations Japanese will hold and the kinds of consciousness these will arise, making reference to previously presented arguments.

**1. The rise of a new strata problem.**
Many of the forms of strata consciousness cited in the previous SSM Surveys and the like have not shown very conspicuous changes in distribution since 1975. The same can be said of strata identification. Of course, there are exceptions such as gender role consciousness. For instance, the ratio of those who criticize the type of division of labour in gender roles that sees 'men outside and women inside' has increased rapidly during the last 20 years, regardless of gender and age (see chapter 5). Of course, male-female inequality based on this division of labour is not a recent phenomenon. While people have actively complained against it for a long time, it was not until the mid-1980s that gender inequality began to attract broad attention. While there has been debate about whether the recent rapid changes in consciousness evince behavioural changes, it at least demonstrates the broadening interest in this issue.

In other words, it highlights the possibility of socially recognising pre-existing forms of inequality and discrimination such as women's and minority issues etc., as a problem of structural inequality (strata). There is also a possibility that the will for and dissatisfaction towards reforms will build up as a new social problem (strata problem) in place of poverty.

**2. Seeking a fair society.**
There are not a few researchers who claim that it is not merely 'affluence' but 'fairness' that will be at the centre of strata-related issues. Then, the 1985 and 1995 SSM Surveys cited 'feelings of fairness' as an important topic. These surveys revealed that about 60% of the respondents believed that Japanese society was unfair. Unlike 'middle' consciousness, which many people similarly claim to possess and is easily linked to satisfaction and conservative consciousness, there appears to be a certain dynamic that anticipates changes in feelings of unfairness.

However, there are some doubts about the claim that 'fairness' is at the centre of strata issues and that 'feelings of fairness' are the focus of strata consciousness. This is because the notion of a 'fair' society and people's living conditions, that is, 'what leads us to believe that it is fair' is not concrete. 'Fairness,' is a social mechanism for the purpose of realising an 'affluent' lifestyle that focuses, for instance, on the allocation of social resources and their use. Until now, realising 'affluence' was considered to be a natural objective. People have presently lost sight of this natural precondition. Claims of 'fairness' and complaints against 'unfairness' are not possible without establishing a concrete image of the hopes and desires people strive to achieve through a 'fair' mechanism (Umino and Saitō 1990; Saitō 1998).

### 3. A new sphere of activities.

The result of rising living standards during Japan's period of high economic growth was that many people came to possess 'middle' consciousness. Although former inter-strata disparities such as occupation, income and academic background by no means diminished, their significance declined. It cannot necessarily be claimed that people ceased to worry about status and inequality. This claim is based on two perspectives. The first is based on postmodern theories. While people may certainly be less concerned about pressure and anxiety over occupation, income and academic background, differentiating oneself from other people in other aspects becomes necessary in order to confirm self-identity. The second is the claim based on empirical data. As discussed in relation to strata identification, it cannot be said that people's concerns and sensitivity towards status have not weakened.

However, there is a possibility at variance to previous notions of strata as a referent for such desires and feelings. That is, people may be aiming to obtain status (the pursuit of prestige) in spheres of activity that were previously believed to be unrelated to social status such as local and volunteer activities and corporate environmental conservation activities (Imada 1998; Shirakura 1998).

### 4. The emergence of a 'de-strata group'

Previous arguments concerning strata consciousness are unconsciously premised on the notion that all people desire a high hierarchical status, although there are some differences in the extent of this. However, does this accord with reality? On the one hand, as symbolised by the overwhelming number asserting 'middle' consciousness, a decent 'affluent' lifestyle has become possible for many people. On the other hand, a certain siege mentality manifested in claims such as 'widening disparities' and the 'entrenchment of strata' centred on the theory of an education-conscious society has intensified. There is the possibility that, against the backdrop of 'affluence,' people with traditional 'middle' consciousness, that is, those who certainly are not losers, and people who 'have no interest in' and are 'unrelated to' pursuing strata and status will emerge as a strata. In other words, it is possible that people who have been guaranteed a certain level of affluence and social status will cease to be status-oriented. These people possess an attitude about life characterised rather by the endeavour to satisfy their own internal values, as well as by their indifference towards the prospects of promotion within social organisations, the necessity of gaining employment in a good company, and desperate efforts to ensure their children's advance to higher education (Tomoeda 1998).

Of course, as the large number of naturalistic literary figures in the Meiji period demonstrates, 'de-' stratified people had long existed in Japan. However, this is strictly an exception, differing from the anticipated 'de-strata group' in that people have to prepare themselves for a poor existence (Hara 1997). This is quite simply a new lifestyle amid 'affluence.'

### 5. Increasing focus on academic background consciousness

This may appear to contradict the above argument, but in comparison with the disparities in 'material' affluence, which are ostensibly difficult to detect, there remain clear differences in people's academic background. Moreover, there has been a significant decrease in the number of people who, for economic reasons, are unable to proceed to higher education or cannot send their children to the next stage of education. Despite this, the interest in academic background and advancing to higher education remains universal. People's perceptions of academic background and their own personal experiences are distorted. For instance, while many people believe that ability and effort are reflected in their academic background, many respond in surveys that there is unfairness, with regard to academic background (see chapter 2).

However, people's attitudes toward academic background are not uniform. There are many people at present who attach importance to specific educational institutions, such as University X and High School Y, as well as those who possess traditional attitudes and attach importance to academic background levels, such as junior high school, senior high school and university. It can also be anticipated that people referred to as the 'de-strata group' will be vehemently opposed to the notion of placing an emphasis on academic background levels and schooling history. Can it not be said that in place of strata identification in an era in which society is moving towards affluence it is indeed consciousness of academic background that reflects the differences in people's hopes and evaluations in an age of affluence? In this sense, it is possible academic background consciousness will become a focal point for strata consciousness.

**Political and satisfaction consciousness systems within strata consciousness**

Looking back to figure 4.1 and table 4.2, in 1955, there were occupational strata and identified classes in which the support rate for the reformist parties was higher than that for the LDP, as well as those in which the support rate for the LDP was higher than that for the reformist parties. However, by 1985, the support rate for the LDP exceeded that for the reformist parties irrespective of occupational strata and identified class. Nevertheless, support patterns based on strata location in which support for the LDP is highest among self-employed white-collar workers and lowest among blue-collar workers in large companies has remained virtually unchanged until 1995 (figure 4.1).

That is, the relationship between 'objective strata' and political party support consciousness has continued to exist since the 1980s, even to this day. Nevertheless, as demonstrated in the first section of this chapter, 'objective strata,' which are concerned with the phenomenon of politics, are pluralistic. At least three types of 'objective strata' can be identified:

1. Vertical hierarchical status characterized by levels in affluent life and social status.
2. Occupational strata demarcation in which business profits and political networks are involved.
3. Strata based on age and academic background in which ideology is involved.

Each of these is related to politics by way of a different political mechanism and their stress/strength has changed with time.

Table 4.2 shows political party support consciousness according to 'subjective strata.' While party support is virtually unrelated to 'strata identification,' it is closely related to 'class identification' within this 'subjective strata.' Certainly by 1985, support for the LDP among each identified class exceeded that for the reformist parties. However, there are clear differences in levels of support for the LDP and reformist parties among the capitalists and middle class, on the one hand, and the working class, on the other. For instance, support for the LDP among the capitalists/middle class and working class was 48% and 37.5%, respectively, whereas support for the reformist parties was 10.3% and 17.6%, respectively. In addition, support for the reformist parties among the working class in particular is worth noting in that it is virtually constant, irrespective of strata identification. There is a weak tendency that the lower people placed themselves in terms of strata, the higher the support rate was. But the difference is negligible. This suggests that for people who consider themselves to be working class and continue to support reformist parties, being 'working class' has an extremely significant meaning. In other words, the notion of 'working class' has assumed importance, not as a something tangible, but as a concept that connotes critical perspectives of the present state of politics and society in terms of stratification theory. This is the concept of 'working class' as 'being reformist' as well as 'belonging to low level strata,' and corresponds to the fourth of the four elements of working class consciousness discussed in section 2.

How should we perceive this relationship between 'objective strata' and 'subjective strata' (especially 'identified class'), on the one hand, and politics, on the other? This also corresponds to the issue of the relationship between consciousness 'according to strata' and consciousness 'in regard to strata' presented at the beginning of this chapter.

Hara (1998b) demonstrates that strata consciousness can be divided into 'political consciousness systems' and 'satisfaction consciousness systems.' 'Political consciousness systems' can be referred to as 'social consciousness systems.' In terms of the items on the SSM Survey, 'political consciousness systems' include various forms of political and social consciousness, beginning with 'party support' centred on 'class identification.' On the other hand, 'satisfaction consciousness systems' include 'work satisfaction' and 'overall lifestyle satisfaction' centred on 'strata identification.' Moreover, this has remained virtually unchanged since 1955.

These two groups differ in two respects. The first difference pertains to whether they include the element of conflict. In the case of 'satisfaction consciousness systems,' the level of 'satisfaction' is very much a problem. Of course, people might make comparisons with the others and pursue the causes of 'satisfaction' and 'dissatisfaction.' However, as manifested in the claims that 'life will not be easy because I have not made enough effort,' and 'my husband's wage will not rise because he is an incapable person,' as long as these causes remain at the individual level, conflict is not possible (this problem is linked to the second difference).

In the case of 'political consciousness systems,' they contain some conflicting elements. For instance, as discussed previously, because the phenomenon of politics is a game of power seizure in which symbols are held aloft, it is conceivable that in the future some kind of political rift will emerge and political parties will subsequently undergo realignment. In addition, while working class consciousness is extremely diverse in its meaning, it has been noted that it contains some kind of conflicting emotions (antipathy) towards 'capitalist class' and middle class.' Seen in this light, political phenomena and class identification have an affinity with each other.

Second, 'political consciousness systems' correspond to 'public' or 'social' life-worlds, while 'satisfaction consciousness systems' accord with 'private' or 'individual' life-worlds. Politics is a public event. The policies and laws decided in the political realm prescribe the system and structure of the national community and influence every aspect of people's lives. The pluralistic entity we call strata is concerned with politics through the public aspect of each of its many dimensions. In other words, being positioned in a certain strata is linked to some kind of ideal associated with how the community, as a whole, ought to be. This depends on the type of meaning we attach to strata.

'Objective' strata can be conceptualised in many ways, for instance, in terms of income levels, the amount of assets, academic background levels, intra-company status and occupation etc. The meaning we attach to each of these differs between individuals. These are socially significant insofar as they are of public value. Although body height has never constituted strata, income and assets do. For body height does not create public problems, whereas opportunity disparities based on poverty and income do.

Seen in this light, the relationship between class and politics is the complete opposite to the Marxist hypothesis; class is not something that pre-exists and constitutes politics. Hierarchical phenomena which appear in the form of something significant in the public space we call politics have been presented as 'class.' Japanese 'working class' consciousness can be said to represent the public aspect of strata.

# 5 Gender and Stratification

There is no denying that until the 1970s, all research on stratification ignored women. This is not because scholars believed women lived in a world unrelated to the issue of stratification. The reason is simpler and more deep-rooted. It is because stratification research did not question both the premise of 'household communality' and the premise of 'male representativity.' In other words, the reason for women being ignored was simply that it was assumed that the phenomenon of stratification could be understood by focusing only on men. The same logic also applied to children and the elderly.

It is only natural that from the 1970s doubts began to emerge regarding this male-centric approach to stratification research. While industrial advancement led to a steady increase in the number of female company employees and those working for themselves in professional occupations, it also gradually diminished the role of women working in family businesses such as agriculture.

Among the main theories purporting to explain the social factors restricting female employment opportunities was the 'theory of statistical discrimination' in economics and the 'theory of patriarchy' in feminism. The theory of statistical discrimination claims that because at least a certain number of women are inclined to retire prematurely and become full-time housewives, it is rational for companies to adopt a discriminatory employment policy against them. On the other hand, patriarchy theory posits that the inclination to become full-time housewives is itself the result of 'patriarchy,' a male-dominated and completely ideological system (Walby 1986; Ueno 1990). Both theories point out some important aspects of what actually occurs. However, it is unreasonable to base on a single theory our attempt to understand the various forms of male–female opportunity disparities and the related entire ideological systems, where the disparity is, not infrequently, approved for women's sake.[1]

In fact, the structure of female employment opportunities is intricately linked to such factors as industrial structure, the family system, statutes and culture, and has undergone significant historical change. Especially in postwar Japan remarkable changes have taken place, and it seems highly unlikely that they are explained by a single theory. The complex and unintentional results of various factors and other contingencies of the time should have been at work there.

This chapter examines, through an accurate understanding of the changes in female employment opportunities, what kind of relevance gender structure has for stratification.

## Changes in working conditions

### From an agricultural family worker to employee

While some may be under the impression that the changing position of women in the postwar Japanese labour market is characterised mainly by their continually increasing participation in society brought about by the popularisation of higher education, the fact is more complex. Although we cannot ignore the impact of far-reaching changes in constitutional and civil law reforms on the family system, it can be said that what clearly shaped the underlying fundamental trend was the relative decline in the agricultural population.

Table 5.1 shows the overall changes in female working conditions from 1950 to 1995. While the total number of female workers increased 1.86 times from 14.08 million to 26.14 million, the female population of those aged 15 (14 for some survey years) and above also rose about 1.87 times from 28.87 million in 1950 to 54.02 million in 1995. Hence the workforce rate has remained virtually unchanged. However, the number of those in agriculture and forestry continually declined during this period. In the 1950s, 8.78 million women were working in these sectors, which accounted for 62.3% of Japan's total female workforce, but by 1995 these figures had declined to a mere 1.62 million and 6.2%, respectively. In absolute terms, this was a decline of 7.16 million people and was a percentage drop of 81.5%. At the same time the number of non-agricultural-forestry workers increased. The number of employed female workers, in particular, rose from 3.00 to 20.34 million, an increase of 17.34 million. Looking at this change in terms of the percentage of the total workforce, it represented a dramatic increase from 21.3% to 77.8%.

The basic tone of this change was that it was a transition from a time in which family workers in farming households constituted an over-whelming share of workers in the agricultural and forestry sectors to a time when non-agricultural-forestry employees represented a commanding share. This is the most significant change to have taken place in women's labour during the 45-year postwar period. Sweeping changes took place in 'women's labour' during this period.

*Table 5.1: Trends in the numbers of female workers and their break-downs (unit: 10,000)*

| Year | Work participation rate | Number of workers | Agriculture and forestry | Non-agricultural and non-forestry employed | Non-agriculture and non-forestry in total |
|---|---|---|---|---|---|
| 1950 | 48.8 | 1408 | 878 | 300 | 531 |
| 1955 | 54.0 | 1705 | 823 | 475 | 881 |
| 1960 | 53.6 | 1807 | 661 | 701 | 1146 |
| 1965 | 50.0 | 1878 | 553 | 893 | 1325 |
| 1970 | 49.3 | 2003 | 442 | 1086 | 1558 |
| 1975 | 45.0 | 1953 | 323 | 1159 | 1627 |
| 1980 | 46.7 | 2142 | 272 | 1345 | 1867 |
| 1985 | 47.4 | 2304 | 232 | 1539 | 2066 |
| 1990 | 49.0 | 2536 | 205 | 1823 | 2326 |
| 1995 | 48.4 | 2614 | 162 | 2034 | 2451 |

Source: Labor Force Survey conducted by the Management and Co-ordination agency.

The working conditions for female farmers in the past were harsh beyond imagination by today's standards. To a somewhat lesser extent, the same can also be said of males. Every member of the family who could work was mobilised as labour, and most farm young housewives worked in the fields while carrying their babies. Day after day women in farming families were engaged in gruelling farmwork and housework from before dawn until late at night and were only able to rest on rainy days and in winter. This was the lifestyle of many women in Japan until the early 1960s when harvester machines and electrical household items began to spread to Japan's farming regions.

The composition of female jobs in the non-agricultural-forestry sectors, which had shown remarkable expansion, also changed significantly. Although not shown in table 5.1, among the 7.01 million non-agricultural-forestry workers in the 1960s, 50.6% were in the blue-collar stratum such as skilled and service workers, labourers and security personnel. This figure dropped to 36.5% by 1995. Looking at it the other way round, only 19% of all female workers in 1960 were workers in professional, technical, clerical and sales occupations, which tacitly constitute the contemporary focus of issues relating to male–female employment disparities. After the period of rapid economic growth, it had reached 49.4% by 1995 with an increase of 5.35 million in the number of women engaged in clerical occupations and 2.44 million in the professional and technical occupations.

Thus, shortly after the war an overwhelming majority of women in the workforce were engaged in agriculture, and even in the 1960s a great majority of them were in agriculture or in the blue-collar stratum. But the percentage steadily declined after that and was replaced by white-collar employment.

## The age of housewife ideology

Neither agriculture nor blue-collar occupations were involved with the M-shaped work model. In order for M-shaped work to be possible, first, a certain degree of affluence must exist: the ability of housewives to make ends meet without having to work when raising a child is a necessary condition. Second, a family business is inexpedient for M-shaped work, since family businesses are often run by married couples and their families, and all family members are expected to cooperate and collaborate to pursue a common form of economic activity. However, this is not to say that family businesses are all tied to the notion of housewives working to earn a living. For example, pre-modern samurai and merchant households can be seen as a type of family business, but women from relatively prosperous strata did not work for a living.

That non-M-shaped work was sustained to some extent by the poverty and spirit of family business suggests that, for married women, withdrawing from the labour market to become full-time housewives was believed to be linked to affluence and the modernisation of family and lifestyle. In fact, women from urban middle stratum families, where the husband was a white-collar employee working for either a large company or the government, increasingly became full-time housewives from an early point in time, because this type of lifestyle manifested a certain hierarchical superiority. In her book entitled *Housewife* Ann Oakley (1974) claimed that it was propagated by men in late Victorian England when wives staying at home without working was considered proof they were middle class, i.e., 'full-time housewives were a symbol of being middle class' to cite Yamada (1994: 164). However, this was by no means a male-only ideology; the idea was keenly supported by females themselves.

During the period of postwar reconstruction, Japan's economy began to move in the direction of full-scale modernisation. Large numbers of children from the farming villages poured into the four main industrial zones to serve as a young white-collar and blue-collar workforce. When they created new families, the image of the full-time housewife who looks after the family by devoting herself to housework and raising the children captivated, along with the nuclear family system, many people as a new family ideology. An increasing number of women, mainly from the generation who were in their 20s in 1955, began to leave work after marriage in order to concentrate on the housework This phenomenon can be called 'housewifisation' and was one of the first changes that occurred in the career models of women in postwar Japan.

Above all else, housewifisation meant liberation not only from farm work but also from other harsh production activities, including factory work. For young women working in textile and electrical machinery assembly factories and living in the controlled environment of large female dormitories, a lifestyle in which upon marriage they could acquire an independent and free living space – even in wooden small housing – and be able to devote themselves to raising the children and performing housework during the daytime at their own discretion while awaiting the return of their husbands from work might not have been as luxurious as that of the American middle class depicted on television dramas at the time, but was a first step towards this ideal. While this was, of course, an ideology that accepted a perceived gender-based division of labour as a truism and bound women to the house and cemented economic subordination to their husbands, it was nevertheless truly emancipatory at the time.

As is evident from figure 5.1, from the 1960s to 1975, the labour force participation rate among young females continued to decline. In other words, during and shortly after the period of high economic growth 'housewifisation' was an underlying trend in Japanese society until the baby boomers, who were born between 1946 and 1950, began to enter the labour market. After then, this trend was soon reversed and the labour force participation rate among those aged between 25 and 29 began to rise sharply. As is commonly known, this phase is congruent with the period in which the total fertility rate, which had been maintained at around 2.1, began to decline gradually. In other words, the generation of women born after 1951 began to undergo a concurrent process of 'de-housewifisation' and 'marrying later.'

On three occasions housewife disputes were fought over the issue of whether women and housewives should have an occupation. The last of these began in 1972 and it was precisely at this time that the 'women's liberation' movement was active in Japan, as it was elsewhere. As already discussed in each of the chapters thus far, the early 1970s was, in many ways, a significant watershed in Japanese society and the same can also be said of the gender structure. It was a period in which the housewifisation of Japanese women, which had progressed smoothly until that time, ground to a halt and the labour force participation rate among the young began to rise.

*Figure 5.1: Trends in female labor force participation rates*

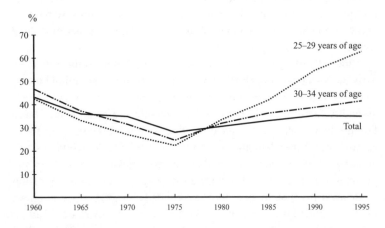

Source: Labor Force Survey conducted by the Management and Coordination Agency.

It was also a period in which the 'casualisation' of employment increased significantly in Japan. Throughout the period of high economic growth, the percentage of women over the age of 15 working part-time (temporary and day work) slowly increased. However, from 1975 to 1980, this figure rose at a stroke by a conspicuous 3.4 points. What brought about the increase in part-time work during this period was the generation of women who preceded the baby boomers. While those women, who were born between 1936 and 1945, were the main bearers of housewifisation during the period of high economic growth, after 1975 when, in other words, these women had reached their 30s and their children were no longer infants, large numbers of them began to work part-time. This was also a period of low economic growth after the first oil crisis, and Japanese companies, seeking an inexpensive labour force, began to build their factories in the locales. For families, the incomes derived from housewives' part-time work played a role in maintaining an affluent lifestyle amid rising costs for childcare and education. Since then, an increasing number of baby boomers and those from later generations have been engaged in part-time work.

**An overview of changes in the postwar gender structure**

As we can see from figure 5.2, the increasing popularisation of higher education among women has lagged behind that for males. In 1955, when statistical data began to be compiled, the advancement rate of males to university was 13.6%, while the figure for women was only 2.5%. Only 15% of university students were females. Even if we combine this with the figure for junior colleges, the advancement rate for females to tertiary education was only 5.1%. The advancement rate for both males and females has risen gradually since 1961, and this figure peaked once in 1975. While the advancement rate for males to university during this time rose by about 25 points from 15% to 40%, for women it increased by only 10.5 points from 2.5% to 13%. Nonetheless, the proportion of women among university students increased to 25% and colourful clothing became conspicuous on many campuses. The following section examines more closely the changes in the post-war gender structure by focusing, in particular, on trends in the advancement rate for females to tertiary education.

**The postwar recovery period: from wartime defeat to 1960**

Japan's socio-economic environment before the period of high growth did not merely fail to rebound sufficiently from wartime devastation but was, on the whole, still strongly redolent of the pre-modern era. Certainly, civil law reforms had already been carried out, the demographic transition was complete, the number of children per couple had settled at two or three and a new educational system was inaugurated. Nevertheless, a number of traditional elements (among

*Figure 5.2: Trends in the advancement rates to higher education*

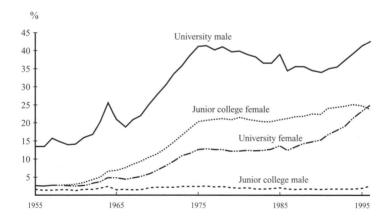

Source: Calculated from the Basic School Surveys conducted by the Ministry of Education.

which were those that were consolidated after the Meiji period) such as family norms and norms pertaining to gender roles stubbornly remained. An overwhelming number of people basically lived in an 'agricultural society.' Apart from those in professional occupations such as school teachers and nurses, married women working 'outside the house' were the exception. Academic backgrounds, which served as qualifications for entry into the modern occupational system, were still alien to most women. That the advancement rate for women to four-year universities did not rise was linked, apart from economic reasons, to the still feeble meaning of academic background.

During this time, Japan's industrial structure also underwent a steady transformation and what took a hold on women was the notion of a 'housewife ideology.' While this idea had already spread to women from the middle class and above before the war, this represented only a fraction of the overall population. With the increase in the urban workforce during the postwar process of development of the heavy and chemical industry sectors, housewife ideology became an available option for most wives. This was further supported by a process in which these women established nuclear families and their burden of housework was alleviated as a result of the diffusion of electrical household appliances.

### The high growth period: 1961–1975

Under the Ikeda cabinet, Japan's large-scale industrial transformation, which had been proceeding smoothly, was actively promoted as an explicit government policy. Educational opportunities were also increasingly expanded in concert with this transformation.

The advancement rate to high school continued to rise from the time the new educational system was inaugurated. The 11.3 point gap between males and females that existed in 1950 had been largely eliminated by 1960. However, even during the period of high growth, the gender disparity in tertiary education opportunities and the employment situation expanded rather than decreased. Alternatively, junior colleges, which were established in 1955, became the standard 'tertiary education' attainment target for women.

There is a reason why advancing to junior college became the key component of tertiary education for women. It maintained the modern family ideal of housewifisation by supplying female personnel to meet the rising demand for clerical workers in a highly industrialising society and, at the same time, providing prospective spouses for the increasing number of male university graduates, in accord with the modern family ideal of housewifisation.

On the other hand, the meaning of what it was to be a female university graduate was still vague at this time. While the number of new female entrants in universities had increased to 98,267 by 1976, from only 28,808 in 1961, perhaps more than 30% of new female graduates were out of work and between 30% and 50% of those with jobs were employed as teachers, as graph 5.3 demonstrates. As a result, in 1965, only 36.2% of new female university graduates (apart from those advancing to graduate school) obtained non-teaching jobs, and even in 1980 this figure was still only 46%. In other words, the majority of female university graduates during this time were either teachers or were out of work. It was in the late 1960s that the so-called 'theory that over-educating women will ruin the country' (*joshi gakusei bōkokuron*) became a popular topic of conversation. Against the backdrop of this notion was the fact that an overwhelming number

*Figure 5.3: Career paths of new female graduates from four-year universities*

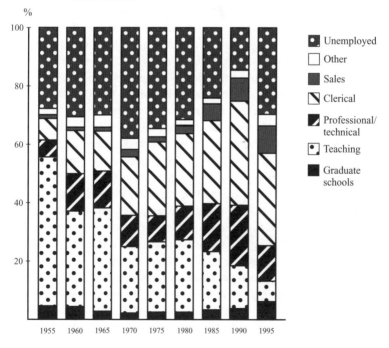

Source: Basic School Surveys conducted by the Ministry of Education.

of female graduates from universities were not taking part in general economic activities.

Apart from professionals such as teachers and public servants, it was only media-related companies that employed female university graduates. But the door for them was firmly shut in the manufacturing industry, as well as trading companies and finance. The possibility of acquiring academic qualifications and following a career path was extremely limited.

Moreover, there was still the widely-accepted belief in Japan that an overly-strong academic background can hinder a woman's chances of marriage.² Iwao Sumiko (1993: 38) highlights an episode in which the father of one female baby boomer made his daughter abandon plans to enter university, claiming 'nobody wants to marry a woman that is too clever.' From our experiences [as belonging to the baby boomer generation], this woman's father was probably an overly-traditional type even at that time and, in fact, it was not difficult for female university graduates to get married. And yet, it cannot be denied that this belief still existed.

This was an age that was far removed from the idea of female university graduates forging a career for themselves. However, this period of high economic growth, during which we observed the student revolts, was also one in which preparations were underway that would create a basis for changes that would present themselves later. First, there was a significant shift from arranged marriages to love-based marriages. At the beginning of the post-war era, when statistics became available, most marriages were arranged. Since this time, love-based marriages have been gradually increasing. In the 1960s, the percentages of arranged and love-based marriages were on a par. After then, especially from 1975, the percentage of love-based marriages rose sharply. There are various meanings attached to this change, but in the context of this chapter the following two are particularly important. First, unlike arranged marriages, love-based marriages are less influenced by the idea of 'balancing family ranks' (*ie no tsuriai*) or hypergamy factors such as academic background, but rather by 'individual-level similarity' (*kojin reberu de no dōshitsusei*). Second, socially alike individuals deciding to get married on their own volition implies their equality at the time of marriage. In the case of arranged marriages, an awareness is easily engendered that marriage be arranged depending upon the potential earning capacity and career lifestyle of a prospective husband who is working. However, in the case of love-based marriages, a prospective wife's current or would-be career lifestyle should also be considered.

The second epochal change is the emerging tendency for women to either marry later or not at all. The total fertility rate, which was close to a stable 2.1, began to decline from 1974, dropping to 1.8 in 1977. Those who brought about this decline were females of the baby boom and post-baby boom generations, who were the generations of those graduating from universities in the early 1970s.

The third change was that graduating from university was no longer the exception for women. In the 1960s, there were a limited number of people who knew female acquaintances who had advanced to university. This was no longer the case by 1975. While a good many women were still unemployed after graduation, female graduates began moving into quite a wide range of occupations, especially in the mass media. By 1975, it was certainly not unusual for young women to aim for university and it came to be recognised that it was a matter of course for this to be determined by ability.

The extremely important social changes outlined above occurred gradually throughout Japan's period of high economic growth and were complete by 1980. This period was one in which an increasing housewifisation occurred and a modern gender-based division of labour was consolidated. At the same time, a foundation that could reverse these trends had also been tacitly prepared.

## The low growth period: 1976–1986

As a result of the first oil shock that began in late 1973, Japan's high economic growth, which was already experiencing a downturn, had come to an end. In 1975, Japan was in the midst of a depression. While the advancement rate for males wishing to attend university reached an all-time high of 41% during this year, it declined thereafter and did not reach this level again until 1996. The female advancement rate also began to stagnate. The desire to undertake tertiary education was influenced by the state of the economy. This is because tertiary education is, in a sense, a kind of long-term investment.

In the advanced industrialised countries feminism and the feminist movement arose from the ashes of leftist ideology following the student uprisings from 1968 to 1970. This ideology, which was initially thought to be that of a few 'highly eccentric women,' was gradually adopted by those women with higher education working in academia. It then captivated many other women. While there is considerable diversity among feminist arguments and theory, it is basically a protest against the modern gender-based division of labour. Today, where harsh working conditions for women in agriculture and industry are a thing of the past, the exclusion of women from production activities amounts to a deprivation of opportunities for them. Moreover, the relative importance of domestic labour diminished due to Japan's demographic transition and home mechanisation against the backdrop of which has been a relative decline in the value of family life.

Amid these developments, two expansive underlying trends in the labour of young females began after 1975. First, the female labour force participation rate, which had been declining during the high growth period, reached its lowest point in 1975 for all generations, and began to rise again. This is especially notable for those between 25 and 29 years of age, as shown in figure 5.1. Second, there was a steady decline after 1975 in the percentage of those not working among female university graduates, as well as an emergent and wide-scale increase in the percentage of those entering various occupations. Looking at this type of data, it can be argued that 1975 was an important watershed for women's working behaviour. The housewifisation of women that had been progressing up to that time came to an end and the labour force rate generally began to rise.

**After the bubble economy: 1987 to the present**

Against the backdrop of the spread of feminist thinking and the increase in female university graduates was a shift in the female labour policy from protectionism to egalitarianism. The Equal Opportunity Law was established in 1984 and following the 1985 Plaza Accord, the Japanese economy began to pick up again and female employment expanded. During the five-year period from 1985 to 1990, the number of total female workers increased by 2.32 million and those employed in the non-agricultural-forestry sectors rose by 2.84 million. [Those in the agricultural or forestry sectors decreased.] This was the greatest rise ever over a five-year period. The advancement rate for females to tertiary education also began to rise again.

Looking at the shift towards an increase in female employment after 1975 according to academic background, we find that university graduates have exhibited the most significant change. If we look at the situation following graduation according to the Basic School Survey, the percentage of non-working junior college graduates in 1975 was 24.4%, while 34.7% of new university graduates were out of work. The percentages in 1990 decreased to 9.3% and 14.4%, respectively. While the percentage of non-workers remains smaller for new junior college graduates, the extent of the decrease is greater for new university graduates.

Next, figure 5.4 shows the employment rate according to academic background and age based on the Basic Employment Structure Survey. With 1974 as a base point, for women between the ages of 25 and 29, the order of education levels in terms of the extent of the expansion of the employment rate is: university, junior college, high school and junior high school. It is the same for females aged between 30 and 34. Those under 34 years of age in 1992 were of the generation in which university graduates generally entered university in 1976 and graduated in 1980. One can argue that it was from this generation that the attitude of university graduates toward occupation became stronger than that of junior college or high school graduates. However, it is necessary to examine with caution whether this signifies that highly-educated women have become increasingly career-oriented. This will be considered in the next section.

## One's life course and strata differentiation

### Changes to people's life course

While the employment opportunities for women have expanded in various ways since 1975, the M-shaped labour force rate curve, which has already flattened out in the West, still clearly exists in Japan, suggesting that many difficulties remain for women continuing work while raising their children. In considering this problem, it is important to distinguish between the following two factors. The first is the subjective preferences among women regarding careers. In other words, a preference between getting married and basically focusing on housework; continuing to work as much as possible while married; and not placing much emphasis on marriage and child-rearing from the beginning. The other factor is the exogenous conditions for each of these three lifestyles: in other words, social conditions that facilitate or prevent marrying, not marrying or continuing to work while married.

As a matter of fact, these two factors are intertwined. For instance, the 'housewifisation' and 'housewife ideology' that progressed from the early postwar years to the high growth period was basically a preference exercised by women generally. On the other hand, this preference was sustained by various conditions (such as that a household budget was able to be sustained only by the husband's income or that labour outside the home was harsh) which facilitated a

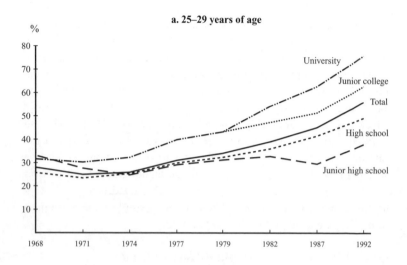

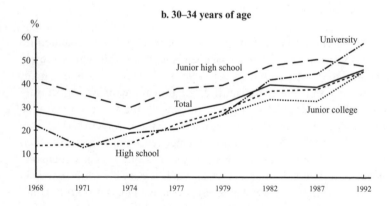

Source: Basic Survey of Employment Structure conducted by the Statistics Bureau.

lifestyle in which women were full-time housewives and made it more acceptable than other preferences and alternatives.

Let's look at the changes in the preferences among women based on data from the 1985 and 1995 SSM Surveys. Figure 5.5 shows the percentage of those who agree with the idea that 'men should work outside and women should look after the house.'[3] From 1985 to 1995,

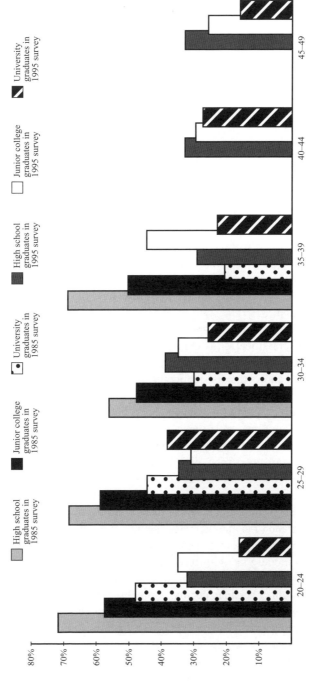

*Figure 5.5:   Approval rates of the opinion that men should work and women should stay home*

Source: SSM Survey data. Only for females.

there was a substantial drop among respondents from most academic backgrounds and cohorts. In addition, while in 1985 there were clear differences based on academic background in which there was a tendency for the approval percentage to be lower the more highly educated a person was, in 1995, the academic background differences had virtually disappeared. The same can be said of age-group and age differences. However, we know that even in 1995, close to 30% of women still supported the notion of a division of labour based on gender roles.

These changes ultimately pertain to 'consciousness.' But what type of course do women choose to follow in life? This can be divided into four categories.[4]

1. Unmarried model: those who have never married.
2. Work continuation model: those who continue to work after marriage.
3. Housewife transition model: those who move into the out of work category following marriage. This also includes those who decide to work again later.
4. Marriage precedence model: those who have never worked before marriage.

Each of the four courses emphasise images and are named accordingly. Since this classification is extremely broad, it should be noted that there may be considerable diversity within the same category.

Table 5.2 shows the distribution based on age according to the 1995 SSM Survey. It should be noted that the observation that the large number of those from the young cohorts belonging to the unmarried model does not necessarily mean that they have chosen this path; it could be the case that they are simply still unmarried. As far as the other points are concerned, first, we know that it was in the generation of those aged 55 or above that quite a few belonged to the marriage precedence model. People of this age are mostly graduates of high school or below and about 20% of them spent the three to seven years between graduation and marriage 'helping with the housework' without working outside. Next, while in the old generations the housewife transition model vied with the work continuation model, the former became gradually ascendant, and after peaking among the 40–44 year old generation, it began to decline. From this, we know that the peak of 'housewifisation' was in the generation following the baby boomers.

Looking at this based on academic background, the following characteristics, which are not shown in the table, can be observed.[5] First, among the 40 to 49 year olds, there are more university graduates than those with different academic backgrounds who

*Table 5.2: Distribution of female life-course patterns by age*

| Age | Single | Married | | | N |
| | | Continued to work | Changed to household domestic work | Married before getting a job | |
|---|---|---|---|---|---|
| 65–69 | 1.7 | 36.4 | 35.5 | 26.5 | 121 |
| 60–64 | 4.9 | 32.2 | 42.7 | 20.3 | 143 |
| 55–59 | 0.0 | 34.1 | 47.0 | 18.9 | 132 |
| 50–54 | 4.6 | 42.5 | 43.7 | 9.2 | 174 |
| 45–49 | 5.2 | 38.1 | 50.5 | 6.2 | 194 |
| 40–44 | 3.4 | 31.8 | 60.2 | 4.6 | 176 |
| 35–39 | 5.3 | 39.3 | 50.7 | 4.7 | 150 |
| 30–34 | 11.1 | 34.1 | 52.4 | 2.4 | 126 |
| 25–29 | 33.3 | 25.0 | 40.6 | 1.0 | 96 |
| 20–24 | 80.2 | 4.4 | 13.2 | 2.2 | 91 |

Source: 1995 SSM Survey data, A slip.

belong to the marriage precedence model and, conversely, less to the work continuation model. Among the 30 to 39 year olds, though, there was an increase in university graduates belonging to the work continuation model, reaching about 50%[6] and the share of those belonging to the housewife transition model declined. Among 25 and 29 year olds, the unmarried percentage of 61.5% among university graduates is conspicuously higher than among junior college and high school graduates at 22.7% and 32.2%, respectively. In addition, among this age group, there are about 45% of junior college and high school graduates who belong to the housewife transition model, while for university graduates it is only 7.7%.

In this manner, looking at actual employment behaviour we know that differences based on academic background have exhibited fundamental changes for the generation immediately following the baby boomers and for subsequent younger generations. While among the present middle-aged generation, university graduates were more strongly inclined towards housewifisation than those with other academic backgrounds, among the young generation university graduates became increasingly more career-oriented than those from other academic backgrounds.

**Strata differentiation among women**

In the previous sections the discussion focused upon the increasing popularisation of higher education and traced the epochal changes taking place with regards to family and work. However, this may have given the impression that women in general are in the same position.

This, however, is not the case. While much of the research on the changes in the employment situation has focused on female university graduates in particular, it is important to note that highly educated females, including not just university graduates but also junior college graduates, remain an overwhelming minority.

This section explores the actual situation surrounding stratification differences among women from various perspectives. To start with, figure 5.6 shows the trends in academic background disparities according to origin strata. The data is a combination of SSM Surveys from 1985 and 1995 and examines the tertiary advancement rate above or equal to the junior college level for each birth cohort. We have examined the similar situation for males in figure 1.5. Because it focused on respondents aged between 25 and 34 in each survey year, these two figures are not strictly comparable. Nevertheless, a general comparison is still possible. Based on these graphs, we know that (1) the disparity among origin strata is greater for women than men, and moreover, (2) the disparity has consistently expanded for women over the past 20 years. For instance, among the 25–34 year old generation, in more than 60% of the cases in which the father was a professional and a self-employed white-collar worker, the respondent received a tertiary education, whereas when the father was a blue-collar or an agricultural worker, it was less than 25%. This disparity has clearly widened compared to 30 years ago. This is a manifestation of the 'widening disparity in upper goods' discussed in chapter 1. What type of differences in terms of occupational careers is produced by these differences in academic background and in origin strata? For this problem, we must recognise that women constitute a far more complex structure than men. This is because women's circumstances differ greatly according to whether they marry or not, and, if they do, which strata their husbands belong to. Of course, in terms of logic, the same can be said of men. However, because both the percentage of women who are employed and their average individual incomes are low, the level of influence is fairly limited.

Moreover, among women it is not possible to analyse 'inter-generational mobility' in a manner similar to that for males. This is because for women there is no representative strata axis like the occupational strata for males.

Because of space limitations, it is impossible to elucidate fully the complex structure that exists for women. Moreover, elucidating this would require a far wider sample than that provided by the SSM Surveys. Therefore, this section is limited to providing an overview that focuses on disparities arising from academic background.

Figure 5.6: *Females' higher education advancement rates by origin stratum*

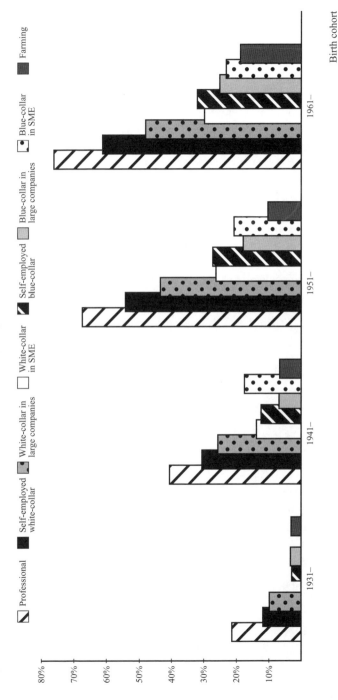

Source: 1985 and 1995 SSM Survey data.

The first opportunity disparity resulting from academic background
is the first job. Table 5.3 shows the distribution of the first job based
on academic background for each birth cohort. While it adopts a
broad job classification, it is possible to observe the following basic
characteristics.

There has been a consistent concentration of university graduates
in professional and white-collar occupations, and since the 1941
birth cohort, regular white-collar jobs have exceeded professional
occupations. This is congruent with the trends observed in figure 5.3.
While junior college graduates evince a virtually similar distribution
to university graduates, among the 1961 (latest) cohort, it came to
more closely resemble a high school graduate rather than a university
graduate. This seems to result from the sophistication of professional
occupations and a kind of 'junior college graduate inflation' that
accompanies the increase in junior college graduate numbers. High
school graduates have consistently found employment mainly in
white-collar occupations, but many have been employed in blue-collar
type jobs in comparison with graduates from the junior college level

*Table 5.3: Distribution of first occupations by educational level (%)*

| Birth cohort | Professional | White-collar | Blue-collar | Self-employed white-collar | Self-employed blue-collar | N |
|---|---|---|---|---|---|---|
| *1931–40* | | | | | | |
| University | 52.2 | 43.6 | 0.0 | 4.4 | 0.0 | 23 |
| Junior college | 42.1 | 31.6 | 10.5 | 15.8 | 0.0 | 19 |
| High school | 6.5 | 60.7 | 18.8 | 7.6 | 6.5 | 356 |
| Junior high school | 2.6 | 19.3 | 47.3 | 4.4 | 26.5 | 457 |
| *1941–50* | | | | | | |
| University | 37.3 | 47.1 | 0.0 | 13.7 | 2.0 | 51 |
| Junior college | 33.7 | 48.0 | 5.1 | 10.2 | 3.1 | 98 |
| High school | 5.2 | 70.3 | 16.6 | 5.2 | 2.8 | 616 |
| Junior high school | 3.8 | 24.2 | 60.0 | 3.0 | 9.4 | 265 |
| *1951–60* | | | | | | |
| University | 38.1 | 45.4 | 2.1 | 14.4 | 0.0 | 97 |
| Junior college | 36.7 | 55.3 | 1.9 | 5.6 | 0.6 | 161 |
| High school | 10.3 | 68.5 | 18.2 | 1.4 | 1.6 | 571 |
| Junior high school | 4.0 | 15.8 | 77.6 | 0.0 | 2.6 | 76 |
| *1961–70* | | | | | | |
| University | 33.3 | 58.7 | 1.6 | 6.4 | 0.0 | 63 |
| Junior college | 17.8 | 72.6 | 6.7 | 3.0 | 0.0 | 135 |
| High school | 13.9 | 68.2 | 17.0 | 0.6 | 0.3 | 330 |
| Junior high school | 9.1 | 45.5 | 36.4 | 9.1 | 0.0 | 11 |

Source: 1985 and 1995 SSM Survey data, but only for females. White-collar and blue-
collar workers include part-timers.

and above. Junior high school graduates have taken mainly blue-collar jobs, either working for others or are self-employed (the latter includes agriculture). However, this trend peaked with the 1951 cohort. Most of the 1961 cohort was employed in white-collar jobs. This is because of the overall decline in blue-collar jobs.

Even for current jobs at the time of the survey, this pattern of first job distribution to professional, white-collar and blue-collar occupations differing according to academic background has continued in the same way. However, concerning current occupations, different situations have arisen pertaining to status such as unemployment and part-time work, which do not appear as occupational strata, in the current classification. These are influenced by such factors as marriage, husband's strata and the household budget, etc. As a result, unlike males, the strength of a woman's academic background does not simply correlate with the height of her occupational status.

In order to examine this situation, table 5.4, focusing on women aged between 35 and 55 in 1995, highlights the relationship between academic background and husbands' current occupation. This age group consists of those who were 18 year olds between 1959 and 1978 (it does not include the most recent cohort who graduated after the bubble economy) who are currently playing a key role in economic activities and family life.

The husbands of female university graduates were mainly either professionals or white-collar workers in large companies. While junior college graduates are quite similar in this respect, there is a tendency for their husbands to be from more diverse strata. Many of the husbands of high school graduates were white-collar workers in SMEs or blue-collar workers. About 60% of the husbands of junior high school graduates were blue-collar workers, either self-employed or working in SMEs, or agricultural workers. While this disparity in academic backgrounds is rather pronounced, it is very similar to the distribution of present occupation according to academic background for males in their 40s in 1995 (see table 2.2).

Next, table 5.5 shows the relationship between academic background and females' current employment situation. From this table, the following structural characteristics can be observed.

1. The out-of-work percentage is positively related to the strength of one's academic background. In other words, the weaker the academic background, the higher the labour force rate.
2. Full-time workers (professionals, full-time white-collar and blue-collar workers), where gender-based employment or discrimination is the great issue, account for only 24.9% of

Table 5.4:  *Husbands' occupational strata by wife's educational level (35–54 years of age) (%)*

| Wife's educational level | Husband's occupational strata | | | | | | | | |
|---|---|---|---|---|---|---|---|---|---|
|  | Professional | White-collar in large company | White-collar in SME | Self-employed white-collar | Blue-collar in large company | Blue-collar in SME | Self-employed blue-collar | Farmer | N |
| University | 45.3 | 29.5 | 7.4 | 12.6 | 0.0 | 2.1 | 3.2 | 0.0 | 95 |
| Junior college | 29.0 | 29.7 | 10.3 | 12.3 | 5.2 | 7.1 | 5.2 | 1.3 | 155 |
| High school | 7.8 | 22.0 | 16.4 | 10.9 | 11.1 | 16.4 | 12.1 | 3.2 | 718 |
| Junior high school | 2.6 | 6.8 | 14.2 | 6.3 | 10.0 | 37.4 | 18.4 | 4.2 | 190 |
| Total | 12.9 | 21.2 | 14.5 | 10.5 | 9.2 | 17.4 | 11.5 | 2.9 | 1158 |

Source: 1995 SSM Survey data, but only for females. The table includes only those who were married and excludes 'unknown'.

Table 5.5:  *Distribution of the respondents' employment situation by educational level (35–54 years of age) (%)*

| Respondent's educational level | Respondent's employment situation | | | | | | | | | |
|---|---|---|---|---|---|---|---|---|---|---|
|  | Professional | Full-time white-collar | Full-time blue-collar | Self-employed white-collar | Self-employed blue-collar | Part-time white-collar | Part-time blue-collar | Unemployed | N | % |
| University | 16.5 | 11.0 | 0.0 | 24.8 | 0.9 | 13.8 | 0.0 | 36.7 | 109 | 8.0 |
| Junior college | 12.0 | 14.2 | 1.1 | 15.8 | 3.3 | 14.2 | 4.4 | 35.0 | 183 | 13.4 |
| High school | 4.0 | 14.8 | 5.7 | 14.5 | 5.6 | 15.3 | 12.6 | 27.6 | 826 | 60.4 |
| Junior high school | 2.4 | 7.2 | 13.6 | 7.2 | 13.2 | 11.2 | 23.6 | 25.6 | 250 | 18.3 |
| Total | 5.8 | 13.0 | 6.1 | 13.9 | 6.3 | 13.5 | 12.5 | 28.9 | 1368 | 100.0 |

Source: 1995 SSM Survey data, but only for females. The table includes the unmarried.

all cases. Self-employed workers, part-time workers and non-workers account for roughly an equal share of the remaining 75% of these cases.

3. The overwhelming majority of full-time workers are those with an academic background below the level of high school graduate, while university graduates only constitute 8.8%. In addition, female university graduates who are full-time workers only account for 2.3% of all women.

4. On the whole, the differences in occupational strata disparities arising from academic background among women are not as significant as the cases of the first job in table 5.3 and males in chapter 2. This is because there was a tendency for females with a strong academic background to leave professional or full-time white-collar jobs to become full-time housewives.

Because the influence of academic background is related not only to the type of occupation women adopt, but also to the occupation of the men they marry, women's strata status cannot simply be expressed according to their own occupational status. Simply looking at the influence on individual incomes is insufficient to understand the ascendancy of the highly educated strata, which comprises many of the non-workers. In this regard, household income, which includes husbands' income, is a kind of overall indicator.

The median of annual household incomes is calculated for each of the three levels of junior high school graduate, high school graduate and junior college/university graduate, and table 5.6 shows the ratio of the two upper levels to junior high school graduate level for each birth cohort.

From this table, it can be argued that disparities in annual household income based on academic background among the age group of 35–54 year olds are considerably greater for women than for men. In other words, the total economic earning rate for those with strong academic backgrounds is higher for women than for men.[7] This is because since more men have received a tertiary education than women, the probability of a highly educated female marrying a highly educated man is greater than *vice versa*. Moreover, a highly educated female has a good chance to maintain a relatively advantageous household income, despite the tendency to be out of work.

Whether this trend also applies to younger generations is unclear according to this survey and is an issue for future research. Nevertheless, from the current data, we can observe the following aspects of female strata differentiation.

*Table 5.6: Household annual income disparities by gender, age and*
         *educational background (1995)*

| Educational | Age | | | |
| background | 25–34 | 35–44 | 45–54 | 55–64 |
|---|---|---|---|---|
| *Male* | | | | |
| Junior college and university | 1.34 | 1.56 | 1.40 | 1.91 |
| High school | 1.13 | 1.28 | 1.22 | 1.22 |
| *Female* | | | | |
| Junior college and university | 1.27 | 1.69 | 2.04 | 1.70 |
| High school | 1.04 | 1.33 | 1.27 | 1.46 |

Note: The figures represent the median values in terms of ratio to the median values
of junior high school graduates.
Source: SSM Survey data.

1. While the hierarchical status of females is similar to that of males
   in that it is prescribed considerably by academic background, it is
   also different in that it cannot be traced to their own occupational
   status.
2. Overall, there is a stronger possibility that disparities based on
   academic background are greater for women than men.
3. Moreover, the disparities involved in attaining an academic
   background based on origin strata are greater for women than for
   men and are expanding.
4. On the other hand, people who are highly educated full-time
   workers only constitute a minimal percentage of women overall.

**The choice of highly educated females**

There is a greater degree of difference in female strata depending
whether one is a university graduate or not than it is for males.
Against the background of this is a situation in which women with
an academic background below the level of junior college are more
frequently and clearly linked to different types of occupations than
males. Of course, this is one of the causes behind the general wage
disparities between males and females. For instance, junior college
and nursing school graduates are tied to 'ancillary jobs.' In addition,
a discrepancy with males has been created through physical skills in
blue-collar occupations and the like. It is only for university graduates
that these obstacles do not exist. Then, one can expect that for them
only universal qualifications such as academic background and ability,
totally unrelated to physical differences, are involved in determining
the chances of taking intellectual jobs.

In this sense, paradoxically, the issue of life chance disparities between the genders should become most acute among university graduates.

It is difficult to anticipate whether female university graduates will become increasingly career-oriented in the future or whether there will be an increase in the number of women who conform to the unmarried model or the work continuation model. There are several relevant factors here. First, in terms of the problem of individual preferences, if female university graduates were able to find employment, there would be a stronger tendency for them to want to continue working in comparison to those with different academic backgrounds. Above all, this is because the wage levels of highly educated women are virtually the same as that for males and that the future benefits forgone by leaving work are considerably large. In fact, this has always been the case. The tendency for those who find work upon graduation to continue working in some form is, to a certain degree, higher among university graduates in their 40s than for those with different academic backgrounds.

On the other hand, the tendency for women with strong academic backgrounds to have husbands with high incomes, paradoxically, works to weaken the will of them to continue working.

Turning to exogenous factors, the conditions for women to continue working while married remains particularly harsh for university graduates in Japanese society. They are related to the family lifestyle opportunities and life courses female university graduates might create after marriage, as well as to the decisions of individuals and companies premised upon them.

1.  In many cases, the family that female university graduates might create tends to live in conurbations centred on Tokyo and Osaka where places of employment for the husband and wife with high education are concentrated. Because they naturally have to live in the city outskirts, their commuting time is extremely long. As a result, it is difficult to reconcile work with housework and raising children.

2.  There is a strong possibility that the husband and the wife employed in a large company or the central bureaucracy will be transferred to various locations domestically and abroad. This is a general personnel management policy in large Japanese organisations that makes it difficult to maintain a family life without either the husband or the wife leaving work. The present employees in large companies or the central bureaucracy who are older than or equal to 40 have accepted this lifestyle. Those who can

stay away from this necessity are limited to self-employed workers, teachers or local government officials.

3. Not only is the practice of lifetime employment for female university graduates in large Japanese companies limited, but it also
   makes women feel out of place, even after they succeed in entering
   a company. This is based on the practice of total commitment
   by the employee to the company. It is more difficult for married
   women than men to apply themselves to work and companionships
   in the company without thinking about the family.

It is the Japanese style of so-called 'companyism' that is at the root
of this situation. To put it in somewhat extreme terms, it can be
argued that the housewifisation phenomenon that arose during the
period of high economic growth was a different manifestation of
this companyism in which women were transformed into the narrow
role of defender of the home front for Japan's corporate warriors.
Under companyism, the possibility of women being able to reconcile
work as a career with family life is extremely limited. In a sense,
companyism 'makes family of secondary importance and prioritises
the company.' In the case of males, it is made possible by the wife
caring for the family, whereas for women, a 'house husband' does
not usually exist.

   There are five theoretical possibilities underlying this fundamental
contradiction.

1. In a bizarre twist, the best way for women to reconcile career and
   family with companyism is to completely subsume family under
   companyism. In other words, the company fully takes care of the
   housework and raising the children. For instance, the husband
   and wife work for the same company and live in housing provided
   by that company. Both prioritise work while the company is
   completely responsible for the housework and raising the children.
   It can be argued that this is one fabulous example of complete
   equality and amounts to corporate communism. Of course, this
   is merely a bad joke.

2. Just as before, women continue to be excluded from the core
   personnel of the main economic organisation that is the company.

3. Premised upon companyism, women take on careers and abandon
   the idea of having a family. This may have been a quietly and
   slowly developing situation. Of course, this does not mean that
   all women will choose this option. However, there is a strong
   possibility that the percentage is rising.

4. Companyism survives in Japan, though somewhat in a diminished way. In this case, in order for highly educated women to reconcile careers with family, they will advance into occupations in which there is little fear of long-distance commutes, such as professional jobs, local government and welfare-related services.
5. Repudiate companyism and raise the possibility of reconciling a career and family.

Many people will think the final choice is desirable. However, this is not that easy. The culture of companyism is highly autogenous. There is little likelihood of it changing to the extent outlined in the Equal Opportunity Law. To the economic entity that is the company, companyism is, of course, rational, and for its members, it is also of cultural significance in terms of wages, lifestyle security, identity and expressions of creativity. It is difficult for agents to attempt intrinsically to change this stable balance. If it does change, it will be as a result of either the company itself no longer being able to act in a manner expected by the culture of companyism in a changing global economy (layoffs and reductions in various allowances) or public policies providing institutional support (child-care and housing) for certain legal regulations[8], or combining the two.

However, finally, in order to avert any misunderstanding, the preceding discussion does not claim that it is only 'companyism' that is the cause behind the M-shaped work model in Japan. One cannot deny that it is the perceptions of family and career, urban structure, the child-care system and, above all else, the preferences of women themselves that are the key.

## Women and stratification theory

### Two contradictory premises

Do women ultimately constitute a stratum that is in conflict with males? Are they situated within a stratum as individuals on a similar footing to males, regardless of sex? Are they situated within a stratum forming a family with a male head of household? There have been no issues that have perplexed stratification researchers as much as these over the last 20 years.[9] There is an inherently acute dilemma here in class and stratification theory.

Class and stratification theory, both the Marxist and Weberian accounts, was originally premised upon the 'basic principle of market conditions' in which 'a person's hierarchical status is prescribed by the market opportunities he/she enjoys in the labour market.' On this premise, stratification theory so far considered hierarchical status mainly in terms of occupational and employee status. However, this premise is incompatible with the notion of 'household communality,' another premise of stratification theory. The latter claims that the household is a life community and the basic unit of strata that cannot be further divided, because it generally has a consumption communism aspect to it. In other words, 'the basic principle of market conditions' considers strata in the context of relations of production activities that is the labour market. On the other hand, the premise of 'household communality' perceives strata mainly in terms of consumption life.

In the event people join together in a family business to engage in production activities, these two notions of strata could be congruent. However, the existence of women, who are today increasingly engaging in production activities independent of their husbands and households exposes a fundamental contradiction between these two premises in stratification theory.

Several empirical approaches have been previously adopted to address questions relating to whether it is the household or the individual that is the unit of strata and also whether it is the household, the husband or the woman that determines the issue of her strata (the major studies are Felson *et al.* 1974; Velsor *et al.* 1979; Erikson 1984; Naoi 1990 and 1994; Akagawa 1998). These studies all have in common a methodology that draws out indicators that are believed to reflect the strata circumstances of women, and which of the following, the household, the husband or the woman's attributes, best explains the distribution of this statistically. Subjective class and strata identification are often used as indicators in these studies. And, both Western and Japanese research demonstrates that it is basically the husband or the household's circumstances that has far greater explanatory power, and that the influence of the woman's circumstances is weak.

Nevertheless, it is difficult to come to the conclusion, based on this, that one should consider the concept of strata mainly in terms of the husband's attributes or the household. That is to say, this problem is not simply one of empirical relevancy, but rather a problem in which theoretical relevancy has crumbled. Incidentally, this problem was not conspicuous so much among stratification researchers, because few of them noticed the contradiction between 'the basic principle of market conditions' and 'household communality.' However, even if it is not conspicuous, this does not mean that stratification theory is in a sound state. Whether there are many or few women who work independently of their husbands – in fact, if we consider incomes, it is still insignificant in statistical terms – there is no changing the fact that stratification theory contains theoretical contradictions.

We can examine the degree of incompatibility in the data at the actual individual level brought about by the contradiction between 'the premise of household communality' and 'the premise of the basic principle of market opportunities.' Table 5.7 shows the combined distribution of the employment circumstances for women and their husbands from the perspective of women. The following points are observed.

1. When premised on the basic principle of market opportunities, non-working females are excluded from the strata classification and their percentage amounts to 39.5%. Also, it is difficult to see the part-time work carried out by women who have working husbands as a primary indicator of a woman's strata classification. These people numbered 431 or 15.5%. In total, 55% of women are excluded from the strata classification when market opportunities are primarily considered.

2. Looking at the problem brought about by the premise of household communality, there is the issue of women in a different type of employment to their husbands. Because the male and female categories differ in table 5.7, we will consider the following four categories as being common to both genders: 'white-collar employee (including part-time workers),' 'blue-collar employees (including part-time workers),' 'self-employed white-collar workers' and 'self-employed blue-collar workers.' If the husband and wife belong to the same category, there is no problem with household communality. However, it is inconsistent if they belong to different categories. One may assume that there are no problems when the woman is unmarried or when the woman or the husband are out of work. The bold figures in the table represent an inconsistent combination. This is often called a 'cross-class family,' and numbers 520 or constitutes 18.6% of all families. Among married women it is 23.5%, and among those women who are married and working it is 40.4% that constitute 'cross-class' families.

Feminist scholars have presented a different and far more radical issue. They claim that women constitute a different stratum or class to men. First, if we consider strata as status within market conditions,

Table 5.7: Combination of wives' and husbands' employment situations (%) (Column total = 100%)

| Wives' employment situation | Husbands' employment situation | | | | | | | | | |
|---|---|---|---|---|---|---|---|---|---|---|
| | Unmarried | White-collar in large company | White-collar in SME | Self-employed white-collar | Blue-collar in large company | Blue-collar in SME | Self-employed blue-collar | Unemployed | Total | N |
| Full-time white-collar | 37.0 | 18.5 | 16.3 | 7.4 | 16.4 | 15.3 | 5.6 | 8.1 | 17.9 | 499 |
| Full-time blue-collar | 7.0 | 1.5 | 4.0 | 1.5 | 5.9 | 8.3 | 5.0 | 4.6 | 4.8 | 135 |
| Self-employed white-collar | 7.1 | 3.2 | 4.0 | 53.0 | 2.3 | 3.6 | 19.0 | 2.7 | 10.8 | 301 |
| Self-employed blue-collar | 4.2 | 1.7 | 1.2 | 4.4 | 1.8 | 5.4 | 34.4 | 4.2 | 7.1 | 199 |
| Part-time white-collar | 9.6 | 19.0 | 13.5 | 4.1 | 8.2 | 11.1 | 5.0 | 5.8 | 10.3 | 287 |
| Part-time blue-collar | 4.9 | 7.5 | 12.9 | 4.1 | 18.1 | 19.4 | 6.5 | 8.4 | 9.5 | 266 |
| Unemployed | 30.3 | 48.5 | 48.0 | 25.6 | 47.4 | 36.8 | 24.3 | 66.3 | 39.5 | 1102 |
| Total | 20.6 | 16.6 | 11.7 | 9.7 | 6.1 | 13.8 | 12.1 | 9.4 | 100.0 | |
| N | 575 | 464 | 325 | 270 | 171 | 386 | 337 | 261 | | 2789 |

Note: The table excludes those cases in which the employment situations of either the husband or the wife are unknown. 'Professionals' are included in either of the white-collar strata according to company size and employment status. 'Self-employed blue-collar' includes self-employed agricultural, forestry and fishery workers.

source: 1995 SSM Survey data. Only for females aged 20–69.

it is clear that in the market women are given opportunities owing to their gender that differ from men. The types of jobs open to women differ to those available to men and the degree to which these are open also differ. Even in the same occupation the chances for promotion and career prospects differ, as does remuneration. In principle, this situation is similar to one where someone with a different academic background is given different market opportunities. Second, similar to academic background, status (*mibun*) differences are often associated with gender. Here, status (*mibun*) refers to a social category, classified according to an innate or innate-like attribute, which is given different market and lifestyle opportunities through the particular course one adopts in life. What produces this are general and basic perceptions of superiority and inferiority, exclusionary and discriminatory treatment in various settings and an overall world of social meaning that sustains these elements. Of course, in the case of gender, unlike race and discrimination against outcast people, it is wrong to perceive women as being unilaterally placed in a subordinate role in all aspects of social life. However, it is undeniable that in terms of social standings, as determined by an individual's placement through market labour characteristics in an industrial society, women on the whole have been given an inferior status (*mibun*).

In response, Goldthorpe (1983: 469) claims that the fact that women are placed in a situation in which they are given few opportunities can be traced to an economic dependency on their husbands and that 'lines of class division and potential conflict run between, but not through, families.' In other words, he thinks, class categories and gender disparities are separate. However, the problem is 'in what theoretical rationale are gender based opportunity disparities, in principle, distinguished from class opportunity disparities?' Goldthorpe does not address this question.

In this manner, the basic principles of market opportunities and household communality do not sufficiently conform to reality and are theoretically problematic. The next chapter examines what we should make of this.

# 6 The Prospects for a New Stratified Society

## The modern in stratification

What is stratification? What is class? This book has sought to address these questions. Another important issue pertains to why 'class,' which has been the topic of fierce debates over the last 200 years, has come to be seen as unimportant today? Answering these questions requires a new understanding of the nature of society that has developed in modern times.

The term post-modern has been widely used over a long period of time. In Japanese, it is translated as 'de-modern' (*datsu kindai*). More precisely, the term refers to 'after the modern' and denotes a new era following the end of an age that was modern. In sociological terms, many scholars such as Lyotard (1979) spoke of the post-modern in connection to 'the loss of grand narratives.' The term 'modern' originally derived from the French word *moderne* (fashionable). It was used to refer to 'something contemporary,' particularly from the late seventeenth to eighteenth century during which arguments emerged over whether contemporaneous culture and especially literature were superior to that of the classical and renaissance periods. Thereafter, the term gradually came to denote a periodisation different to the classical and middle ages. That said, it also differs according to genre and even among historians there is no established theory as to when the modern era began. However, the sense that society as a whole, including its political and economic structure, has entered a new era distinguishable from preceding periods has been transformed into a firm belief equivalent to the notion of the earth being round.

Despite longstanding sociological attempts dating from before the time of Comte, we do not yet have a precise answer to the question of how to separate what is really modern from preceding periods. Scholars have employed various dichotomies or trends such as *Gemainschaft – Gesellschaft*, community – association, rationalisation, and individualism – universalism. These certainly highlight the characteristics of modernity, but are not strictly inherent to it. For instance, even super-modern corporate organisations contain obvious *Gemainschaft*-type elements.

Only the following two elements can be said to be clearly related to the essential features of modernity. One of these is, evidently, modern industry and technology. Railroads, automobiles, aeroplanes, televisions and personal computers clearly neither existed nor were conceived in the pre-modern era. In addition, a social system that could produce and consume these items only developed in the modern era.

The other element is modern historical consciousness, in other words, modern self-consciousness as a historical particularity. This can be called 'a grand narrative.' While the substance of this self-consciousness takes many forms, this consciousness itself is a common feature of modern societies. At the heart of this is historical consciousness and in most cases it is linked to the concept of historical development.

## Industrialisation and class/strata

The concept of class arose from the amalgam of these two features of modernity: industry and history. Immediately following the French Revolution, Claude Henri de Saint-Simon created the category of 'industrialist class' and emphasised that it is precisely this class that would play a leading role in the coming industrial society. It was Saint-Simon's protégé and the founder of modern sociology, Auguste Comte, who carried on this line of thinking. It was Marx who fused this idea with Hegelian philosophy and classical economics to create his own, unique theory of historical development. Marx and Engels audaciously proposed that 'all history is the history of class conflict' – a thesis that indeed greatly contributed to global thinking thereafter. This theory was posited about 150 years ago, in 1848, with the outbreak of the February and March Revolutions in Paris and Vienna, respectively.

The meaning of class, which emerged in this manner, was as 'the standard bearer of historical transformation.' This was certainly not a static conceptual framework that simply classified people according to socio-economic differences, but perceived 'class as an agent' that guides the modern self-consciousness (story) that is history.

However, class has another meaning. This was discovered by the exiled Russian sociologist Pitirim A. Sorokin. He perceived industrial society not as an arena for class conflict, but as a space for hierarchical status attainment and mobility. This is referred to as 'strata as attainment.'

To be sure, the phenomenon of mobility is an indispensable part of industrialisation, which is one of the basic trends of modernity.

Industrialisation certainly does not denote merely the development of specific individual industries such as manufacturing industrialisation or informatisation, but generally just the emergence of new industries. What type of industry will develop is a creative issue and cannot be determined in advance. In the past, the so-called secondary industries such as mining and manufacturing had developed first. This was accompanied or followed by development in commerce, beginning with retail and finance, and then in the service industries catering to individuals and business enterprises corresponding to the various needs of a developed industrial society. Economic growth, in the long-term perspective, is nothing other than the development of production and consumption of new products and services. When this happens, from where do the people who produce these new goods and services emerge? These people are either those who were employed in old industries and changed occupations (intra-generational mobility) or are the children of those employed in old industries who have found new employment (inter-generational mobility).[1]

This leads to the following, compelling proposition regarding industrialisation: 'strata mobility is indispensable for society to achieve industrialisation.'

At a glance, this proposition resembles the orthodox theory of industrialisation. It was originally believed that strata mobility opportunities and industrialisation would continually and eternally expand in the long-term. And, in a related manner, other various strata disparities would also continually diminish while the trend towards equalisation would continue. Against the backdrop of such speculation is the functionalist theory of evolution. Industrialisation theory perceives industrialisation as an endless, expansive process of efficiency and rationality. In addition, it sees strata disparities primarily as an obstacle to the efficiency and rationality of industrial society. Hence, the goal of industrialisation theory is manifested in the thesis of attainment in which all people work according to their abilities and aptitude. Industrialisation is seen as an eternal process leading to this utopia.

However, if we argue that industrial society is economically rational, this is only in the more short-term sense that rational companies will survive the selective pressures of short-term markets. It does not mean that society as a whole becomes more rational in the long-term sense. What is important for industrial society is the opening up of new economic opportunities. Therefore, it is necessary neither for opportunities to be completely equalised nor for equalisation to be everlasting.

For both strata mobility and industrialisation, they must be sustained by motives at the individual/micro-level. These involve people taking advantage of the opening up of new economic opportunities and pursuing individual attainment. Hence, we believe that the following basic thesis regarding the relationship between modern society and strata holds true: 'A modern society is one that can link the strata attainment motives and creative destruction (Schumpeter) of individuals to macro-economic development by opening up, in principle, strata mobility opportunities.'

In the case of Japan, there have been two significant and discontinuous expansions of opportunities. Needless to say, one was the Meiji Restoration during which the pre-modern status (*mibun*) system was abolished and strata mobility was institutionalised through school education. However, the various limits of this transformation were gradually exposed during the Shōwa era. Relations between the landowners and tenant farmers in the farming villages became rigid and the opportunities for tenant farmers were curbed significantly. Moreover, as a result of the substantial economic costs associated with secondary and tertiary education, the advancement opportunities for the low-income strata remained limited. As for the second discontinuity, the various postwar reforms such as those pertaining to the educational system and agricultural land had the effect of breaking the shackles. This was further promoted by an expansive education policy geared towards high economic growth, beginning in 1960, and the human resource development that accompanied this.

## The illusion of equalisation

The period of high economic growth transformed the lifestyle of the Japanese people. Previously, the average household did not contain a television, refrigerator, automobile or telephone. People worked from early in the morning until late at night. Relatively high income families sent, if they could afford, their children to institutions of higher education, and dreamt that the next generation would come to enjoy a more affluent and cultured life.

By the time of the first Oil Shock, the world had undergone a fundamental transformation. Japanese engineers developed the bullet train, university campuses suffered student revolts and Japan hosted the 1964 Olympics and 1970 World Expo. Japan's GDP grew rapidly to become the second largest in the free world. Urban workers moved from wooden apartments into 2DK (2 bedrooms with a dining-kitchen) housing complexes in the suburbs. The number of salaried workers increased. City trams disappeared and absolute poverty was essentially eradicated. That people began to emphasise environmental issues and exclaim 'go to hell GNP' was nothing other than proof that Japan had attained affluence. With international developments such as the Sino–Soviet split, China's Cultural Revolution and the Soviet invasion of Czechoslovakia, socialism rapidly lost its appeal.

Looking at the undoubted advances in lifestyle affluence in Japan, it was not unreasonable for many sociologists to believe that 'equalisation had progressed.' In fact, in many aspects, equalisation did expand. The following examples can be cited to support this argument:

1. The spread of consumer durables.
2. Diminishing urban-rural lifestyle differences.
3. The elimination of inter-strata and inter-regional disparities in the high school advancement rate.
4. The elimination of relations between former land owners and tenant farmers, as well as family lineage consciousness.
5. A certain degree of reduction in individual and household income inequalities.
6. As a whole, these five trends resulted in a general levelling off of lifestyles.

To demonstrate this, figure 6.1 reveals the trends in the spread of refrigerators and telephones according to strata. Even beyond these items, many consumer durables such as washing machines, televisions and automobiles etc. spread rapidly to all households during the high growth period. As can be seen from the typical example of refrigerators, this spread of consumer durables passes through the following stages: equal poverty → expanding disparities → equal affluence. This is the process by which upper goods are downgraded to basic goods. There is no doubt that this spread of consumer durables has brought about a basic 'equalisation of lifestyles.' In terms of all households benefiting from the consumer revolution, equalisation has advanced to a notable degree.

The equalisation of lifestyles resulting from the overall rise in affluence led to a decline in the prominence of strata and class differences. Amid the increase in the number of those pursuing side jobs in rural villages, the disparities in living standards between the former land owners, old-established families and tenant farmers have been eliminated completely. Any child can now attend high school

## *Figure 6.1: Diffusion process of durable consumer goods by stratum*

### a. Refrigerators

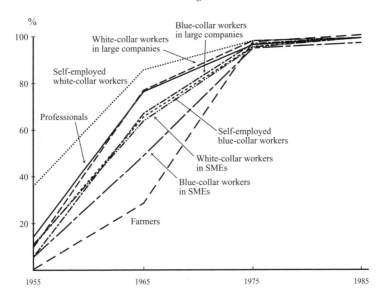

### b. Telephones

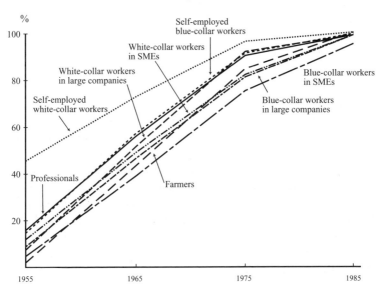

Note: Data on telephones for 1965 are unavailable.
Source: SSM Survey data. Only for males aged 20–69.

while there is an understanding that advancement to university
is determined largely by scholastic ability. While the people in
residential areas on the outskirts of large cites are heterogenous
in occupational strata, they live in proximity to each other and are
comparatively similar in ages and incomes. With the transformation
of many of the inner-city areas of Tokyo into commercial districts, the
former hierarchical distinction among them between the uptown and
the downtown has declined in significance.

This elimination or diminution of strata disparities is an undeniable
social fact – one that is widely acknowledged. In the 1960s, the
Marxist theory of class rapidly lost its credibility. Class (whether or
not it previously existed) has now disappeared as an agent. The theory
of industrialisation appears to have been victorious. However, in fact,
amid this process of equalisation and levelling, non-diminishing or
gradually expanding disparities clearly exist as outlined below:

1. Opportunities for tertiary education. Since 1955, the disparities
   for male university advancement rates according to origin strata
   remain mostly unchanged. Using the data from 1965 as a base, the
   disparities have grown slightly. They have grown even further for
   women.
2. Income disparities. The overall disparity in individual and
   household incomes declined somewhat until 1975, and while it
   basically remained stable thereafter, disparities at the household
   level grew.
3. Occupational disparities based on academic background. Compared to junior high school graduates, the possibilities of a university or high school graduate landing a high-ranking white-collar
   job have increased since 1955.
4. Inter-generational circular mobility. While mobility has partially
   increased, there are also short-term fluctuations. In general,
   and over the long-term, the mobility pattern can be said to be
   stable. In other words, it is difficult to argue that relative mobility
   opportunities have continued to expand.

These points prove that industrialisation theory is inappropriate.
Equalisation has certainly progressed, but not to the extent predicted
by industrialisation theory.

## The semantics of strata

There are a significant number of strata researchers today who make
claims about 'de-stratified society,' 'de-classed society' or 'classless

society.'[2] While they all attempt to articulate important epochal changes in contemporary advanced societies, the concepts they have introduced are ambiguous. What kind of important changes have strata undergone? In order to answer this question correctly, we must first assess what strata and class have basically denoted up until now.

## Class as agents and strata as attainment

As previously suggested, the 'class as an agent' and 'strata as an attainment' dichotomy is useful.[3] This concept comprises multiple elements, which can be classified internally.

The concept of class as an agent comprises the following elements: (a) fundamental conflict of interests; (b) political agent; and (c) historical agent. A fundamental conflict of interests refers to the notion of class as an exclusive collective with inherently conflicting interests. Above all, the original Marxist theory of exploitation, which is based on the theory of labour value, and the generalised theory of exploitation through the works of nco-Marxists such as John Roemer and Erik O. Wright, underpins this collision of interests. The theory of domination expounded by Ralf Dahrendorf and the (mistakenly named) neo-Weberian closure theory also serves as a theoretical basis for this conflict of interests.[4] The Feminist theory of patriarchy and its claims of unpaid labour is an adaptation of this.

A political agent refers to the concept of class as a major actor in the macro-political process. In this context, the concept of class is premised on a tacit classification based on occupational or industrial lines. The 'theory of pluralistic group interests' and the concept of 'corporatism' posit that classes in the form of political actors exist and have attempted to understand politics as an arena for the mediation of potentially conflicting interests among these classes.

A historical agent denotes class as an emergent agent that plays a role in the unfolding of the grand narrative that is history. The materialist concept of history is representative of this notion, which posits that history is characterised by dramatic spectacles such as the birth of a new class, its conflict and struggle with older classes and the decline and disappearance of the pre-existing class. The concept of class here is also premised on a tacit classification based on occupational or industrial lines.[5]

The preceding discussion has highlighted the three main elements comprising the concept of class as an agent. These three elements have combined to exert a powerful influence on the typical conceptualisation of class. From the nineteenth until after the mid-twentieth century, this influence was dominant and its legacy continues until the present day.

On the other hand, the concept of strata as an attainment can be understood in terms of various different images. First, (d) there is inequality in lifestyle opportunities. Apart from economic opportunities such as income, assets and consumer durables, there have been persistent inequalities related to the opportunity to benefit from 'social goods' such as occupational status, job description, education, qualification, social status and honour. This has been conceptualised as 'being stratified' or 'stratification.' Next, is the notion that such inequality (e) constitutes a single hierarchy. According to analyses of status attainment, such a hierarchy has been assumed to constitute the core of 'occupational prestige' and 'socio-economic status.'

There is also the concept that strata are not a persistent hierarchy but (f) a cluster. There is variation among them in the sense that some strata have clear boundaries and are highly significant in terms of all people belonging primarily to one while others have undefined criteria and do not evoke a strong 'typical image.' A great deal of empirical research treats strata as clusters as such, and while their boundaries have been made explicit in an operational sense, their theoretical underpinnings are weak. In addition to occupational strata, it is also possible to conceptualise strata as academic background strata, income strata and asset strata, etc. Moreover, it is often assumed that these correspond to differentiated 'lifestyles.'

Finally, (g) there is the concept of strata as prestige. In people's subjective consciousness strata are an evaluative scale that people use to position themselves *vis-à-vis* other people.[6] A subjective approach to strata such as the *Yankee City* research series conducted by Warner *et al.*, and research into occupational prestige and strata identification are based on this concept. Many of these studies are tacitly based on the assumption that people, for the most part, share a common, subjective evaluation scale.

There are diverse conceptualisations and images of class and strata. The question is: 'which one of these is correct?' To state our conclusion in advance, such diversity reflects the diversity pertaining to the manner in which phenomena related to class and strata emerge empirically. Hence, it is not an issue of which one is correct. Nevertheless, there is still contention over the issue: 'are any of the ways in which class and strata emerge intrinsic?' This is concerned with the theoretical opposition in the issue of 'how does such strata and class differentiation arise?'

## What was 'the conflict of interests'

The notion of 'the death of class' and 'de-class' as claimed by Western sociologists today can basically be said to be an expression of the recognition that class as a historical agent – and not general strata – has disappeared. This is already an indisputable fact. Of course, even today the intellectual tradition of attempting to understand society using a Marxist framework is still deep-rooted, especially among the intelligentsia. Therefore, the word class is used with the tacit expectation that it is an independent unitary actor. However, as discussed, for instance, in chapter 2, even in Bourdieu's reproduction theory 'class' has disappeared as an independent actor. Wright's theory of class (1985; 1987), which is the self-proclaimed representative of contemporary Marxist class theory, is, in effect, a product of stratification theory (Seiyama 1992).

What was the conflict of interests that sustained this notion of class as an agent? A reconstruction of stratification theory must first begin with a theoretical reflection of this issue.

In the case of Marxism, it was the theory of 'exploitation' that sustained this notion of conflicting interests. This maintains that workers have not received the value of what they possess by rights. The issue of what, by rights, belongs to who is explained by the labour theory of value. However, setting aside the case of an independent, self-employed and self-owning worker producing rice, or making bamboo baskets, for example, and then selling them, no standard exists regarding how much of the value of products produced belongs to each worker in the complex sphere of economic activities today. Unless such standards exist, it is impossible to conceptualise 'exploitation.'

Instead, here we present the hypothesis that conflicting interests arising as an economic relationship among occupational strata are both temporary and inadvertent, and that a structural collision of interests could arise only in a political or pre-modern status (*mibun*) system-type of relationship. This hypothesis fits well with the facts pertaining to the historical transformation of 'class.'

Economic relations are bargaining relations. Bargaining is not settled unless both sides profit. Even capitalists and workers have a relationship in which one injects capital and attempts to gain profits while the other contributes labour and tries to receive wages. Under a market economy based on a division of labour, an occupational stratum is a set of people who provide particular goods and services. The various occupational strata are tied together by mutually profitable bargaining relations. It is possible to withdraw from an unfavourable deal. It is naturally mutual profits and not conflicting interests that are at the heart of this. This is, we believe, fundamental to relations between each occupational stratum in a modern industrial society.

At the same time, in a pre-modern pre-industrial society, the economic system is subordinate to relations of political dominance. The political power of the king and aristocracy was based only not on the fact they were the large land owners but on the hereditary possession of political power in the form of a dominion. In the case of feudal Japan, the economic development of agriculture, commerce and industry was only possible within the framework of and under subordination to the political system. The pre-modern classes of aristocracy, bourgeoisie, warriors and farmers were not based on mere occupational strata but on political power and the pre-modern status (*mibun*) system. Modern society has broken down this pre-modern status (*mibun*) system and political domination, and liberated the economy from the shackles of politics, under the political framework of the nation state.

Weber believed that, unlike pre-modern status (*mibun*), modern class emerges as a party with conflicting interests within the market. However, the situation surrounding interest in the market is certainly not inherent. In addition, the pre-modern status (*mibun*) system is not simply one characterised by an inequality of honorary goods as Weber claimed. It featured an inequality of political and civic rights prescribed by law, norms and customs. Even in modern society, various forms of the pre-modern status (*mibun*) system exist in part. This applies to relations between landowners and tenant farmers in farming villages and within the company between management, factory workers and apprentices; regular and part-time employees; career track and rank and file employees; workers employed by head office and the branch office; and male and female employees. Such status (*mibun*) strata of pre-modern types do not simply constitute economic relations but legal and political discrimination. Among the forms of discrimination, though, are those that accompany protection and responsibility, such as that between parent and child. Hence, it cannot be immediately claimed that all forms of discrimination are disadvantageous to the lower strata. But generally they possess the potential for a conflict of interests. Most of the phenomena described using the word 'class' for pre-modern societies denoted pre-modern status (*mibun*) and not simply occupational strata.

The modernisation of society was a process that had gradually diminished this pre-modern status (*mibun*) system. People confronting each other in modern market conditions were already being liberated from the yoke of the pre-modern status (*mibun*) system.

What was the conflict between capitalists and workers? We believe that it has been a conflict of interests across three areas that were not intrinsically economic in nature. First, it is a conflict of interests as between a buyer and seller in economic transactions. There are always 'negotiations' in economic transactions between two parties. The interests of capitalists and workers conflict at the point of such negotiations. Second, in many countries, a substantial population increase preceded substantial industrialisation. The existence of a so-called potential industrial reserve of unemployed people resulted in the relative suppression of wages while the gap between the rich and poor continued to grow. 'Freedom from poverty,' which has become a basic good today, was still an upper good in the early-modern era. This led to rising dissatisfaction among workers on low wages. Third, the process of industrialisation, for the most part, inevitably led to the rise and fall of industry and industrial technology and intermittently created people who struggled with adversity. Beginning with the Luddite movement in earlier times, the large-scale labour protests involving workers at the Mitsui Miike coal mine and Japan's National Railways, which in effect were localised in a particular industry and short-term, resulted from this process of industrial conversion. The same can be said of the protests during recessionary times. The tenancy disputes in the early Shōwa period were mainly caused by the agricultural slump during the Great Depression. In this case, that strata continued to carry various remnants of the pre-modern status (*mibun*) system was an important factor.

It is not only former class but also feminist and ethnic issues that can be understood as problems relating to the status (*mibun*) system of the pre-modern type. Since there are also market failures, political protection, regulations, and hence, the status (*mibun*) system linked to strata do not completely disappear. Industries and strata that are politically protected are in potential conflict with other elements in society. One of the causes of the French Revolution was the conflict between the aristocracy and religious hierarchy on one hand, whose tax burden was alleviated as a result of vested interests and who received special political privileges, and common people on the other. A similar pattern exists in Japan today. However, this is not one between occupational strata but is an issue of separate industries and is no longer a pattern of conflict on a global scale.

**What was class?**

Who or what is an agent of historical change? Does it involve taking the political initiative during periods of important political change? Causing events (riots and social movements) that will accelerate political change? Or, adopting 'new types of behaviour' in historical change in a sense that differs from political change? The industrial class envisaged by Saint Simon was recognised as an agent of change in the third sense, 'playing a role in industrial activities.' Concerning political change, there were also occasions when strata were agents in a number of riots and movements. However, political change itself is not always an extension of riots and movements but unfolds in a way that eliminates the causes generated by these. In fact, since the American War of Independence, important political changes that have taken place in world history have been basically led by the political intelligentsia. In modern times, even if a particular economic class becomes a support base for the newly emerging forms of political power, there is no historical evidence to suggest that it will itself seize political power.

However, it cannot be said that the notion of class as a political agent is completely erroneous. Peasant movements and trade unions have existed and even today there is still some kind of relationship between class and politics. There are several factors explaining this. The first point that must be noted is that the lower class has been mired in poverty for a long time and there was a great deal of meaning attached to the political desire to escape poverty. Second, after the mid-nineteenth century, ideologies such as Marxism have provided a concept of class that was linked to politics and reality accorded with this. Of course, one of the major reasons why such ideologies attracted people from lower class lies in their poverty. Third, against the background of the structure of election-based politics, political networks were constructed through the medium of occupational and economic organizations.

Traditional theories of class, beginning with Marxism, assumed the existence of class as an entity that was based on a conflict of interests and posited that the class consciousness and political attitude adopted is contingently shaped. However, since the modern era, the truth has probably been the opposite. Class has been instead a concept designed to interpret and place the strata problem of poverty onto political statements.

Why has modern society been obsessed with class? It is because modernity opens up economic opportunities and links people's attainment motives to macro-economic and political development.

On the other hand, it also derives from the fact that individualistic resources for the use of these newly-created opportunities are divided unequally. Class was a concept linking the model of the free market with the reality that is the pronounced segregation of living standards and lifestyles based on the unequal distribution of resources. That class was, in a sense, efficacious for a long period of time was because of the continuing reality that was the severe inequality of living standards and lifestyles.

However, following the Second World War, especially from the late 1950s to the early 1970s, the period of rapid economic growth in the advanced industrialised societies brought about a substantive resolution to 'the poverty problem' afflicting them. Of course, this did not mean that these societies had achieved total equalisation but had basically attained 'equalisation in basic goods.' Most people now had adequate food, shelter and clothing. Moreover, it was possible for anyone to obtain a wide variety of consumer durables, food and clothing, which were once considered to be luxury goods and symbols of an upper class lifestyle. It was not only compulsory education, but also secondary education to which access was equalised. The distribution of basic goods was also substantially equalised.

In this respect, 'class' had lost its social significance. The decline of reformist political parties in Japan is one manifestation of this.

What is the situation regarding strata? Unlike the concept of class based on a conflict of interests, the notion of strata expresses an inequality of lifestyle opportunities in terms of a hierarchy or a set of clusters. Therefore, unless inequality is eliminated, it is impossible for strata to disappear. In addition, as discussed in the previous section, whether it is post-modern or whatever, an industrial society inevitably creates inequality. However, this is not to say its mode remains the same as in the past. What kind of strata structure is gradually developing in Japan?

## The age of new strata

### Women and strata again

It is essential to resolve the issue of women's hierarchical status when considering how strata are evolving. As suggested in the last section of chapter 5, stratification theory was traditionally premised on contradictory assumptions: the basic principle of market opportunities and household communality. In fact, against the backdrop of this is the hidden, major premise that 'society is enveloped by a single strata division and individuals belong to one of these in a unique way.' This consists of two assumptions: 1. 'the total uniformity of strata division' and 2. 'the uniqueness of strata affiliation.' It is, in fact, these two assumptions that researchers of women's strata problems question.

These assumptions are clearly the vestiges of class theory as an agent. Both Marxists and non-Marxists have attempted to allocate as many people as possible in society to one of the uniformly constituted classes.[7] However, the notion of class as an agent is illusory. It is a hypothetical notion against the backdrop of empirical phenomena such as politically-oriented collective action and is a virtual image. While there is a certain reality to collective action, the same cannot be said of class. All people do not participate in collective activities and individuals take part in many different forms of collective action.

Having eschewed the concept of class as an agent, we will now focus on strata as something attained. Individuals construct strata subjectively, which they aspire to achieve. In principle, the scale of the strata is:

1.  not uniform but pluralistic
2.  not extensive but localised
3.  above all else, not objectively universal but subjectively in-
    dividualistic

To say that it is pluralistic means, for instance, that academic background, occupation and income constitute their own strata scale. To say that it is localised suggests, for instance, that occupational strata scale does not encompass all occupations. Rather, for the individual in question, it only comprises the parts that are significant for him/her.

Even though the scale is inherently pluralistic, this does not mean that each dimension is of equal value. For many employed people, an occupation, above all, carries weight in the following sense. First, an occupation identifies a person and is the most significant factor that defines an individual in society. When responding to the question: 'What are you?' people cite their occupation. Second, an occupation is the most significant means of obtaining an income. An occupation, in this sense, constitutes the most important strata scale. We can confirm this without appealing to theories of relations of production and the value of labour.

However, not all people have occupations. There are some people who, although employed, do not place any importance on their occupation. For these people, something other than their own occupation has meaning in terms of strata. This might be their husband's occupation, children's education record, or the strata of their family of origin. Or, among the employed/unemployed scale, unemployment might be ranked higher. In these matters, an individual's idiosyncrasies loom large and it is difficult to ascertain general trends.

Given this perspective, the following reply can be given to the question about what strata means for women. First, gender has properties akin to the pre-modern status (*mibun*) system. Various social norms and expectations have been assembled on top of the inherent attribute – sex. Therefore, there is a latent structure of conflict between women as a whole and men as a whole, which can be said to be a type of 'class'-like condition. Of course, this is not because men 'exploit' and 'exclude' women and force them to perform 'unpaid work.' Instead, differences in preconceived ideas, role expectations, behavioural norms and feelings of superiority and inferiority etc. based on gender force upon women different lifestyle opportunities to men.

Aside from this, strata scale exists for women in the form of two types of attainment. One that they have in common with males is a strata scale that is gender-neutral but male-oriented depending on one's perspective. Attainment in terms of a professional, corporate and bureaucratic organisation hierarchy is representative of this. On the other hand, for women, there exist women-only strata scales. It is composed of, for example, whether one is employed or not, or to which stratum her husband belongs.

These three strata axes, that is, strata as gender, gender-neutral strata and intra-gender strata also potentially exist among men. However, because gender-neutral strata such as academic background, occupation and income carry far more weight for men, the others are mostly meaningless.

We will now sort out the problems of household or individual and production or consumption within this framework. Strata scale is primarily subjective. There is no guarantee that it is common among people. Moreover, diverse strata scales exist even within an individual. In their everyday life, people choose any of these three strata axes as something meaningful and evaluate and rank themselves and others, as well as behave, based on this. The objective of stratification theory is to explore and elucidate how people's subjective and stratified world of meanings is generally or individually structured, how it is linked to people's conduct and various forms of social consciousness, as well as how it is related with a more 'objective' social structure, institutions and norms.

From the perspective of the fundamental subjectivity of strata scale, we should consider that the issue over whether the household or individual is the basic unit of the strata has not been objectively decided. When asked about strata identification, there are both occasions when people reply based on household attributes, and when they respond only on the basis of their own circumstances (Seiyama 1998c). This is the reality. The notions of 'the communality of the household,' 'the basic principle of market conditions,' 'the total uniformity of strata division,' and 'the uniqueness of strata affiliation' are all works of fiction conveniently concocted by stratification theory. The dispute surrounding 'class for women' has been fought by those disputants who share a common assumption of 'total uniformity' and 'uniqueness,' over which of the following notions is valid: 'the communality of households' or 'the basic principle of market conditions,' as an additional premise. However, such an axiomatic approach is destined to fail. To put it somewhat amiably, these are either models designed to comparatively simplify and draw out people's complex strata circumstances or hypotheses. The dereism associated with these hypotheses is obvious today.

This is not to say, however, that they were not originally significant as models. Therefore, only focusing on and exploring occupational strata at the individual level of father and son has meaning when addressing the issue of 'social mobility,' for instance. From a different perspective, considering the distribution of household income is also important. We may choose different models in accordance with the problems we examine.

As noted above, there are at least three axes of strata for women. Among these, strata between genders are generally an issue between women and men. If we exclude this, there are four-fold combinations arising from whether gender-neutral strata or intra-gender strata and whether the unit is household or individual. They are all possible strata scales. If we were to illustrate this combination with examples, it would look like table 6.1.

## Individualism and pluralisation

As discussed previously, while the distribution of basic goods has been equalised substantially resulting from advancing affluence, inequality in terms of upper goods remains. This clearly makes

*Table 6.1: Two stratification scales and stratification units*

| Stratification sale | Household unit | Individual unit |
| --- | --- | --- |
| Gender neutral | Household income | Educational background |
| | Combination of husband's and wife's occupations | Occupation/career |
| | | Individual income |
| | Family business | |
| Intra-gender | Husband's occupation and family business | Respondent's educational background |
| | Husband's income | Occupation including housewife |
| | Educational background of children | |

stratified inequality less conspicuous. Yet, this is because inequality in basic goods is an object of concern for everyone, whereas, unlike basic goods, a preference for upper goods is quite uncommon among people and, as a result, a hierarchy is not conspicuous. For instance, the difference between owning and not owning a private vehicle is about 1.5 million yen, whereas there difference between owning a regular car and a luxury car is several millions of yen. But, the former is clearly a more conspicuous difference. When inequality in basic goods exists, strata appear to be consistently one-dimensional. However, inequality in upper goods is pluralistic and does not constitute a single hierarchy.

This has had the following impact on people's subjective consciousness and perceptions. First, people have diverging evaluations regarding 'upper and lower' goods and lifestyles. That is to say, in accordance with people's diverging interests in the inequality of various upper goods, the subjective evaluation regarding which of these to emphasise also diverges. In addition, as an extension of this, there have emerged those people who, for the most part, do not evaluate 'upper and lower.' These represent a differentiation of 'strata concepts' among people. Second, the 'strata and class are unnoticeable' phenomena have arisen. It is not only that the concept of class as something possessing a historical mission has been forgotten. It has even become difficult to have a clear image of how strata, which are classified according to lifestyle opportunity disparities, exist. Because this is even true of researchers with specialist knowledge, it is understandable that the public will find this difficult to grasp. Third, together with the first two points, the notion of 'strata as something to be attained' has become individualised and diverse lifestyles are asserting their own unique consciousness. The 'de-stratification' discussed in chapter four is a generic designation of this phenomenon. These influences certainly correspond to important epochal changes in strata phenomena. What we must be cautious of is, however, that while this suggests class has lost its meaning, it does not mean that 'strata have disappeared' let alone that 'inequality has been eliminated.'

The collective features of strata are diminishing while becoming more individualistic. This is an inevitable consequence of the diversification of the value dimensions of people's lifestyles and pluralisation of attainment values. Imada and Hara (1979) once pointed out that 'the status inconsistency' of strata scales such as academic background, occupation and income is increasing. This demonstrates that the one-dimensional model is for a fact being dismantled. However it is not only the model but its meaning that is also being dismantled. The 'equivalence class concept of strata' as an exclusive and encompassing collective to which people primarily belong – leaving aside it being an operational academic construction – no longer holds true as a social reality and is not sustained by people's common understanding of its meaning.

Even though strata have become pluralised, two rigid common social value scales continue to, in fact, exist. It goes without saying that one is 'income.' Income represents purchasing power or currency and is a one-dimensional measure of the ability to purchase all goods and services introduced into the economic market. While it is one social construct, it is also a common measure. All individuals and households, in principle, are located on this one-dimensional scale. The other scale is 'academic background.' This one-dimensional feature is, in fact, not as certifiable as income. What sustains this one-dimensional image is the notion that academic background is determined through a process of one-dimensional nationwide scholastic competition among those belonging to the same generation. This notion, however, is not necessarily completely true. Nevertheless, the reality, more or less, approximates this and upon it a one-dimensional measure of academic background permeates society.[8]

As a result of increasing segregation of academic background and income and pluralisation of upper goods, the hierarchic value of income has declined in Japan. The guarantee of equalised affluence in basic goods has reduced the financial incentives in attainment. The practice whereby the business community does not publicise information pertaining to employee incomes has been sustained through collusion with the mass media, which also conceals such information, which has also prevented 'income from being a symbol of status attainment' in the main sphere of economic activities. It is not income but corporate affiliation and position that are the symbols of status attainment. This has created strata conditions that, at least, differ significantly to America. It is only among show business people and professional athletes, who attract public attention when their income ranking is announced every year, that income has become a status symbol.

As a result, since around the period of low growth, the hierarchic value of income has diminished in Japanese society. It is academic background that became salient in terms of hierarchic value.

Due to the universalisation of competition over academic background, academic background has developed an independent meaning. Academic background has assumed its own value rather than being for the purpose of maximising income and occupational prestige. In a globalising society, academic background is establishing itself as the international lingua franca and the prestige associated with where people receive a MBA or PhD has become a global standard.

## Stability and change in occupational hierarchies

What is the situation surrounding occupation, which has theoretically assumed no less importance as a strata scale than income and academic background? At a glance, we have one piece of paradoxical data. As discussed in chapter three, according to the SSM Surveys of occupational prestige conducted at twenty-year intervals in 1955, 1975 and 1995, the correlation coefficient of the occupational prestige score was an extremely high 0.93 – 0.98. In other words, it can be argued that the manner in which occupations have been ranked in relative terms has remained virtually unchanged over the last 40 years. This appears to contradict previous assertions that the strata hierarchy has become pluralised and that strata are no longer substantive as collectives.

This puzzle can be interpreted in the following way:

1. Prestige is fundamentally a relative and not absolute measure. Even if disparities in income, living standards and lifestyles are reduced, there will be no change to the prestige structure, if the vertical hierarchy is maintained.
2. The notion of strata as collectives was originally sustained by a divergent image of lifestyles based on income disparities. In

particular, it was based on the typical lifestyle image of the vast number of peasants, the very significant number of factory workers and the small number of urban middle class. But, this typical lifestyle image dissipated amid the overall process of equalisation while maintaining an occupational hierarchy.

3. However, that a macro-level hierarchy of relative scales was maintained implies the continued social validity of an interpretive schema that gives meaning to individual occupational attainment.

Whatever the case may be, while pluralistic and non-collectivist, people still adhere to the notion of a strata hierarchy, which is not expected to fade away. The reason is that it is a notion that forms the bedrock of an industrial society.

The notion of macro-hierarchy among occupations is not created based on the concrete experiences of people, but is formed as a result of people accepting it as conventional social wisdom or as shared notions permeating society. Unless it is clearly at variance with people's concrete experiences, and as long as it explains empirical phenomena well, such a shared notion is reproduced as a social concept. Then, what are the various phenomena sustaining the inter-occupational macro-hierarchy in contemporary society? Drawing upon Tsuzuki's analysis (1998: 78), these phenomena are academic background and income (believed to be) linked to each occupation and the notion of a type of public value such as 'the degree of social responsibility.'

As discussed frequently, an industrial society is one that is able to link people's individual attainment motives with macro-development. Attainment motives are created by individual values pertaining to the various possibilities that are open to individuals in social realities. If reality cannot be seen to constitute meaningful configurationality, attainment motives will not be established. The modern educational system was a key institution mediating individual motives and social strata hierarchy. It has shown what and how values are imbued socially and, at the same time, it has provided motivation regarding 'which to strive for' from among the value hierarchies. It is very much a matter of course that this system highly valued a strong educational background as something modern. Further, the school education system has been sustained by the creation of a reality in which modern elements and strong academic background are highly valued.

As shown previously, the pattern of relative social mobility among occupational strata has, despite some fluctuation, undergone a relatively stable persistence. The basis of this is the continuing attainment motives through the stability of occupational hierarchy and school education. Although the economic and cultural disparities associated with people's origin strata have also been stable and they have restricted attainment motives and attainment resources to that extent, it has not been too great 'to cause strata to become rigid and closed.'

However, the strata system, which has previously driven modern society, is now undergoing various gradual changes and will be slowly forced to undergo further modifications. As mentioned before, no one-dimensional value hierarchy may be presented under pluralistic configurationality. Then, the problem of how to motivate individuals in this situation is substantial. It is perhaps this that lies at the heart of the various acute problems faced by the school education system today. On the other hand, it can be argued that the ideas of 'deregulation' and 'neo-liberalism' aim to link with macro-development by revitalising people's motives, raising the prominence of strata values such as income.

## Strata and public value

The claim that the nation state is an imaginary, fictional or created entity has gained currency in recent years. It is not incorrect, if we consider this as a case of a general characteristic of a social institution.[9] However, if we make this statement about the nation state, it is more appropriate to claim instead that it is 'class' that is imagined. Needless to say, poverty, working conditions, occupation, academic background and income are not imaginary but real. However, 'class' as a theoretical device that reads into the commonality and communality of lifestyle opportunities has 'been created' by theorists and ordinary people. The same can also be said of the notion of strata as collectives. As discussed in chapter two, Bourdieu shares this view.

Modernity has been characterised as an age in which class and the nation state have been in conflict. While this is true in some respects, modernity has a history as a movement that created inclusive communality of people dating back at least to the sixteenth century and the idea of the nation state that has established a degree of substance is at its core. It can be argued that the idea of the nation state dismisses the notion of a political pre-modern status (*mibun*) system and implies that citizens have equal entitlements and constitute a political community. It can also be said that the notion of class was complementarily significant in that it recognised the lack of equal entitlements and activated social movements toward obtaining equal entitlements. T.H Marshall's three-stage theory of citizenship articulates this situation well. While the lower classes have gradually obtained legally as well as politically equal entitlements, it has taken a long time to receive socio-economic rights. This was finally attained around 1970 when poverty was basically eradicated from the advanced industrialised countries.

During this process, the notion of class assumed an important public value as something sustaining the movement to establish equal entitlements. The attempt to escape from the lower tiers of society, not only individually but also collectively and systematically, was significant in that it basically eliminated social poverty and expanded equal entitlements. Accordingly, the subgroups of members classified according to 'class' being represented in the political process was also one concrete way of achieving this.

There is one more aspect to the public nature of strata. As already discussed, the equilibrium in the world of strata signification is directed towards adjusting relations between individual motives and macro-development. Here, apart from 'income' and 'academic background,' the notion of 'social responsibility' is significant. It was a conceptual device designed to promote industrial society as part of the project to construct nation states and also to link egoistic individual attainment motives to public values in society. The more prominent strata become, the more they are required to be of public value.

However, as a result of strata becoming individualistic, we have lost the opportunity to look at the various social problems previously expressed in terms of strata and no longer discuss concrete policies to resolve these issues. Individuals who seek and succeed in attainment have become less conscious of the public value entailed with it. The so-called 'reproduction theory,' which concomitantly emerged as a newcomer to stratification research, has also closed the door on a realistic examination of social problems by unnecessarily presenting actual opportunity disparities as something enormous and unchangeable.

This book has sought to emphasise the following two points. First, the modernistic notion is still meaningful that it is desirable to rectify strata disparities. In particular, we should endeavour to reduce the disparities that prevent people from sufficiently developing their capabilities. An industrial society is one that utilises people's individual capabilities for the purpose of personal attainment as well as of social public-spiritedness. Even though opportunity restrictions arising from the pre-modern status (*mibun*) system and poverty have been largely reduced today, they still exist to some extent. There is even the possibility that the burden of giving one's children a tertiary education has risen in relative terms compared to thirty years ago. There is still the substantial task of expanding opportunities for women, the disabled and foreigners.

Second, at the same time, utilising opportunities and achieving is ultimately a person's individual responsibility. As a result of strata becoming difficult to detect today, values worthy of attainment have become difficult for people to discern. But achievable values are not simply limited to income and academic background: they include serving people close to you and the public at large, art, performing arts, science and technology, the development of new technologies and products, justice and fairness etc. That strata have become pluralised means that values have become pluralised. However, this is not to say that both have disappeared.

To put it in Kantian terms: 'Individual strata attainment should also be the pursuit of universal values.' While constituting the mechanism that makes this possible is a societal responsibility, it is ultimately individual people with strong personalities who will assume some role in strata. It is under this mechanism that a stratified society will find new dynamism and public spiritedness.

# Glossary

## Occupational Strata

In this book various classificatory categories of occupational strata are used. An occupational classification forms the basis of these occupational strata categories. For this, the SSM surveys employ the 'SSM occupational classification' devised at the time of the 1975 survey. This is based on the occupational classification scheme adopted in the 1970 Census and consists of 288 occupations . The 1955 and 1965 SSM survey data were also recoded in accordance with this. In addition, at the time of the 1995 survey, a new classificatory scheme was created comprising 188 occupations, to which the above 288 occupations were integrated in consideration of work content similarities and changes in numbers employees.

A broad SSM occupational strata scheme, built from the SSM occupational classification, has been used comprising the eight strata categories of professional, managerial, clerical, sales (including services), skilled, semi-skilled, non-skilled and agriculture (Odaka 1958). In the case of a small sample, a still more coarse strata scheme comprising non-manual (professional, managerial, clerical and sales), manual (skilled, semi-skilled and non-skilled), and agriculture, or another one comprising white-collar (professional, managerial and clerical), gray-collar (sales), blue-collar and agriculture, is used, both of which are constructed by merging the above eight. These categories are based on work content similarities, as well as the nature and degree of the necessary knowledge and skills.

However, it is well known that income and prestige differ according to employment status (employer or employee) and company size. Consequently, a so-called general classification scheme, which incorporates these standards, is often used as a strata category. The eight- and 12-level classificatory schemes in tables 1.1 and figure 3.1, respectively, are representative of this. Table G.1 shows each of the eight categories in terms of job description (SSM major occupation divisions), employment status and company size (employee numbers) (See Yasuda and Hara 1984).

*Table G.1: Components of eight general categories*

| Eight general categories | Occupational categories (SSM major occupational classifications) | Employment status | Firm size (Number of employees) |
|---|---|---|---|
| Professional | Professional | | |
| White-collar in large companies | Managerial, clerical and sales | Administrators and executives | Government |
| | | Employees | Government, 300 or more |
| White-collar in SME | Managerial, clerical and sales | Employees | Less than 300 |
| Self-employed white-collar | Managerial, clerical and sales | Administrators and executives | Other than government |
| | | The self-employed, independent professions and family workers | Less than 300 |
| Blue-collar in large companies | Skilled, semi-skilled and unskilled | Employees | Government, 300 or more |
| Blue-collar in SME | Skilled, semi-skilled and unskilled | Employees | Less than 300 |
| Self-employed blue-collar | Skilled, semi-skilled and unskilled | The self-employed, independent professions and family workers | |
| Farmer (Agriculture) | Agriculture | | |

Note: 'Agriculture' includes forestry and fishery. We sometimes treat 'managerial' (which comprises those who engage in managerial jobs as employees) as an independent category (see Figure 4.1 and Table 4.3a). 'Professional' and 'agriculture' are classified as occupations regardless of their 'employment status' and 'firm size.'

## Occupational Prestige Score

This is a score pertaining to the general ranking of occupations. At the time of the 1975 SSM survey, an occupational prestige survey was conducted separately to the main survey. This survey asked respondents to classify 82 typical occupations as either 'highest,' 'somewhat high,' 'average,' 'somewhat low' and 'lowest.' Each evaluation was given a corresponding score (100 for highest, 75 for somewhat high, 50 for average, 25 for low and 0 for lowest). Average scores of all respondents were calculated. If all respondents rated a particular occupation as 'the highest,' it would be given a score of 100, and if they rated it as 'the lowest,' it was given a score of 0. Moreover, this score was extended to the remaining occupations and the score given to all of these was called the 'SSM occupational prestige score.' Beginning with the path analysis, this score was used as a quantitative measure of occupational status in many analyses.

In 1955 and 1995, surveys were conducted of 31 and 56 types of occupations, respectively, under the same format. However, as demonstrated in this book, the mutual score correlation is extremely high and the ranking of people's occupational evaluations has remained virtually unchanged through this time. In addition, it is known that the correlation with similar survey results in other advanced industrialised societies is also high and that they share a common occupational evaluation ranking (See Naoi 1979).

## Path Analysis

This is a method of statistical analysis designed to estimate the scale of the causal link among variables in a complex causal system comprising many variables. Figure 3.2 is referred to as a path diagram as it is a model showing the causal relationship among variables linked to occupational careers. Among these variables, one's father's academic background and main occupation are external variables that are given as predetermined in this analysis. The remaining variables are internal variables that are determined by other variables within the system. A multiple regression equation for each internal variable appears as follows:

$$X_3 = p_{31}X_1 + p_{32}X_2 + p_{3R}R_3$$

$$X_4 = p_{41}X_1 + p_{42}X_2 + p_{43}X_3 + p_{4R}R_4$$

$$X_5 = p_{51}X_1 + p_{52}X_2 + p_{53}X_3 + p_{54}X_4 + p_{5R}R_5$$

$$X_6 = p_{61}X_1 + p_{62}X_2 + p_{63}X_3 + p_{64}X_4 + p_{65}X_5 + p_{6R}R_6$$

In addition to external variables, the dependent variables of the former equations become independent variables of the latter and these are called recursive regression equations. Here, $X_1$ = father's academic background, $X_2$ = father's main occupation, $X_3$ = academic background, $X_4$ = first occupation, $X_5$ = occupation at the age of 30 and $X_6$ = occupation at the age of 40. $R_i$ is a variable that expresses unknown factors (residual factors) outside the system, which are assumed to affect the dependent variable randomly. In a path diagram this effect corresponds to the arrows pointing to the internal variables from outside the system. $p_{ij}$ is referred to as a path coefficient and under the model shows the scale of the direct, causal prescribing forces on the dependent variable.[1] A path coefficient is the same as a standardised partial regression coefficient in a common multiple regression analysis. While it can be estimated according to an identical procedure, it is also possible to estimate the indirect causal prescribing forces that are routed through other variables. In this manner, since it is possible to estimate the prescribing forces according to the causal path, this analysis is called a path analysis (See Seiyama 1983).

There is a covariance structure analysis that has often been employed recently. This is said to further develop path analyses by being able to place latent variables in a causal path (Toyoda 1998).

## Log-linear model

A log-linear model is a statistical model designed to explain the frequency of each cell in frequency distribution tables such as cross-classification tables and social mobility tables. Using table 1.1 as an example, it is natural to consider the following model as one that explains the frequency of each cell.

$$\hat{n}_{ij} = \alpha\beta_i\gamma_j\delta_{ij}$$

$\hat{n}_{ij}$ is the frequency (expected frequency) of the cell represented by low $i$ column $j$ predicted by the model. $\alpha$ is the common, basic frequency of each cell. $\beta_i$ is the effect of the scale of low $i$ (In the case of a social mobility table, it is the effect of the scale of the distribution of the father's occupation $i$). $\gamma_j$ is the effect of the scale of column $j$ (the effect of the scale of the distribution of the child's occupation $j$). $\delta_{ij}$ is the interaction effect of row $i$ column $j$ (the effect of the strength of the link between father's occupation $i$ and child's occupation $j$). In other words, the frequency of the cell $\hat{n}_{ij}$ considers that the basic, common frequency $\alpha$ will rise and fall due to the influence of $\beta_i$, $\gamma_j$, $\delta_{ij}$. If we perform a logarithmic conversion of the above model, it would take the form of the following linear model:

$$\log_e (\hat{n}_{ij}) = \log_e (\alpha) + \log_e (\beta_i) + \log_e (\gamma_j) + \log_e (\delta_{ij})$$

This is a log linear model. Normally, in order to avoid complications, each of the items on the right side is re-written in the following manner[2]:

$$\log_e (\hat{n}_{ij}) = \lambda + \lambda_i^R + \lambda_j^C + \lambda_{ij}^{RC}$$

Of course, this is only one example, and there might be alternative models. An analysis using a log-liner model is called a log-linear analysis. It (1) determines the adequacy of the model based on a $\chi^2$ test between the actual frequency $n_{ij}$ and the expected frequency $\hat{n}_{ij}$, and (2) conducts an estimate of the parameter $\lambda$. The fixed opportunity model introduced in chapter 3 is expressed as:

$$\log_e (\hat{n}_{ijk}) = \lambda + \lambda_i^R + \lambda_j^C + \lambda_k^Y + \lambda_{ik}^{RY} + \lambda_{jk}^{CY} + \lambda_{ij}^{RC}$$

The $Y$ refers to the year the survey was taken. Among the parameters, $\lambda_{ik}^{RY}$ is the effect of the different distributions for the father's occupation in every survey year, while $\lambda_{jk}^{CY}$ is the effect of the different distributions for the child's occupation in every survey year. And $\lambda_{ij}^{RC}$ is the effect of the strength of the link between the father's and child's occupation irrespective to the survey year $Y$ (See Upton 1978; Hara 1983).

## Event History Analysis

As occupational changes, marriage and death demonstrate, it is not unusual to change from one situation to another during one's life. One of the methods used to analyse the factors that prescribe the ease with which such changes occur is an event history analysis. It is only in sociology that this is called an event history analysis. It is generally referred to as a 'survival time analysis' or an 'occurrence time analysis.'

For instance, with regards to two groups of people, those with attribute *A* and those with attribute *B*, temporal changes in the percentage of people who continue working in a company are demonstrated in the graph below. It is more likely for those in group *B* to retire than it is for those in group *A*. This curve is called a 'survival function' and is expressed as $S(t)$. $F(t) = 1 - S(t)$, which is the result of subtracting this from 1, represents 'the percentage of people who retired by a certain point in time $t$.' It holds a similar meaning to a probability distribution function. In addition, $f(t) = dF(t) / dt$, which is derived from $F(t)$, corresponds to a density function. See figure G.1.

If we consider 'the probability of retirement for those who did not retire by $t$, which will occur in the subsequent $\Delta t$', and if we denote its instantaneous value by $\lambda(t)$ when reducing $\Delta t$, the following relationship is established:

$$\lambda(t) = \frac{f(t)}{S(t)}$$

This $\lambda(t)$ is referred to as a 'hazard function' and represents the degree of likeliness by which retirements occur at $t$.

In an event history analysis $\lambda(t)$ is believed to differ according to people's attributes $x_1, x_2, ..., x_m$. Expressing the linear combination

*Figure G.1: Graph of survival function*

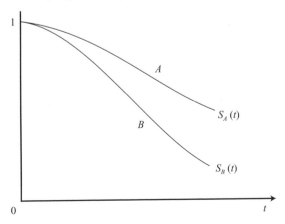

by $\mu = \beta_1 x_1 + \beta_2 x_2 + ... + \beta_m x_m$, it is assumed that the hazard function is prescribed by $\mu$. In other words, it becomes the following equation:

$$\lambda(t) = \lambda(t, \mu)$$

It is believed that the difference in the $\mu$ value between groups $A$ and $B$ in figure G.1 influences the hazard coefficient, parameters $\beta_1, \beta_2, ...,$ $\beta_m$, and they are estimated from the data concerning people who experience change and those who do not. In a statistical analysis one must specify the form of some kind of concrete function in $\lambda(t, \mu)$. There are various types of models, of which one of the most simple is:

$$\lambda(t, \mu) = \lambda_0(t) e^{\mu}$$

$\lambda_0(t)$ is common to all people and is not related to $\mu$. $e$ is the base of a natural logarithm (=2.718...). This is called a 'proportional hazard model' or a 'Cox model.'

The model Inada employed, which was introduced in chapter 3, is called a 'Weibull model' and is rather complex:

$$\lambda(t, \mu) = e^{-\mu \gamma} \gamma t^{\gamma-1}$$

As $\gamma$ is a positive parameter in this model, it is important to note that when $\mu$ moves largely in a positive direction, the hazard function diminishes, and it is difficult for 'retirement' to occur (See Gross and Clark 1975; Allison 1982).

# Notes

## Preface to the Japanese edition

1. Their institutional affiliations listed are those at the time of the surveys

## Preface to the English edition

1. Strata identification is given a score from 5 to 1 for the response categories of 'upper,' 'upper middle,' 'lower middle,' 'upper lower' and 'lower lower.'

## Chapter 1

1. A *kotatsu* is a table-like foot warmer that has a quilt draped over it.
2. The works of Sieyès (1789), Saint-Simon (1823–24), Marx and Engels (1848) and Marx (1868–84) represent the basic literature on class. There are several Japanese-language translations of each of these books.
3. Weber does not necessarily provide a systematic theory of stratification. There are basically two sections of his book *Economy and Society* (5th edition) that deal with stratification. The first is chapter four 'Status and Class.' The second is section six 'The Distribution of forces in the *Gemeinshaft*: Class, Status and Factions' from chapter eight 'Political Community.'
4. While power elite theory occupies a somewhat peripheral position among theories of class and stratification, it provides a body of thought that relates stratification and power with each other, and cannot be ignored. Its early proponents were Pareto, Mosca and Michels. Mills (1956), Dahrendorf (1959) and Bottomore (1964) are the intellectual successors of power elite theory.
5. Basic goods are not only economic goods, but also include all lifestyle resources and conveniences.
6. This is the result of incorporating wide-scale age strata. It is necessary to analyse the disparities between age groups and also within each cohort.
7. For details on the first SSM Survey, see Odaka (1958; 1995).
8. Refer to chapter 3 for details regarding the gross mobility percentage and mobility indicators.
9. Japanese scholar Yasuda Saburō (1964; 1971) dubbed these contrastive concepts 'forced mobility' and 'pure mobility.'

## Chapter 2

1. For research on the theoretical background of feelings of inequity, see Umino and Saitō (1990).

2. Takeuchi (1995) and Kariya (1995) conceptualise the present situation in Japan as a 'meritocracy.' However, in this manner, the issues of 'credentialism' and 'ability-ism' in Japanese will be confused with the notion of 'academic background' equating to 'ability'.

3. This quote is contained in *Fukuzawa Yukichi on Education*, Eichi Kiyooka ed., trans., Tokyo: University of Tokyo Press, 1985, p. 66.

4. For an explanation of this statistical indicator, refer to chapter 3.

5. This is referred to as 'substitutive employment.'

6. For males aged between 40 and 59 in 1995, approximately 25% of high school graduates and 10% of university graduates receive less than the median value of individual incomes for junior high school graduates and, conversely, approximately 10% of junior high school graduates and 20% of high school graduates receive more than the median value of individual incomes for university graduates.

7. Davis and Moore (1945) are the major proponents of the functional theory of stratification. For a detailed introduction, see Tumin (1964).

8. Deviation Score is a scholastic scale devised to indicate one's relative position in an achievement test. This is defined as $10 \times (x - \mu) / \sigma + 50$, where x is one's raw score, $\mu$ is the mean, and $\sigma$ is the standard deviation of individual raw scores.

9. This page number is that of the Japanese translation.

10. If we call the advancement rate for the upper and lower strata $x$ and $y$ respectively, the parallel rise in both means that a relationship signified by $x = y + a$ has been maintained. If we designate the percentage of university graduates who land upper stratum white-collar jobs by $b$, the relative reproduction rate is represented by:

$$\frac{bx}{by} = \frac{y + a}{y} = 1 + \frac{a}{y}$$

This decreases as the advancement rate for the lower strata ($y$) rises.

11. The Japanese mass media claims 'the very high salaries of the parents of Tokyo University students' is evidence both of strengthening of reproduction of academic background of increasing effect of investment in extra-school education (combined junior high and high schools, cram schools and home tutoring) for the purpose of academic background attainment. This is thought to demonstrate the validity of the theory of cultural reproduction, which is based on economic strength. However, there are various leaps of logic in this explanation. First, one cannot make a comparison of the salaries of the parents of Tokyo University students with the average wage for salaried workers, which include those under 40 and young, single people. Second, while it is true that the salaries of parents of Tokyo University students are high compared to those from other national universities, according to the research findings of one of this book's authors (Tokyo University Public Relations Committee 1987), this is not a recent phenomenon. That the children of those from the upper stratum who are blessed with good salaries are relatively well-off when it comes to attaining an academic background, is a long-term and established fact as demonstrated in table 2.4. Third, the extent of the effect of extra-school investment is not clear (see Seiyama 1981; Seiyama and Noguchi 1984). Certainly, since the late 1970s, the relative importance of (private or national) integrated junior-high schools

for examination competition has increased. This is clearly disadvantageous for the low-income strata. This was caused by the school-group system in which students must attend local schools unless they go to private or national schools. This system is said to be just a foolish policy (it would have been a different story if education subsidies were provided for the low- and middle-income strata). However, the enormous investment in extra-school education seems to have only increased education costs for all social strata. In particular, the authors do not believe that it has created a favourable environment for those from the upper stratum who wish 'to buy scholastic ability with money'. Fourth, hypothetically, if extra-school education for the wealthy had an effect, this means it would be contrary to the assertions made by cultural reproduction theorists and that economic capital, not cultural capital, would have an effect on strata reproduction.

# Chapter 3

1. An extremely small number of retail and service employees are included among white-collar 'clerical' workers in large companies.
2. A negative number means a negative relationship. This does not appear in the chart.
3. Seiyama and Tsuzuki et al. (1990) have reached a similar conclusion using a Markov chain model. The Markov chain model is a stochastic model of sequences of events where the probability of an event occurring at certain times depends only upon the situation at the time just before and not upon other preceding situations (Hara 1973). According to Seiyama et al., the data for occupational careers mostly accords with the Markov chain model. In other words, people's occupational careers are prescribed not by factors evident before one commences work, but by the structure of labour markets. Seiyama et al. refer to this as 'the Markov feature of occupational careers.'
4. Strictly speaking, this is a parameter minimising the value of hazard function, which indicate the possibility of quitting a company.
5. Strictly speaking, because there are many instances in which the father's occupation in inter-generational mobility is measured in terms of 'main occupation' or 'the occupation at the respondent's age of 15,' it is desirable to limit the age of respondents to between 45 and 54. However, there is a drawback in that the time scale reflected by the data becomes too broad.
6. Each of SSM Surveys examines detailed occupational career from the time respondents first entered the workforce to the time of the survey. The 1945 data would derive from the occupations the sample of 35–44 year olds held 10 years prior before the 1955 survey while 1935 data would be based on the occupations the sample of 45–54 year olds held 20 years before this survey (this corresponds to the occupations of 25–35 year olds at the time). However, this data does not include what should have been included if the actual surveys were conducted in 1935 and 1945, that is, information about the large number of those who died during the war, either soldiers on the battlefield or civilians. Therefore, it is important to note that this data is somewhat biased.
7. Hara (1998a) carried out a test of the invariant opportunity model using the four categories of upper class white-collar (professionals and management),

average white-collar (clerical, sales and services), blue-collar and
agriculture. According to the results, the risk ratio over the seven points in
time was 3% and over six points in time, excluding 1955, 24%. This shows
the anomalous nature of the 1955 data clearly.
8. The analyses conducted by Imada (1999), Seiyama and Naoi et al. (1990),
Tominaga (1992) and Kanomata (1997) are representative of this body of
thought. For the relationship between the peculiarities of the coefficient of
openness and the log-linear model, see Seiyama (1986; 1991).
9. However, the changes from 1955 to 1975 should not be underestimated.
What an analysis using a log-linear model shows is long-term and potential
'invariance in the opportunity structure.' If we compare these two points
in time, the gross, structural and circular mobility rates each rose sharply,
which clearly contradicts the 'invariant opportunity model' based on the
log-linear analysis. During this time, there was a mass movement of people
from agriculture to other occupations and from rural villages to the cities
(Hara 1971). This has had an overwhelming impact on people's strata and
political consciousness.
10. The American data derives from Featherman and Hauser (1978) and the
English data from Goldthorpe (1980).
11. However, this is limited to societies in which private ownership of the means
of production is approved.

# Chapter 4

1. These groups may also be referred to as urban residents.
2. As discussed in the preface, females were surveyed in the SSM Surveys
from 1985. Because this chapter mainly examines changing strata
consciousness from 1955, the data only refers to males. However, there are,
of course, subtle differences in the awareness of male-female relations such
as gender roles consciousness and other aspects of male-female relations.
One example of this is party support rates (1995). shown in table N.1.
Concerning the characteristics of political consciousness among females,
refer to Hara (1995).

*Table N.1:  Support for political parties 1995 (%)*

|  | Liberal Democratic Party | New Frontier Party | Socialist Party | Communist Party | Other | None | Unknown |
|---|---|---|---|---|---|---|---|
| Male | 24.5 | 8.8 | 7.1 | 2.4 | 2.6 | 52.3 | 2.3 |
| Female | 21.2 | 5.7 | 5.9 | 1.8 | 3.0 | 59.4 | 3.0 |

Source: 1995 SSM Survey data. Ages 20–69.

3. This refers to the high support rate for the reformist parties among the young
generation and the highly educated strata.
4. This refers to the high support rate for the LDP among the self-employed
and agricultural strata, and the high support rate for the reformist parties
among workers in large companies.
5. However, as far as contemporary politics and people's political consciousness
are concerned, this does not mean that political ideology is completely devoid

of meaning (Kabashima and Takenaka 1996). Using SSM Survey data from 1995, Kobayashi Hisataka (1998) conducted a fascinating analysis of the relationship between social strata and politics.

6. The concept of 'status politics' was originally developed by Hofstadter and Bell (Bell 1960), and denoted a pattern of political behaviour in which dissatisfaction with status and anxiety casts a shadow over politics. This occurred against a backdrop of the rise of the radical right wing in America exemplified by McCarthyism. However, the implications of this are not that strong in the research of Imada and Hara, in which concern over status and political orientation towards the status quo are linked.

7. For instance, the House of Councillors election in 1989 in the lead up to which the introduction of a consumption tax became an issue and the 1998 House of Councillors election in the lead up to which policies to stimulate the economy became an issue.

8. For instance, this element is a feature of the party/anti-party conflict that is often seen in elections for heads of local government in each region.

9. 'Ditch plank politics' is a term used to refer to a government's focus on the interests of specific social groups.

10. Of course, the percentage of those claiming to belong to the 'lower' strata declined.

11. In 1977, when the increase in 'middle' consciousness was conspicuous, the arguments put forward by scholars such as Murakami Yasusuke, Tominaga Ken'ichi, Kishimoto Shigenobu, Takabatake Michitoshi and Mita Munesuke about what this meant filled the pages of Japanese newspapers. This was referred to as the 'middle consciousness dispute' (*chūishiki ronsō*) (Murakami 1984; Tominaga 1988; and Kishimoto 1978). For a discussion of the 'middle consciousness dispute' see Imada (1989). While it appears that there was no broad social interest in strata identification in the West, Jackman and Jackman (1983) did conduct an empirical analysis of this issue.

12. Many excellent analyses have been conducted of strata identification. Among these, the studies of Mamada (1990) and Kikkawa (1998b) have produced noteworthy results. In addition, Kōsaka and Miyano (1990) have pursued the issue surrounding the bloating of 'middle' consciousness using a mathematical model.

# Chapter 5

1. It should be noted that there have been bodies of thought that place women at the top of the hierarchy.

2. While Brinton (1993) traces the low advancement and employment rates among Japanese women mainly to traditional family norms and norms pertaining to gender roles, she fails to understand the changes that have occurred after 1975 (Seiyama 1998b).

3. Junior high school graduates were excluded because they represent a young cohort and also because there were a small number of cases.

4. An operational definition based on the data is as follows. The 'unmarried model' (a) refers to those who have never married. The 'marriage precedence

model' (d) denotes those who have never worked before marriage. It therefore includes those who have worked after marriage. The 'housewife transition model' (c) refers to those who have experienced working before marriage and within three years of marriage are out of work and after then continue to be so for more than three years. The 'work continuation model' (b) denotes those who have experienced working before marriage and not experienced within three years of marriage becoming out of work and remaining so for more than three years.

5. Because the number of cases of junior college and university graduates amounts to about only 12 to 31, one should be cautious.
6. Among junior college and high school graduates, the figure was between 25.8% and 38.1% respectively.
7. For more on the high level of the earning return rate (individual incomes) for female university graduates, see Yano (1996).
8. Such as substantial limits to overtime, limiting the time spent socialising outside the company, and guarantee of an unconditional return to the same job for those who leave work temporarily.
9. For the problem of 'female strata,' see the reviews by Okamoto (1990) and Seiyama (1994c).

## Chapter 6

1. Although strata are not congruent with industry, the two correlate. The farming stratum is only located within agriculture and the factory workers in secondary industries.
2. There have been a myriad of debates in recent times in the West regarding the concept and existence of class. A study by Crompton (1993) provides an easily comprehensible overview of these debates. Pakulski and Waters' study (1996) is representative of the theory of 'the death of class.'
3. Seiyama (1998d) developed this based on the earlier arguments made by Satō (1995)
4. See Roemer (1982), Wright (1985), Dahrendorf (1959), Parkin (1979) and Murphy (1988).
5. It is not class but ethnicity that is the central character in the powerful historical story that counters this.
6. According to research conducted by Warner et al. (see Warner 1949), an evaluation of mutual status and ranking form the basis of strata. This constitutes a starting point for American stratification research that is linked to the theory of functionalist stratification and research into prestige.
   Studies by Ōhashi (1971) and Hashimoto (1986) examine class in Japan empirically from a Marxist perspective.
8. This can be said to be a 'code' in Luhmann's sense of the word.
9. See Anderson (1987), Seiyama (1995) and Satō (1999).

## Glossary

1. Figure 3.2 only shows the arrows that correspond to the statistically significant path coefficients.
2. The $R$ and the $C$ refer to a row and column, respectively.

# Bibliography

Abegglen, James C., 1958, *The Japanese Factory: Aspects of Its Social Organization*, New York: Free Press (Urabe, Kuniyoshi, trans, *Nihon no Keiei*, 1958, Daiyamondosha).

Acker, Joan, 1973, 'Women and Social Stratification: A Case of Intellectual Sexism,' *American Journal of Sociology*, vol. 78, no. 4.

Akagawa, Manabu, 1998, 'Josei no Kaisōteki Chii o Meguru Yottsu no Moderu: Josei no Chii Dokuritsu Moderu wa Yūkōka? (Four Models Explaining Women's Strata Status: Is the Women's Independent Status Model Valid?), in Watanabe, Hideki and Shida, Kiyoshi (eds.), *1995-nen SSM Chōsa Sirīzu 15: Kaisō to Kekkon/Kazoku* (*1995 SSM Research Series 15: Marriage, Family and Stratification*), 1995-nen SSM Chōsa Kenkyūkai.

Akiyama, Toyoko, 1985, 'Seiji' (Politics), in NHK Public Opinion Division (ed.), *Gendai Nihonjin no Ishiki Kōzō* (*The Consciousness Structure of Contemporary Japanese*), 2nd ed., Nihon Hōsō Shuppan Kyōkai.

Allison, Paul D., 1982, *Event History Analysis: Regression for Longitudinal Event Data*, Beverley Hills: Sage.

Anderson, Benedict, 1983, *Imagined Communities: Reflections on the Origin and Spread of Nationalism*, London: Verso (Shiraishi, Takashi and Shiraishi, Saya, trans, 1987, *Sōzō no Kyōdōtai: Nashonarizumu no Kigen to Ryūkō*, Riburopōto (expanded edition, 1997, NTT Shuppan).

Becker, Gary S., 1975, *Human Capital*, 2nd ed., New York: NBER (Sano, Yōko, trans, 1976, *Jinteki Shihon: Kyōiku o Chūshin toshita Rironteki Keizaiteki Bunseki*, Tōyō Keizai Shinpōsha).

Bell, Daniel, 1960, *The End of Ideology: On the Exhaustion of Political Ideas in the Fifties*, New York: Free Press (Okada, Naoyuki, trans, 1969, *Ideorogī no Shūen: 1950-nendai ni okeru Seiji Shisō no Kokatsu ni tsuite*, Tōkyō Sōgensha).

Blau, Peter M. and Otis D. Duncan, 1967, *The American Occupational Structure*, New York: Free Press.

Bottomore, T., 1964, *Elites and Society*, London: C. A. Watts (Watanuki, Jōji, trans, 1965, *Erīto to Shakai*, Iwanami Shoten).

Bourdieu, Pierre, 1979, *La distinction: Critique sociale du jugement*, Paris: Éditions de Minuit (Ishii, Yōjirō, trans, 1990, *Disutankushion: Shakaiteki Handanryoku Hihan*, I. II, Fujiwara Shoten).

————, 1987, *Choses dite*, Paris: Éditions de Minuit (Ishizaki, Harumi, trans, 1991, *Kōzō to Jissen: Burudyū Jishin ni yoru Burudyū*, Fujiwara Shoten).

————, et J. – C. Passeron, 1970, *La reproduction: Éléments pour une théorie du système d'enseignement*, Paris: Éditions de Minuit (Miyajima, Takashi, trans, 1991, *Saiseisan: Kyōiku, Shakai, Bunka*, Fujiwara Shoten).

————, 1990, *In Other Words: Essays Towards a Reflexive Sociology*. Polity Press.

Bowles, S. and H. Gintis, 1976, *Schooling in Capitalist America: Educational Reform and the Contradictions of Economic Life*, New York: Basic Books

(Uzawa, Hirobumi, trans, 1986–1987, *Amerika Shihonshugi to Gakkō Kyōiku*, I. II, Iwanami Shoten).

Brinton, Mary C., 1993, *Women and the Economic Miracle: Gender and Work in Postwar Japan*, Berkeley: University of California Press.

Crompton, Rosemary, 1993, *Class and Stratification*, Cambridge: Polity Press.

Dahrendorf, R., 1959, *Class and Conflict in Industrial Society*, Stanford: Stanford University Press (Tominaga, Ken'ichi, trans, 1964, *Sangyō Shakai ni okeru Kaikyū oyobi Kaikyū Tōsō*, Daiyamondosha).

Davis, Kingsley and Wilbert E. Moore, 1945, 'Some Principles of Stratification,' *American Sociological Review*, vol. 10, no. 2.

Djilas, M., 1957, *The New Class*, London: Thames & Hudson (Harako, Rinjirō, trans, 1957, *Atarashii Kaikyū*, Jiji Tsūshinsha).

Dore, Ronald, P., 1976, *The Diploma Disease: Education, Qualification and Development*, London: George Allen & Unwin (Matsui, Hiromichi, trans, 1978, *Gakureki Shakai: Atarashii Bunmeibyō*, Iwanami Shoten).

Erikson, Robert, 1984, 'Social Class of Men, Women and Families,' *Sociology*, vol. 18, no. 4.

——————, and John H. Goldthorpe, 1992, *The Constant Flux: A Study of Class Mobility in Industrial Societies*, Oxford: Clarendon Press.

Featherman, David L. and Robert M. Hauser, 1978, *Opportunity and Change*, New York: Academic Press.

Featherman, David L., F. Lancaster Jones and Robert M. Hauser, 1975, 'Assumptions of Social Mobility Research in the United States: The Case of Occupational Status,' *Social Science Research*, vol. 4.

Felson, Marcus and David Knoke, 1974, 'Social Status and the Married Woman,' *Journal of Marriage and the Family*, vol. 36, no. 3.

Flanagan, Scott C. and Bradley M. Richardson, 1977, *Japanese Electoral Behavior*, Beverly Hills: Sage (Nakagawa, Tōru, trans, 1980, *Gendai Nihon no Seiji*, Keibundō).

Goldthorpe, John H., 1980, *Social Mobility and Class Structure in Modern Britain*, Oxford: Clarendon Press.

——————, 1983, 'Women and Class Analysis: In Defence of the Conventional View,' *Sociology*, vol. 17, no. 4.

——————, and Gordon Marshall, 1992, 'The Promising Future of Class Analysis: A Response to Recent Critiques,' *Sociology*, vol. 26, no. 3.

Gross, A. J. and R. L. Clark, 1975, *Survival Distributions: Reliability Applications in the Biomedical Sciences*, New York: Wiley (Igaku Tōkei Kenkyūkai, trans, 1984, *Seizon Jikan Bunpu to sono Ōyō*, Kaien Shobō).

Hara, Junsuke, 1971, 'Jinkō no Irekae Idō to Keiyu Idō' (Interchangeable and En Route Population Mobility), *Shakaigaku Hyōron*, vol. 22, no. 2.

——————, 1973, 'Marukofu Rensa to Shakai Idō' (The Markhov Chain and Social Mobility), in Yasuda, Saburō (ed.), *Shakaigaku Kōza 17: Sūrishakaigaku (Sociology Course 17: Mathematical Sociology)*, Tōkyō Daigaku Shuppankai.

——————, 1979, 'Shokugyō Keireki no Bunseki' (Analysis of Occupational Careers) in Tominaga, Ken'ichi (ed.), *Nihon no Kaisō Kōzō (Japan's Strata Structure)*, Tōkyō Daigaku Shuppankai.

——————, 1981, 'Kaisō Kōzōron' (Theories of Strata Structure), in Yasuda, Saburō, Shiobara, Tsutomu, Tominaga, Ken'ichi, and Yoshida, Tamito (eds.),

*Kiso Shakaigaku IV: Shakai Kōzō (Fundamentals of Sociology IV: Social Structure)*, Tōyō Keizai Shinpōsha.

—————, 1983, 'Shitsuteki Dēta no Kaisekihō' (Quantitative Data Analysis Method), in Naoi, Atsushi (ed.), *Shakai Chōsa no Kiso (Fundamentals of Social Research)*, Saiensusha.

—————, 1986, 'Shokugyō Idō no Nettowāku' (Occupational Mobility Networks), in Naoi, Atsushi, Hara, Junsuke and Kobayashi, Hajime (eds.), *Rīdingusu Nihon no Shakaigaku 8: Shakai Kaisō, Shakai Idō (Readings of Japanese Sociology 8: Social Strata and Social Mobility)*, Tōkyō Daigaku Shuppankai.

—————, 1988, 'Shakai Kaisō to Seiji Ishiki' (Social Stratification and Political Consciousness), in 1985-nen Shakai Kaisō to Shakai Idō Zenkoku Chōsa Iinkai (ed.), *1985-nen Shakai Kaisō to Shakai Idō Zenkoku Chōsa Hōkokusho 2: Kaisō Ishiki no Dōtai (Report of the 1985 National Survey of Social Stratification and Social Mobility 2: Dynamics of Strata Consciousness)*.

—————, 1990, 'Joron: Kaisō Ishiki Kenkyū no Kaidai' (Preface: Issues in the Research of Strata Consciousness), in Hara, Junsuke (ed.), *Gendai Nihon no Kaisō Kōzō 2: Kaisō Ishiki no Dōtai (Strata Structure in Contemporary Japan 2: Dynamics of Strata Consciousness)*, Tōkyō Daigaku Shuppankai.

— —————, 1993, 'Seijiteki Taido no Hen'yō to Kaisō, Jendā: 1955–85-nen SSM Chōsa no Kekka kara (Changes in Political Attitudes and Strata and Gender: Results from SSM Surveys, 1955–85), in Naoi, Atsushi, Seiyama, Kazuo and Mamada, Takao (eds.), *Nihon Shakai no Shinchōryū (New Trends in Japanese Society)*, Tōkyō Daigaku Shuppankai.

—————, 1994a, 'Political Attitude and Social Strata,' in Kosaka, Kenji (ed.), *Social Stratification in Contemporary Japan*, London: Kegan Paul International.

—————, 1994b, '"Kindaishugisha" no Kaisōkan' (View of Stratification of the 'Modernists'), *Riron to Hōhō*, vol. 9, no. 2.

—————, 1997, 'Sengo Nihon no Kaisō to Kaisō Ishiki: SSM Chōsa 1955–1995-nen no Kiseki (Strata and Strata Consciousness in Postwar Japan: In trace of the SSM Surveys, 1955–1995), *Kōdōkeiryōgaku*, vol. 24, no. 1.

—————, 1998a, 'Ryūdōsei to Kaihōsei: Sedaikan Shakai Idō no Sūsei (Shōwa Shoki-1995-nen) (Fluidity and Openness: Trends in Inter-generational Social Mobility [early Shōwa period-1995], in Ishida, Hiroshi (ed.), *1995-nen SSM Chōsa Sirīzu 1: Shakai Kaisō, Idō no Kiso Bunseki to Kokusai Hikaku (1995 SSM Research Series 1: Basic Analysis and International Comparison of Social Stratification and Mobility)*, 1995-nen SSM Chōsa Kenkyūkai.

—————, 1998b, 'The Invariant Structure of Class Consciousness in Postwar Japan,' in Yosano, Arinori (ed.), *1995-nen SSM Chōsa Sirīzu 21: Sangyōka to Kaisō Hendō (1995 SSM Research Series 21: Industrialisation and Strata Transformation)*, 1995 SSM Chōsa Kenkyūkai.

—————, 1998c, 'SSM Chōsa no Rekishi to Tenbō' (History and Prospects for SSM Research), *Yoron*, vol. 82.

—————, 2002, 'Sangyōka to Kaisō Ryūdōsei' (Industrialisation and Strata Fluidity), in Hara, Junsuke (ed.), *Kōza Shakai Hendō 5: Ryūdōka to Shakai Kakusa (Social Change 5: Fluidization and Social Disparities)*, Mineruva Shobō.

———, and Hiwano, Yoshiko, 1990, 'Seibetsu Yakuwari Ishiki to Shufu no Chii Hyōka' (Gender Role Consciousness and Evaluation of Housewife's Status), in Okamoto, Hideo and Naoi, Michiko (eds.), *Gendai Nihon no Kaisō Kōzō 4: Josei to Shakai Kaisō* (*Strata Structure in Contemporary Japan 4: Women and Social Stratification*, Tōkyō Daigaku Shuppankai.

Hashimoto, Kenji, 1986, 'Gendai Nihon Shakai no Kaikyū Bunseki' (An Analysis of Class in Contemporary Japanese Society), *Shakaigaku Hyōron*, vol. 37, no. 2.

Imada, Takatoshi, 1989, *Shakai Kaisō to Seiji* (*Social Stratification and Politics*), Tōkyō Daigaku Shuppankai.

———, 1998, 'Shakai Kaisō no Shinjigen: Posuto Busshitsu Shakai ni okeru Chii Hensū' (New Dimensions of Social Stratification: Status Variables in a Post-materialist Society), in Imada, Takatoshi (ed.), *1995-nen SSM Chōsa Sirīzu 20: Shakai Kaisō no Shinjigen o Motomete* (*1995 SSM Research Series 20: Seeking New Dimensions of Social Stratification*), 1995 SSM Chōsa Kenkyūkai.

———, and Hara, Junsuke, 1979, 'Shakaiteki Chii no Ikkansei to Hiikkannsei' (Consistency and Inconsistency in Social Status), in Tominaga, Ken'ichi (ed.), *Nihon no Kaisō Kōzō* (*Strata Structure in Japan*), Tōkyō Daigaku Shuppankai.

Inada, Masaya, 1998, 'Chōki Antei Koyō wa Itsu Seiritsu shitanoka: Sedaibetsu to Jitenbetsu ni mita sono Seidoka Katei no Kenkyū' (When was Long-term Employment Established?: A Study of its Institutionalisation According to Generation and Time), in Satō, Toshiki (ed.), *1995-nen SSM Chōsa Sirīzu 2: Kindai Nihon no Idō to Kaisō: 1896–1995* (*1995 SSM Research Series 2: Mobility and Strata in Modern Japan: 1896–1995*), 1995 SSM Chōsa Kenkyūkai.

Ishida, Hiroshi, 1998, 'Intergenerational Class Mobility and Reproduction: Cross-national and Cross-temporal Comparisons,' in Ishida, Hiroshi (ed.), *1995-nen SSM Chōsa Sirīzu 1: Shakai Kaisō, Idō no Kiso Bunseki to Kokusai Hikaku* (*1995 SSM Research Series 1: Basic Analysis and International Comparison of Social Stratification and Mobility*), 1995-nen SSM Chōsa Kenkyūkai.

———, 2000, 'Sangyō Shakai no naka no Nihon' (Japan's Place among Industrial Societies), in Hara, Junsuke (ed.), *Nihon no Kaisō Shisutemu 1: Kindaika to Shakai Kaisō* (Stratification System in Japan 1: Modernization and Social Stratification), Tōkyō Daigaku Shuppankai.

Iwao, Sumiko, 1993, *The Japanese Women: Traditional Image and Changing Reality*, New York: Free Press.

Jackman, Mary R. and Robert W. Jackman, 1983, *Class Awareness in the United States*, Berkeley, University of California Press.

Jeong, Hyeon Suk, 1998, 'Jieigyōsō no Kaisōteki Dokujisei ni kansuru Kenkyū: sono Keisei to Hen'yō' (A Study of the Self-employed as a Unique Strata: Its Formation and Change), *Tōkyō Daigaku Daigakuin Jinbunshakaikei Kenkyūka Hakushi Ronbun*.

Kabashima, Ikuo and Takenaka, Yoshihiko, *Gendai Nihonjin no Ideorogī* (*Political Ideology in Japan*), Tōkyō Daigaku Shuppankai.

Kanomata, Nobuo, 1997, 'Sengo Nihon ni okeru Sedaikan Idō no Hendō' (The Transformation of Inter-generational Mobility in Postwar Japan), *Kōdōkeiryōgaku*, vol. 24, no. 1.

————, 2001, *Kikai to Kekka no Fubyōdō: Sedaikan Idō to Shotoku/Shisan Kakusa* (*Inequality in Opportunities and Results: Inter-generational Mobility and disparity in Incomes/Assets*), Mineruva Shobō.

Kariya, Takehiko, 1995, *Taishū Kyōiku Shakai no Yukue: Gakurekishugi to Byōdō Shinwa no Sengoshi* (*The Future of a Mass Education Society: A Postwar History of Credentialism and the Myth of Equality*), Chūō Kōronsha.

————, 2001, *Kaisōka Nihon to Kyōiku Kiki: Fubyōdō Saiseisan kara Iyoku Kakusa Shakai e* (*The Education Crisis in Stratified Japan: From Reproducing Inequality to a Motivational Disparity Society*), Yūshindō.

Kishimoto, Shigenobu, 1978, *'Chūryū' no Gensō* (*The Illusion of the 'Middle Class'*), Kōdansha.

Kikkawa, Tōru, 1998a, 'Kaisō Hyōka Kijun no Shizukana Hen'yō: Kaisō Kizoku Ishiki no Kitei Yōin no Jikeiretsu Hikaku' (The Quiet Transformation to Strata Evaluation Standards: A Time-series Comparison of Factors Regulating Strata Identification), in Mamada, Takao (ed.), *1995-nen SSM Chōsa Sirīzu 6: Gendai Nihon no Kaisō Ishiki* (*1995 SSM Research Series 6: Strata Consciousness in Contemporary Japan*), 1995-nen SSM Chōsa Kenkyūkai.

————, 1998b, *Kaisō, Kyōiku to Shakai Ishiki no Keisei: Shakai Ishikiron no Jikai* (*Stratification, Education and the Formation of Social Consciousness: The Magnetic Field of the Theory of Social Consciousness*), Mineruva Shobō.

Kobayashi, Hisataka, 1998, 'Shakai Kaisō to Ideorogī' (Social Stratification and Political Ideology), in Katasc, Kazuo (ed.), *1995-nen SSM Chōsa Sirīzu 7: Seiji Ishiki no Genzai* (*1995 SSM Research Series 7: Contemporary Political Consciousness*), 1995-nen SSM Chōsa Kenkyūkai.

Koike, Kazuo and Watanabe, Yukirō, 1979, *Gakureki Shakai no Kyozō* (*Virtual Image of an Educational Credentialism Society*), Tōyō Keizai Shinpōsha.

Kojima, Kazuto, 1978, 'Gendai Seinen no Shakaikan, Seijikan' (Social and Political Perceptions of Contemporary Youths), in Yoshida, Noboru, Kadowaki, Atsushi and Kojima, Kazuto (eds.), *Gendai Seinen no Ishiki to Kōdō* (*The Consciousness and Behaviour of Contemporary Youths*), Nihon Hōsō Shuppan Kyōkai.

Kondō, Hiroyuki, 1997, 'Kyōiku to Shakai Idō no Sūsei' (Trends in Education and Social Mobility), *Kōdōkeiryōgaku*, vol. 24, no. 1.

————, 2002, 'Gakurekishugi to Kaisō Ryūdōsei' (Educational Credentialism and Strata Fluidity), in Hara, Junsuke (ed.), *Kōza Shakai Hendō 5: Ryūdōka to Shakai Kakusa* (*Social Change 5: Fluidization and Social Disparities*), Mineruva Shobō.

Kosaka, Kenji, 1994, 'Introduction,' in Kenji Kosaka (ed.), *Social Stratification in Contemporary Japan*, London: Kegan Paul International.

Kōsaka, Kenji and Miyano, Masaru, 1990, 'Kaisō Imēji: Imēji Keisei Katei e no Sūriteki Apurōchi' (Strata Images: A Mathematical Approach to the Image Formation Process), in Hara, Junsuke (ed.), *Gendai Nihon no Kaisō Kōzō 2: Kaisō Ishiki no Dōtai* (*Strata Structure in Contemporary Japan 2: The Dynamics of Strata Consciousness*), Tōkyō Daigaku Shuppankai.

Linton, Ralph, 1936 [1964], *The Study of Man*, New York: Appleton-Century-Crofts.

Lipset, Seymour M. and Reinhard Bendix, 1959, *Social Mobility in Industrial Society*, Berkeley: University of California Press (Suzuki, Hiroshi, trans, 1969, *Sangyō Shakai no Kōzō*, Saimaru Shuppankai).

Lipset, Seymour M. and H. Zetterburg, 1959, 'A Theory of Social Mobility,' *Transactions of the Third World Congress of Sociology*, London: ISA.

Lyotard, Jean-François, 1979, *La condition postmoderne*, Paris: Éditions de Minuit (Kobayashi, Yasuo, trans, 1986, *Posuto Modan no Jōken: Chi, Shakai, Gengo Gēmu*, Suiseisha).

Mamada, Takao, 1990, 'Kaisō Kizoku Ishiki: Keizai Seichō, Byōdōka to "Chū" Ishiki' (Strata Identification: Economic Growth, Equalisation and 'Middle' Consciousness), in Hara, Junsuke (ed.), *Gendai Nihon no Kaisō Kōzō 2: Kaisō Ishiki no Dōtai* (*Strata Structure in Contemporary Japan 2: The Dynamics of Strata Consciousness*), Tōkyō Daigaku Shuppankai.

Marshall, Gordon, Howard Newby, David Rose and Carolyn Vogler, 1988, *Social Class in Modern Britain*, London: Hutchinson.

Marshall, T. H., 1950, *Citizenship and Social Class*, Reprinted in T. H. Marshall and Tom Bottomore, 1992, *Citizenship and Social Class*, London: Pluto Press (Iwasaki, Nobuhiko and Nakamura, Kengo, trans, 1993, *Shitizunshippu to Shakai Kaikyū*, Hōritsu Bunkasha).

Marx, K., 1868–1884, *Das Kapital* (Hasebe, Fumio, trans, 1952, *Shihonron*, Aoki Shoten).

————, and F. Engels, 1848, *Manifest der Kommunistischen Partei* (Ōuchi, Hyōe and Sakisaka, Itsurō, trans, 1951, *Kyōsantō Sengen*, Iwanami Shoten).

Mills, C. Wright, 1956, *The Power Elite*, London: Oxford University Press (Ukai, Nobushige and Watanuki, Jōji, trans, 1958, *Pawā Erīto*, Tōkyō Daigaku Shuppankai).

Minami, Ryōshin, 2000, 'Nihon ni okeru Shotoku Bunpu no Chōkiteki Henka: Sai-shukei to Kekka' (The Long-term Trend in Income Distribution in Japan: Re-calculation and Its Results), *Tōkyō Keidai Gakkai Shi*, vol. 219.

Misumi, Kazuto, 1990, 'Kaikyū Kizoku Ishiki: sono Bunseki Kachi no Shōshitsu' (Class Identification: The Disappearance of its Analytical Value), in Hara, Junsuke (ed.), *Gendai Nihon no Kaisō Kōzō 2: Kaisō Ishiki no Dōtai* (*Strata Structure in Contemporary Japan 2: The Dynamics of Strata Consciousness*), Tōkyō Daigaku Shuppankai.

Miyake, Ichirō, 1971, 'Seitō Shiji no Ryūdōsei to Anteisei,' (Fluidity and Stability in Political Party Support), in Nihon Seiji Gakkai (ed.), *Gendai Nihon ni okeru Seijiteki Taido no Keisei to Kōzō* (*The Formation and Structure of Political Attitudes in Contemporary Japan*), Iwanami Shoten.

————, 1985, *Seitō Shiji no Bunseki* (*An Analysis of Political Party Support*), Sōbunsha.

Morishima, Michio, 1978, *Zoku Igirisu to Nihon* (*Continuities in England and Japan*), Iwanami Shoten.

Morita, Yōji, 1991, *"Futōkō" Genshō no Shakaigaku* (*The Sociology of Truancy*), Gakubunsha.

Murakami, Yasusuke, 1984, *Shinchūkan Taishū no Jidai* (*The Age of the New Middle Mass*), Chūō Kōronsha.

Murphy, Raymond, 1988, *Social Closure: The Theory of Monopolization and Exclusion*, Oxford University Press (Tatsumi, Shinji, trans, 1994, *Shakaiteki Heisa no Riron: Dokusen to Haijo no Dōtaiteki Kōzō*, Shin'yōsha).

Muchaku, Seikyō (ed.), 1951, *Yamabiko Gakkō* (*Echoes from a Mountain School*), Seidōsha.

Nakamura, Takashi, 1988, 'SSM Chōsa Dēta no Kōhōto Bunseki' (A Cohort Analysis of SSM Survey Data), in 1985-nen Shakai Kaisō to Shakai Idō Zenkoku Chōsa Iinkai (ed.), *1985-nen Shakai Kaisō to Shakai Idō Zenkoku Chōsa Hōkokusho 1: Shakai Kaisō no Kōzō to Katei (Report of 1985 National Survey of Social Stratification and Social Mobility 1: The Structure and Process of Social Stratification)*.

Naoi, Atsushi, 1979, 'Shokugyōteki Chii Shakudo no Kōsei' (*The Composition of the Scale for Occupational Status*), in Tominaga, Ken'ichi (ed.), *Nihon no Kaisō Kōzō (Japan's Strata Structure)*, Tōkyō Daigaku Shuppankai.

Naoi, Michiko, 1979, 'Kaisō Ishiki to Kaikyū Ishiki' (Strata Consciousness and Class Consciousness), in Tominaga, Ken'ichi (ed.), *Nihon no Kaisō Kōzō (Japan's Strata Structure)*, Tōkyō Daigaku Shuppankai.

—————, 1990, 'Kaisō Ishiki: Josei no Chii Shakuyō Moderu wa Yūkōka' (Strata Consciousness: Is the Women's Status Borrowing Model Valid?), in Okamoto, Hideo and Naoi, Michiko (eds.), *Gendai Nihon no Kaisō Kōzō 4: Josei to Shakai Kaisō (Strata Structure in Contemporary Japan 4: Women and Social Stratification)*, Tōkyō Daigaku Shuppankai.

—————, 1994, 'Women's Changing Status and Status Identification,' in Kenji Kosaka (ed.), *Social Stratification in Contemporary Japan*, London: Kegan Paul International.

Nihon Shakaigakkai Chōsa Iinkai (ed.), 1958, *Nihon Shakai no Kaisōteki Kōzō (Stratified Structure in Japanese Society)*, Yūhikaku.

Nomura, Masami, 1994, *Shūshin Koyō (Lifetime Employment)*, Iwanami Shoten.

Oakley, Ann, 1974, *Housewife*, London: Allen Lane (Okajima, Tsubana, trans, 1980, *Shufu no Tanjō*, Sanseidō).

Odaka, Kunio (ed.), 1958, *Shokugyō to Kaisō (Occupation and Strata)*, Mainichi Shimbunsha.

—————, 1995, 'Shakai Kaisō to Shakai Idō Chōsa no Kaiko to Tenbō' (Recollections and Future Perspectives on Social Stratification and Social Mobility Surveys), *Odaka Kunio Senshū 3: Shakai Kaisō to Shakai Idō (Odaka Kunio's Collected Works 3: Social Stratification and Social Mobility)*, Musōan.

Ōhashi, Takanori, 1971, *Nihon no Kaikyū Kōsei (Japan's Class Composition)*, Iwanami Shoten.

Ojima, Fumiaki, 1994, 'Rōdō Shijō ni okeru Nijū Kōzōsei no Saikentō: SSM Shokureki Dēta ni yoru Kigyōkan Idō no Bunseki' (A Reexamination of the Dual Structure of the Labour Market: An Analysis of Inter-firm Mobility based on SSM Occupational Career Data), *Keieikeizai* (Osaka Keizai Daigaku), no. 30.

Okamoto, Hideo, 1990, 'Joron: Josei to Shakai Kaisō Kenkyū no Tenkai' (Preface: The Evolution of Research into Women and Social Stratification), in Okamoto, Hideo and Naoi, Michiko (eds.), *Gendai Nihon no Kaisō Kōzō 4: Josei to Shakai Kaisō (Strata Structure in Contemporary Japan 4: Women and Social Stratification*, Tōkyō Daigaku Shuppankai.

Onai, Tooru, 1995, *Saiseisanron o Yomu: Bānsutin, Burudyū, Bōruzu-Gindisu, Uirisu no Saiseiron (Reading Reproduction Theories: Bernstein, Bourdieu, Balls-Gindis and Willis' Reproduction Theory)*, Tōshindō.

Pakulski, Jan and Malcolm Waters, 1996, *The Death of Class*, London: Sage.

Parkin, Frank, 1979, *Marxism and Class Theory: A Bourgeois Critique*, London: Tavistock Publications.

Parsons, Talcott, 1951, *The Social System*, New York: Free Press (Satō Tsutomu, trans, 1974, *Shakai Taikeiron*, Aoki Shoten).

Roemer, John, 1982, *A General Theory of Exploitation and Class*, Cambridge: Harvard University Press.

Saint-Simon, Claude Henri de, 1823–24, *Catéchisme des industriels* (Sakamoto, Keiichi, trans, 1980, 'Sangyōsha no Kyōri Mondō,' *Sekai no Meicho 42: Ouen/San-Shimon/Fūrie*, Chūō Kōronsha).

Saitō, Yuriko, 1998, 'Jasutisu no Shakaigaku: Seisakuron no Keifu' (The Sociology of Justice: The Genealogy of Policy Theory), in Kōsaka, Kenji and Kōtō, Yōsuke (eds.), *Kōza Shakaigaku 1: Riron to Hōhō* (*Sociology Course 1: Sociological Theory and Methods*), Tōkyō Daigaku Shuppankai.

Satō, Toshiki, 1995, '"Kaisō" Gainen no Saikōchiku: Kaisōron wa nani o katatte kitaka/ nani o katariuruka' (Reconstructing the Concept of 'Strata': What has Stratification Theory Told us? What can it Tell Us?), in Satō, Toshiki (ed.), *Kaisō/Idō Kenkyū no Genzai* (*Current Research into Strata and Mobility*), (Monbushō Kagaku Kenkyūhi Seika Hōkokusho).

———, 1999, 'Kokumin Kokka to iu Shisutemu: "Kokumin" to "Shimin" no Nijūtai' (The Nation State System: The Duality of 'Nation' and Citizen'), in Inoue, Tatsuo, Shimazu, Itaru and Matsuura, Kōji (eds.), *Hō no Rinkai II: Chitsujozō no Tenkan* (*The Criticality of Law II: The Shift in Images of Order*), Tōkyō Daigaku Shuppankai.

———, 2000, *Fubyōdō Shakai Nihon: Sayonara Sōchūryū* (*Japan as an Unequal Society: Farewell to the All-Middle Class*), Chūō Kōron Shinsha.

Seiyama, Kazuo, 1979, 'Jinteki Shihonron to Sukurīninguron: Shakaiteki Saitekisei to Shiteki Kinkō o megutte' (The Human Capital Theory and the Screening Theory: Social Optimality and Personal Balance), *Shakaigakuhyōron*, vol. 29, no. 4.

———, 1981, 'Gakkōgai Kyōiku Tōshi no Kōka ni kansuru Ichi Kōsatsu' (Considering the Effects of Investing in Extracurricular Education), *Hokkaidō Daigaku Bungakubu Kiyō*, vol. 30, no. 1.

———, 1983, 'Ryōteki Dēta no Kaisekihō' (Quantitative Data Analysis Method), in Naoi, Atsushi (ed.), *Shakai Chōsa no Kiso* (*Fundamentals of Social Research*), Saiensusha.

———, 1986, 'Shakai Idō no Sūsei Hikaku Bunseki ni okeru Rogurinia Moderu to Yasuda Keisū' (The Log-linear Model and Yasuda Coefficient in Comparative Analyses of Trends in Social Mobility), in Tominaga, Ken'ichi (ed.), *Shakai Kaisō no Sūsei to Hikaku* (*Trends and Comparisons of Social Mobility*), SSM Sūsei to Hikaku Kenkyūkai.

———, 1990, 'Chū Ishiki no Imi: Kaisō Kizoku Ishiki no Henka no Kōzō' (The Meaning of 'Middle' Consciousness: The Structure of Change in Strata Identification), *Riron to Hōhō*, vol. 5, no. 2.

———, 1991, 'Shakai Idō Kenkyū ni okeru Yasuda no Kaihōsei Keisū no Igi' (The Significance of the Yasuda's Coefficient of Openness in Social Mobility Research), *Riron to Hōhō*, vol. 6, no. 1.

———, 1992, 'Kaikyū e no Tankyū no Kōzō to Sakushu Riron' (Structure of the Search for Class and Exploitation Theory), *Gendai Shakaigaku Kenkyū*, vol. 5.

————, 1993, 'Is the Japanese Mobility Pattern Consistent?: Educational Expansion and Its Effects,' *International Journal of Japanese Sociology*, no. 2.

————, 1994a, 'Intergenerational Occupational Mobility,' in Kenji Kosaka (ed.), *Social Stratification in Contemporary Japan*, London: Kegan Paul International.

————, 1994b, 'Labour Market and Career Mobility,' in Kenji Kosaka (ed.), *Social Stratification in Contemporary Japan*, London: Kegan Paul International.

————, 1994c, 'Kaisō Kenkyū ni okeru "Josei Mondai"' ('The Women's Problem' in Stratification Research), *Riron to Hōhō*, vol. 9, no. 2.

————, 1995, *Seidoron no Kōzu* (*The Structure of Institution Theory*), Sōbunsha.

————, 1996, 'Kazoku ka Kojin ka: Kaisō Tan'i to Jendā,' (Family or Individual?: The Unit of Strata and Gender), *Kazoku Shakaigaku KenkYū*, no. 8.

————, 1997, 'Kaisō Kenkyū to Keiryō Shakaigaku' (Stratification Research and Statistical Sociology), *Kōdōkeiryōgaku*, vol. 24, no. 1.

————, 1998a, 'Seiji Ishiki ni okeru 55-nen Taisei no Henka to Keizoku: Seiji to Kaisō no Saikentō no Kokoromi' (Continuity and Change in the 1955 Regime in the Context of Political Consciousness: An Attempt at Reexamining Politics and Stratification), in Katase, Kazuo (ed.), *1995-nen SSM Chōsa Sirīzu 7: Seiji Ishiki no Genzai* (*1995 SSM Research Series 7: Contemporary Political Consciousness*), 1995-nen SSM Chōsa Kenkyūkai.

————, 1998b, 'Trends of Educational Attainment and Labor Force Participation among Japanese Women,' in Seiyama, Kazuo and Imada, Sachiko (eds.), *1995-nen SSM Chōsa Sirīzu 12: Josei no Kyaria Kōzō to sono Henka* (*1995 SSM Research Series 12: Women's Career Structure and its Changes*), 1995-nen SSM Chōsa Kenkyūkai.

————, 1998c, 'Kaisō Kizoku Ishiki no Junkyo Kōzō ni okeru Jendāsa,' (Gender Difference in the Referential Structure of Strata Identification), in Ojima, Fumiaki (ed.), *1995-nen SSM Chōsa Sirīzu 14: Jendā to Kaisō Ishiki* (*1995 SSM Research Series 12: Gender and Strata Consciousness*), 1995-nen SSM Chōsa Kenkyūkai.

————, 1998d, 'Shutaika Tasseika: Kindai ni okeru Kaikyū/Kaisō no Kōzu' (Agent or Achievement?: Class and Strata in the Modern Age), in Yosano, Arinori (ed.), *1995-nen SSM Chōsa Sirīzu 21: Sangyōka to Kaisō Hendō* (*1995 SSM Research Series 12: Industrialisation and Strata Transformation*), 1995-nen SSM Chōsa Kenkyūkai.

————, 2001, 'Shotoku Kakusa o dō Mondai ni suru ka: Nenreisōnai Fubyōdō no Bunseki kara' (How to Problematize Income Disparities?: An Analysis of Intra-age Group Inequality), *Kikan Kakei Keizai Kenkyū*, no. 51.

————, Naoi, Atsushi, Satō, Yoshimichi, Tsuzuki, Kazuharu and Kojima, Hideo, 1990, 'Gendai Nihon no Kaisō Kōzō to sono Sūsei' (Strata Structure and Its Trends in Contemporary Japan), in Naoi, Atsushi and Seiyama, Kazuo (eds.), *Gendai Nihon no Kaisō Kōzō 1: Shakai Kaisō no Kōzō to Katei* (*Strata Structure in Contemporary Japan 1: The Structure and Process of Social Stratification*), Tōkyō Daigaku Shuppankai.

————, and Noguchi, Yūji, 1984, 'Kōkō Shingaku ni okeru Gakkōgai Kyōiku no Kōka' (The Effects of Extracurricular Education in High School Advancement), *Kyōiku Shakaigaku Kenkyū*, no. 39.

194                                                                    *Bibliography*

————, Tsuzuki, Kazuharu and Satō, Yoshimichi, 1988, 'Shakai Kaisō to Idō no Sūsei' (Trends in Social Stratification and Mobility), in 1985-nen Shakai Kaisō to Shakai Idō Zenkoku Chōsa Iinkai (ed.), *1985-nen Shakai Kaisō to Shakai Idō Zenkoku Chōsa Hōkokusho 1: Shakai Kaisō no Kōzō to Katei (Report of the 1985 National Survey of Social Stratification and Social Mobility 1: The Structure and Process of Social Stratification)*.

————, Tsuzuki, Kazuharu, Satō, Yoshimichi and Nakamura, Takashi, 1990, 'Shokureki Idō no Kōzō' (The Structure of Occupational Mobility), in Naoi, Atsushi and Seiyama, Kazuo (eds.), *Gendai Nihon no Kaisō Kōzō 1: Shakai Kaisō no Kōzō to Katei (Strata Structure in Contemporary Japan 1: The Structure and Process of Social Stratification)*, Tōkyō Daigaku Shuppankai.

Shinbori, Michiya, 1977, 'Gakureki Shakai kara Gakuryoku Shakai e' (From an Educational Credentialism Society to a Scholastic Ability Society), in Asō, Makoto and Ushiogi, Morikazu (eds.), *Gakureki Kōyōron: Gakureki Shakai kara Gakuryoku Shakai e no Michi (The Utility of an Academic Background: The Path from an Educational Credentialism Society to a Scholastic Ability Society)*, Yūhikaku.

Shirakura, Yukio (ed.), 1998, *1995-nen SSM Chōsa Sirīzu 17: Shakai Kaisō to Laifusutairu (1995 SSM Research Series 17: Social Stratification and Lifestyle)*, 1995-nen SSM Chōsa Kenkyūkai.

Sieyès, Emmanuel Joseph, 1789, *Qu'est-ce que le Tiers État* (Ōiwa, Makoto, trans, 1950, *Daisan Kaikyū to wa nanika*, Iwanami Shoten).

Sorokin, Pitirim A., 1927, *Social and Cultural Mobility*, Harper and Brothers.

Spence, Michael, 1974, *Market Signaling*, Cambridge: Harvard University Press.

Sudo, Naoki, 1998, 'Gakureki to Kaisō Ishiki: Gakureki ga Kaisō Kizoku Ishiki no Keisei ni Oyobosu Futatsu no Kōka' (Academic Background and Strata Consciousness: Two Effects of Academic Background on Strata Identification), in Mamada, Takao (ed.), *1995-nen SSM Chōsa Sirīzu 6: Gendai Nihon no Kaisō Ishiki (1995 SSM Research Series 6: Strata Consciousness in Contemporary Japan)*, 1995-nen SSM Chōsa Kenkyūkai.

Tachibanaki, Toshiaki, 1998, Nihon no Keizai Kakusa: Shotoku to Shisan kara Kangaeru (Economic Disparities in Japan: Income and Assets), Iwanami Shoten.

Takahashi, Akiyoshi, 1992, 'Joshō: Chōsa no Kadai to Hōhō' (Preface: Survey Tasks and Methodology), in Takahashi, Akiyoshi, Hasumi, Otohiko, and Yamamoto, Eiji (eds.), *Nōson Shakai no Henbō to Nōmin Ishiki: 30-nenkan no Hendō Bunseki (The Transformation of Rural Society and Farmers' Consciousness: An Analysis of 30 years of Change)*, Tōkyō Daigaku Shuppankai.

Takeuchi, Yō, 1980, *Kyōsō no Shakaigaku (The Sociology of Competition)*, Sekai Shisōsha.

————, 1995, *Nihon no Meritokurashī: Kōzō to Shinsei (Meritocracy in Japan: Structure and Mind)*, Tōkyō Daigaku Shuppankai.

————, 1997, *Risshin shusse-shugi: Kindai Nihon no Roman to Yokubō (The Cult of Success: Romance and Desires in Modern Japan)*, Nihon Hōsō Shuppan Kyōkai.

————, 2001, 'Gakureki Chūryū Ganbō no Seisui to Gan'i' (The Rise and Fall and Implications of the Desire for Middle Class through Academic Background), *Kikan Kakei Keizai Kenkyū*, no. 51.

Tanaka, Satoshi, 1999, 'Kyōiku no Hontai' (The Essentials of Education), in Tanaka, Satoshi (ed.), *'Kyōiku' no Kaidoku (Deciphering Education)*, Seshiki Shobō.

Tōkyō Daigaku Kōhō Iinkai, 1987, '1986 (Dai 36 kai) Gakusei Seikatsu Jittai Chōsa no Kekka' (Results of the 1986 Survey of University Students' Lives), *Gakunai Kōhō*, no. 772.

Tominaga, Ken'ichi, 1988, *Nihon Sangyō Shakai no Tenkan (The Transformation of Japan as an Industrial Society)*, Tōkyō Daigaku Shuppankai.

————, 1990, *Nihon no Kindaika to Shakai Hendō: Tyūbingen Kōgi (Japan's Modernisation and Social Change: The Tübingen Lecture)*, Kōdansha.

————, 1992, 'Sengo Nihon no Shakai Kaisō to sono Hendō: 1955–1985-nen' (Social Stratification and its Changes in Postwar Japan: 1955–1985), in Tōkyō Daigaku Shakai Kagaku Kenkyūjo (ed.), *Gendai Nihon Shakai 6: Mondai no Shosō (Contemporary Japanese Society 6: Problematic Aspects)*, Tōkyō Daigaku Shuppankai.

Tomoeda, Toshio, 1998, *Sengo Nihon Shakai no Keiryō Bunseki (A Quantitative Analysis of Postwar Japanese Society)*, Hanashoin.

Tomoda, Yasumasa, 1977, 'Gakureki Muyōron tai Gakureki Kōyōron' (The Ineffectiveness and Ectiveness Theses of Academic Background), in Asō, Makoto and Ushiogi, Morikazu (eds.), *Gakureki Kōyōron: Gakureki Shakai kara Gakuryoku Shakai e no Michi (The Utility of an Academic Background: The Path from an Educational Credentialism Society to a Scholastic Ability Society)*, Yūhikaku.

Toyoda, Hideki, 1998, *Kyōbunsan Kōzō Bunseki (Nyūmonhen): Kōzō Hōteishiki Moderingu (The Covariance Structure Analysis [Introductory Edition]: Structural Equation Modelling)*, Asakura Shoten.

Treiman, Donald, 1970, 'Industrialization and Social Stratification,' in E. O. Laumann (ed.), *Social Stratification: Research and Theory for the 1970s*, Indianapolis: Bobbs-Merrill.

Tsuzuki, Kazuharu, 1998, 'Shokugyō Hyōtei no Moderu to Shokugyō Ishin Sukoa' (The Occupational Evaluation Model and the Occupational Prestige Score), in Tsuzuki, Kazuji (ed.), *1995-nen SSM Chōsa Sirīzu 5: Shokugyō Hyōka no Kōzō to Shokugyō Ishin Sukoa (1995 SSM Research Series 5: The Occupational Evaluation Structure and the Occupational Prestige Score)*, 1995-nen SSM Chōsa Kenkyūkai.

Tumin, Melvin M., 1964, *Social Stratification*, Englewood Cliffs: Prentice Hall (Okamoto, Hideo, trans, 1969, *Shakaiteki Seisō*, Shiseidō).

Ueno, Chizuko, 1990, *Kafuchōsei to Shihonsei (Patriarchy and Capitalism)*, Iwanami Shoten.

Ujihara, Shōjirō, 1966, *Nihon Rōdō Mondai Kenkyū (The Study of Labour Issues in Japan)*, Tōkyō Daigaku Shuppankai.

Umino, Michio and Saitō, Yuriko, 1990, 'Kōheikan to Manzokukan: Shakai Hyōka no Kōzō to Shakaiteki Chii' (Feelings of Fairness and Satisfaction: The Structure of Social Evaluation and Social Status), in Hara, Junsuke (ed.), *Gendai Nihon no Kaisō Kōzō 2: Kaisō Ishiki no Dōtai (Strata Structure in Contemporary Japan 2: Dynamics of Strata Consciousness)*, Tōkyō Daigaku Shuppankai.

Upton, Graham J. S., 1978, *The Analysis of Cross-Tabulated Data*, New York: Wiley (Ikeda, Hiroshi and Okada, Akinori, trans, 1980, *Chōsa Dēta no Kaisekihō*, Asakura Shoten).

Ushiogi, Morikazu, 1977, 'Gakureki no Keizaiteki Kōyō' (The Economic Utility of an Academic Background), in Asō, Makoto and Ushiogi, Morikazu (eds.), *Gakureki Kōyōron: Gakureki Shakai kara Gakuryoku Shakai e no Michi (The Utility of an Academic Background: The Path from an Educational Credentialism Society to a Scholastic Ability Society)*, Yūhikaku.

Velsor, Ellen V. and Leonard Beeghley, 1979, 'The Process of Class Identification among Employed Married Women: A Replication and Reanalysis,' *Journal of Marriage and Family*, vol. 41, no. 4.

Walby, Sylvia, 1986, *Patriarchy at Work: Patriarchal and Capitalist Relations in Employment*, Cambridge: Polity Press.

Warner, W. Lloyd, 1949, *Social Class in America: A Manual of Procedure for the Measurement of Social Status*, Chicago: Science Research Associates.

Watanuki, Jōji, 1976, *Nihon Seiji no Bunseki Shikaku (Analytical Perspectives on Japanese Politics)*, Chūō Kōronsha.

Weber, Max, 1947, *The Theory of Social and Economic Organization*, edited with an Introduction by Talcott Parsons, New York: Free Press.

————, 1948 [1991], *From Max Weber: Essays in Sociology*, edited with an Introduction by H. H. Gerth and C. Wright Mills, London: Routledge.

Weber, Max, 1967, Hamashima, Akira, trans, *Kenryoku to Shihai (Power and Domination)*, Yūhikaku.

————, 1970, Sera, Kōshirō, trans, *Shihai no Shoruikei (Typologies of Domination)*, Sōbunsha.

Wright, Erik Olin, 1985, *Classes*, London: Verso.

————, 1997, *Class Counts*, Cambridge University Press.

Yamada, Masahiro, 1994, *Kindai Kazoku no Yukue: Kazoku to Aijō no Paradokkusu (The Future of the Modern Family: The Paradox of Family and Love)*, Shinyōsha.

Yano, Masakazu, 1996, *Kōtō Kyōiku no Keizai Bunseki to Seisaku (Tertiary Education: Economic Analysis and Policy)*, Tamagawa Daigaku Shuppanbu.

Yasuda, Saburo, 1964, 'A Methodological Inquiry into Mobility,' *American Sociological Review*, vol. 29, no. 1.

————, 1971, *Shakai Idō no Kenkyū (The Study in Social Mobility)*, Tōkyō Daigaku Shuppankai.

————, and Hara, Junsuke, 1984, *Shakai Chōsa Handobukku Dai 3 han (Social Survey Handbook 3rd edition)*, Yūhikaku.

Young, M., 1958, *The Rise of Meritocracy*, London: Thames & Hudson (Kubota, Shizuo and Yamamoto, Uichirō, trans, 1982, *Meritokurashī*, Shiseidō).

# Name index

Abegglen, James C. 69
Acker, Joan 30
Allison, Paul D. 178

Bell, Daniel 9
Bendix, Reinhard 9, 24
Blau, Peter M. 66
Bourdieu, Pierre 48, 51–3, 157, 169
Brinton, Mary C. 183

Clark, R. L. 178
Comte, Auguste 148–9
Crompton, Rosemary 184

Dahrendorf, Ralf 155
de Saint-Simon, Claude Henri 149
Duncan, Otis D. 66

Engels, Friedrich 6, 149
Erikson, Robert 28, 84, 144

Featherman, David L. 27–8, 81, 83
Flanagan, Scott C. 97
Fukutake, Tadashi 11
Fukuzawa, Yukichi 34, 59

Goldthorpe, John H. 8, 28, 84, 147
Gross, A. J. 178

Hara, Junsuke xi–xii, xxiv–xxv, 9, 26, 31, 61–2, 66, 74, 88, 90, 92–3, 94, 96, 100, 105, 107, 111, 113, 115, 166, 172, 176
Hashimoto, Kenji 184
Hauser, Robert M. 27, 81

Imada, Takatoshi xii, 93, 112, 166
Inada, Masaya 70–1
Ishida, Hiroshi 84

Jeong, Hyeon Suk 109

Kanomata, Nobuo xxiv
Kariya, Takehiko xxvi–xxviii, xxix
Kikkawa, Tōru 107
Kobayashi, Hisataka 183
Koike, Kazuo 37, 41, 42
Kondō, Hiroyuki xiii–xiv, xxx, 56
Kōsaka, Kenji xii, 20

Linton, Ralph 34
Lipset, Seymour M. 9, 24, 27
Lyotard, Jean-François 148

Mamada, Takao 183
Marshall, Gordon 109
Marshall, T. H. 170
Marx, Karl 6, 7, 149
Minami, Ryōshin xxi–xxii
Misumi, Kazuto 108
Miyake, Ichirō 94, 100
Miyano, Masaru 183
Morishima, Michio 85

# Subject index